IMAGES
of America

GILA BEND

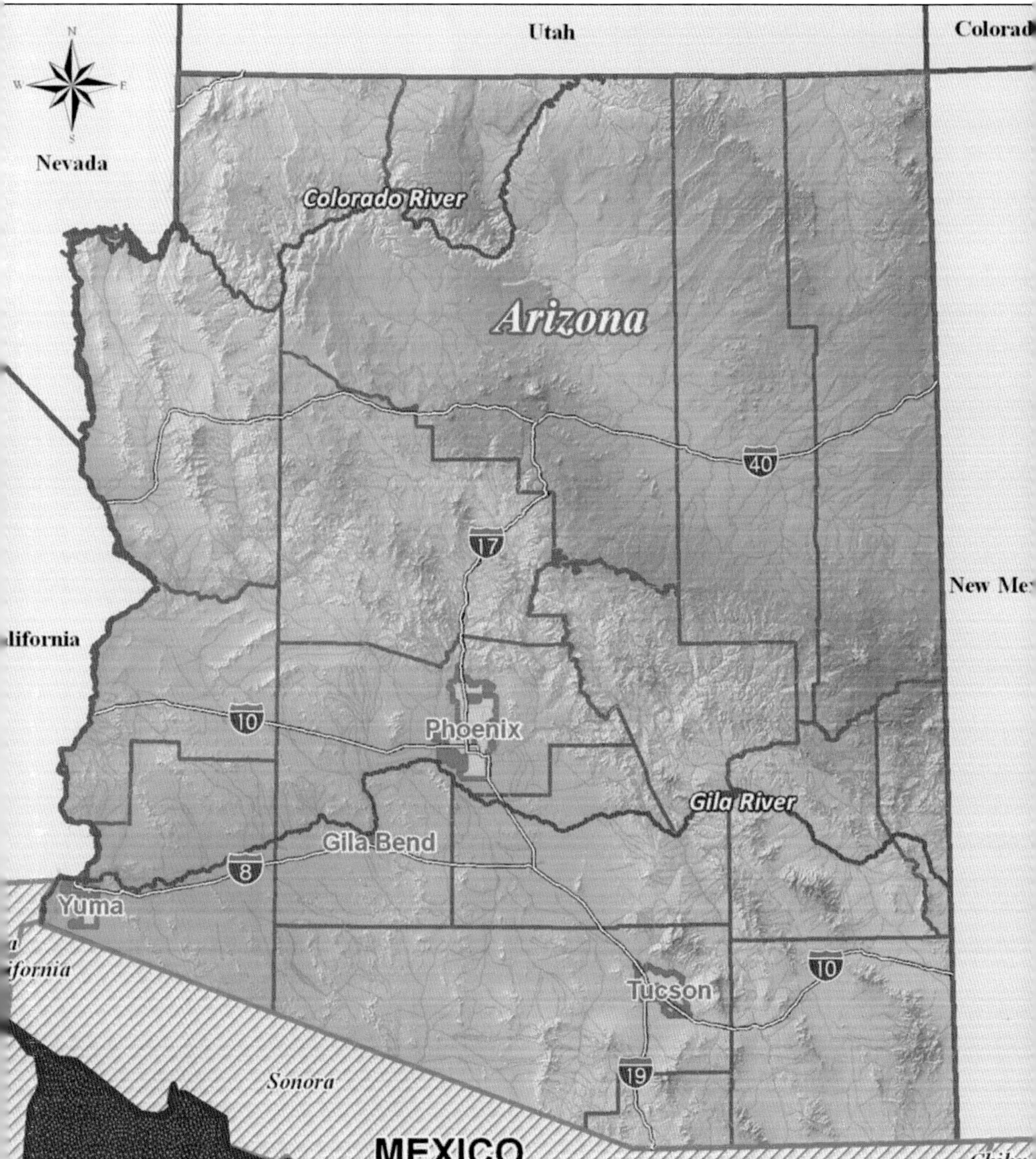

This map of Arizona shows the geographical location of Gila Bend in relation to the state capital, Phoenix, as well as to the cities of Yuma and Tucson. These three communities played an important part in the genesis of the town at the big bend of the Gila River. (Courtesy of Marta Dent.)

On the Cover: The Gila Garage and its neighbor, the Tourist Garage, were early additions to the streetscape in the wake of the realignment of the interstate highway through Gila Bend. (Courtesy of Daisy Bean Policy.)

IMAGES
of America

GILA BEND

Vincent Murray

ARCADIA
PUBLISHING

ISBN 978-0-7385-8475-1

Published by Arcadia Publishing
Charleston, South Carolina

Printed in the United States of America

Library of Congress Control Number: 2011942672

For all general information, please contact Arcadia Publishing:
Telephone 843-853-2070
Fax 843-853-0044
E-mail sales@arcadiapublishing.com
For customer service and orders:
Toll-Free 1-888-313-2665

Visit us on the Internet at www.arcadiapublishing.com

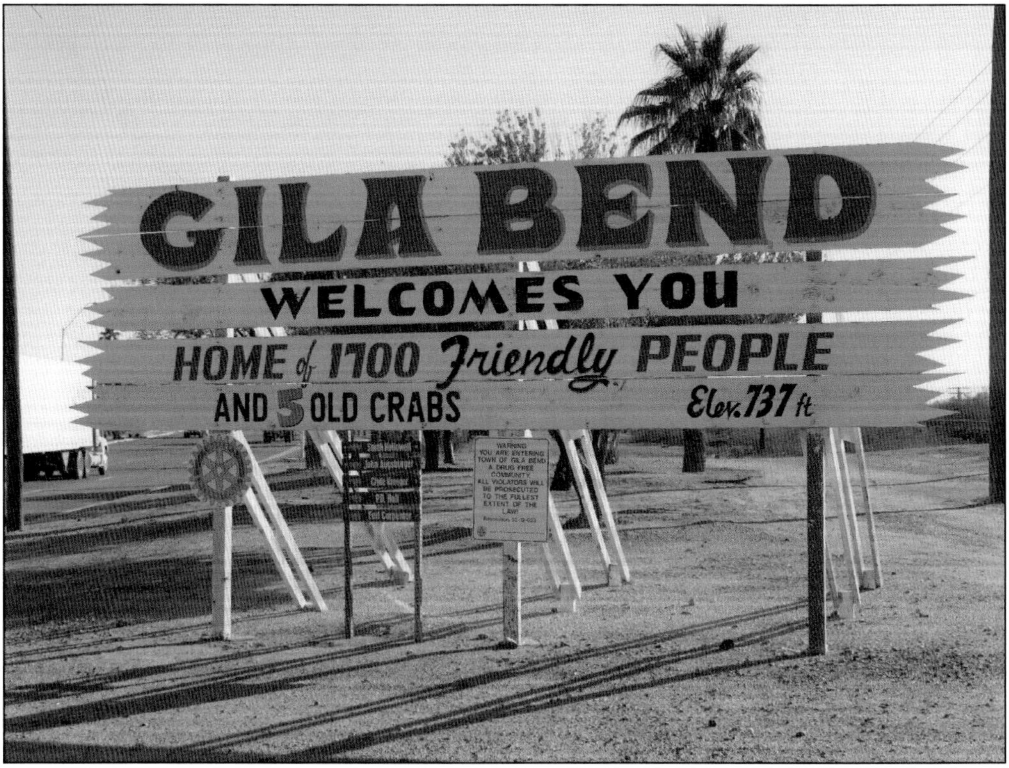

This book is dedicated to the "Gila Benders," those persevering individuals living at the big bend in the Gila River during the past, present, and future. (Courtesy of Cyndi Eisenberger.)

Contents

Acknowledgments

This book would not have been possible had it not been for the assistance of local Gila Benders like Daisy Bean Policy, Gary Miller, Ed Stout, Betty Gills, Betty Sipes, Bonnie Sandoval, Elizabeth Cool, Steven Holt, Mayor Ron Henry, Clyde Kreeger, Natu Bhakta, and Elva Mae McMahon. When I started this project years ago, I received assistance from Johnny Laird, an instrumental figure in the creation of the Gila Bend Historical Museum. Laird, unfortunately, passed away before the book's completion. Also of great assistance were Elva Mae's daughter, Donna Sizemore, who served as an intermediary, as well as a valuable source of knowledge; and Cyndi Eisenberger, who works for the town and made the archives of the Gila Bend Historical Museum—as well as her own personal photographs—available. I also need to thank Marta Dent, who has never hesitated to help me with my mapping needs, and my brother Matt "Dragon" Murray, who was willing to make a number of special trips just to take photographs. Also, Wendell Huffman and Peter Barton are two Nevadans I had contacted for railroad information, only to discover that they have their own huge piece of Gila Bend history. Most of all, I need to thank Heather Goebel, who can make no claim to being a native, like many of those I met in the process of doing this book, but she is, nevertheless, a true Gila Bender. Her sometimes-annoying efforts exemplify her passion for the town, and she went well out of her way in providing immeasurable assistance.

Introduction

"Quirkily resilient" may be the best way to describe this little town located 45 miles southwest of Downtown Phoenix. It derives its name from a large bend in the Gila River to the north of the community. Pronounced "Hee-la Bend," the little town has a population that is relatively static, proudly boasting on a sign at the town's entrance, "Home to 1700 friendly people and 5 old crabs." This is hardly a descriptive appellation for a place some see as the furthest extension of the Greater Phoenix metropolitan area, since Gila Benders all seem to be friendly, and crabs are noticeably absent from the desert. Shrimp, however, are another story. While the population is a few hundred more than the sign proclaims, it is significantly less than most of the communities in central Arizona. Although Phoenix and other communities in the region experienced a population boom, increasing exponentially after World War II, the town of Gila Bend has remained comparatively unchanged.

The town sits at 700 or so feet above sea level in the middle of Arizona's portion of the Sonoran Desert. It has little rain but a lot of heat, hitting a high of over 100 degrees one-third of the year. As it is one of the hottest places in Arizona, if not the country, people from elsewhere often ask, "Why would you want to live here?" The answer, it seems, is Gila Bend's sense of community, where everyone knows everyone, like TV's fictional Mayberry placed among sand, cactus, and creosote. That is where the physical comparison ends. Though it possesses an internal small-town charm—the product of friendly, welcoming citizens—its atmosphere does not give way to the stereotypical nature of a town in North Carolina, the Midwest, or most of Arizona, for that matter. Its Main Street is not its main street, and its downtown is the epitome of highway frontage.

Gila Bend is a historical town by every definition of the word, and while the community may appear unchanging, the first people living at the big bend in the river were setting up homes over 1,000 years ago. When they departed, others came, keeping a steady stream of indigenous occupation that continues on to this day in the San Lucy Village. Though the local population has always been self-sufficient, the location of the community has been the catalyst for an almost biorhythmic cycle of prosperity and privation that seems to be an endemic theme to the history of the bend. However, Gila Benders are a hardy stock, and though the town has boomed and busted, they never bail out.

The earliest permanent inhabitants to the area are commonly referred to as the Hohokam, an archeological term used to describe an ancient culture that covered much of southwestern Arizona, stretching from north of Phoenix southward into Mexico. The Hohokam were canal builders who developed a vast irrigation system, reclaiming countless acres for agricultural use. At the bend in the river, archeological evidence shows that, in addition to irrigated fields, they had a prosperous village with a ceremonial mound and ball courts. Also along a valuable travel route following the Gila River, a short cut from the east across a waterless desert, the bend was prime real estate centuries before people would use that term. Since there is no written record of the Hohokam, we can only speculate as to what motivated them to leave after living at the bend for close to five centuries.

The first written records about the bend come from Catholic missionaries and their military escorts who, during the 17th and 18th centuries, traversed the long-used trade routes in their quest for souls and settlement sites. They found the former but skipped the latter, preferring to continue on to California, like many others who followed. Were the town to have existed back then, Gila Bend would have been located in terra incognita, or unknown land, under Spanish rule and would have been on the northern fringe of Sonora after Mexican independence before becoming part of the United States with the Gadsden Purchase in 1853.

Nonnative settlement at the bend did not occur until 1858 when the Butterfield Overland Mail Company decided to build a stage station at the site. The Butterfield Stage, as it is typically—and inaccurately—referred to, was short-lived due to the Civil War. After the war ended, a new station developed with entrepreneurs who saw the potential in supplying freighters and other travelers along the road to California.

As a community, Gila Bend was officially born in 1871 with the federal government's approval of a post office and then reborn less than a decade later when the railroad passed through a few miles south of the stage station. As the community at the stage station withered away, the new community in proximity to the railroad line prospered. The new community's location between Tucson and Yuma placed Gila Bend in an advantageous position, and the railroad quickly developed the site as a changeover station. Within a short time, the Southern Pacific added a bunkhouse, depot, section house, roundhouse, and coal shed. Soon, speculators laid out a town around the station grounds, and lots quickly sold. In 1891, efforts at a huge reclamation system watering thousands of acres with the help of an upstream dam fueled more speculation.

In 1912, the development of a copper mine at Ajo, 30 miles south of Gila Bend, brought more prosperity to the town, initiating a spur line between the two communities. Though agricultural development was on the minds of early settlers, it required an oil-rich speculator investing over $1 million in the agricultural infrastructure to develop the potential of the area's nutrient-rich soil on a large scale. An added consequence of this infrastructure also changed the dynamics of automobile-based transportation system in the area: rerouting the Phoenix-Yuma highway to Gila Bend where it joined with the Tucson-Yuma highway. Within a short time, the town became a transportation hub between Arizona's two largest communities with Yuma and San Diego, as well as a key stopover on the nation's intercontinental highway system.

Being on an artery in the nation's ground-based transportation structure created Gila Bend's booms and busts. As improvements in highway construction fueled Gila Bend's automotive-based prosperity in the 1950s and 1960s, improvements in railroad technology, specifically the diesel engine, had the opposite effect on the local rail industry. No longer needing the supplies in Gila Bend, the railroad began withdrawing from the town, abandoning the depot, water and oil tanks, and a number of other structures. By 1971, the Southern Pacific discontinued changing crews and eliminated 200 local jobs. Then an oil shortage hit, and combined with the advent of the interstate, the once christened "Fan Belt Capital of the World"—so named because it was almost requisite to stop in Gila Bend when passing through—was relegated to being an exit on Interstate 8.

Gila Bend may have been down, but it was far from out. A dry climate and an ample supply of warm, mineral-rich water provide perfect conditions for aquaculture—specifically, shrimp farming. While the technology is not new, this is usually an industry found near the coast, not in the middle of the Sonoran Desert. Gila Bend is also the location of two new gas-fired electrical generating plants supplying gigawatts of electricity into the Southwest's power grid, and recently, the town was selected as the site of one of the nation's largest solar energy plants.

One

A Big Bend in the River

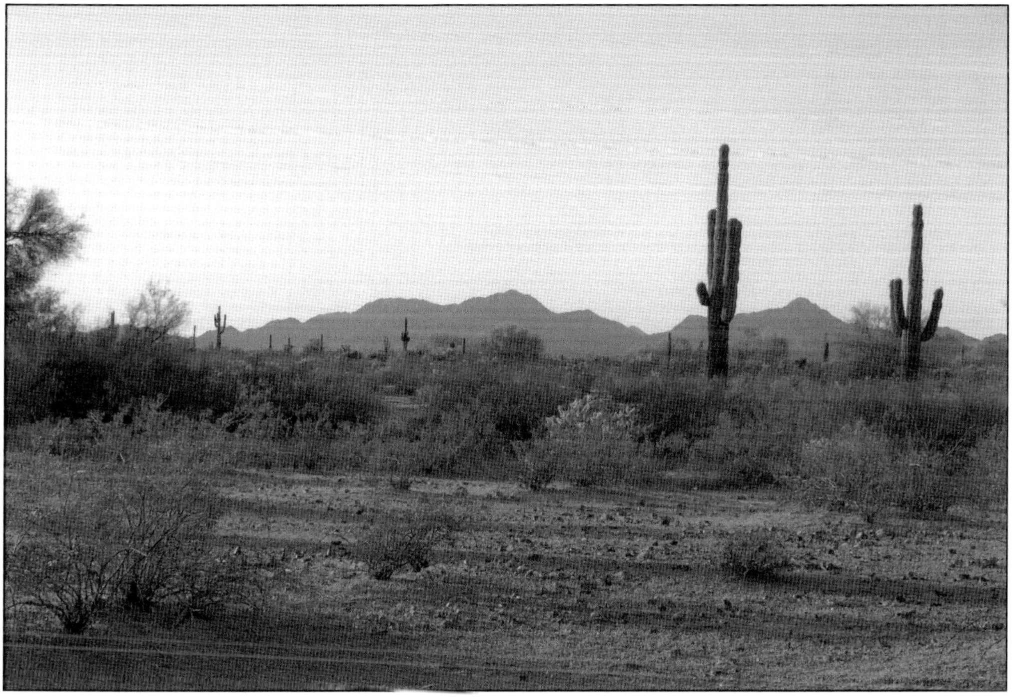

Gila Bend is located in the Sonoran Desert, a region that encompasses much of southern Arizona and southeastern California and stretches southward into the Mexican states of Sonora, Sinaloa, and the two Baja Californias. The only place on earth where the mighty saguaro cactus grows, it is also home to a variety of cacti with less than evocative monikers such as organ pipe, hedgehog, beavertail, and the not-so-cuddly teddy bear cholla. Creosote, ironwood, and jojoba are all natives, as are palo verde, ocotillo, brittle brush, and about three dozen species of wildflowers, which can coat the desert with color as beautiful as any New England fall. A cornucopia of fauna also call the Sonoran Desert home, including bighorn sheep, ringtailed cats, collared peccaries, horned toads, and wily coyotes. (Courtesy of Cyndi Eisenberger.)

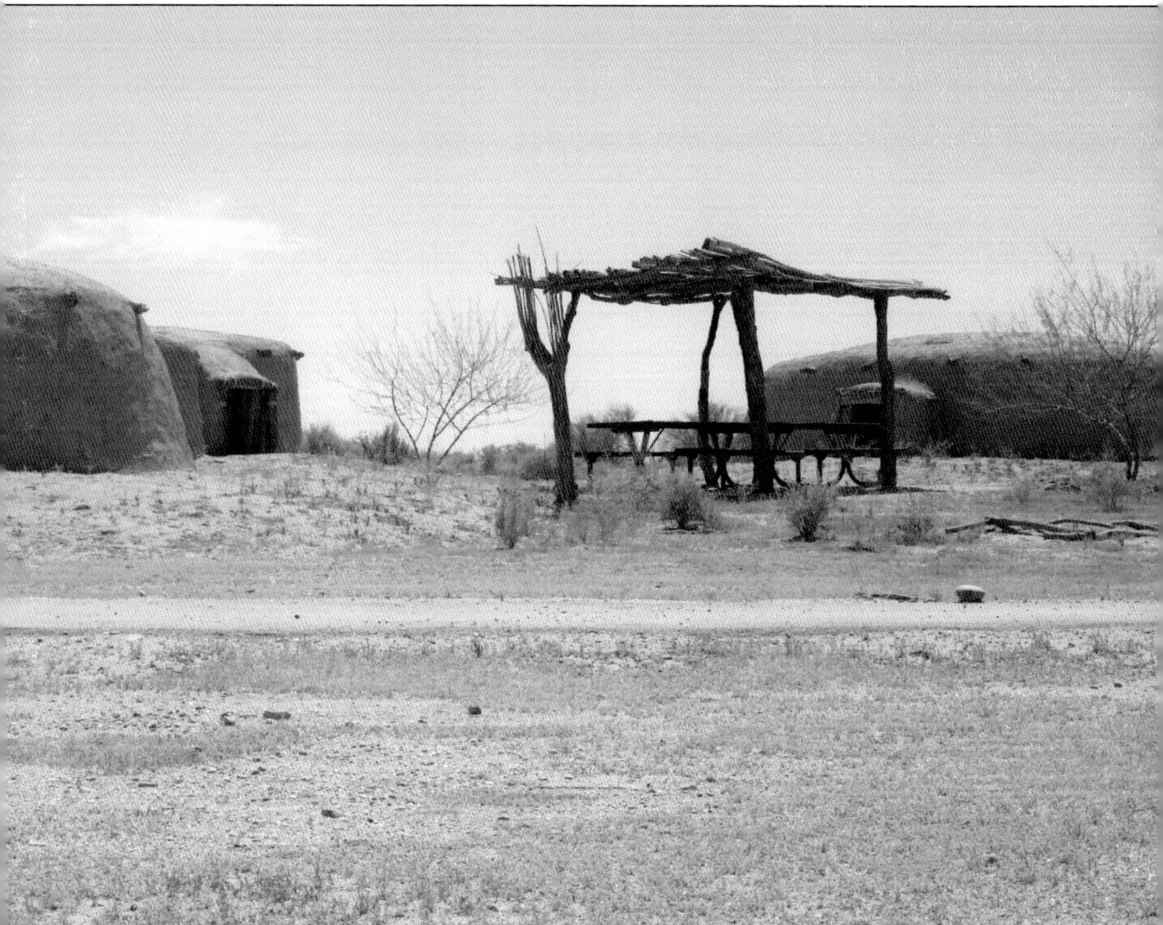

The earliest identifiable residents at the big bend in the river were in the area several millennia ago. As evidenced by the archaeological resources in the vicinity, the Hohokam lived near the river as early as 300 BC. The Gatlin Site, shown here, contains a number of pit houses, a canal, and one of the few documented ceremonial mounds, which was built around 900–1100 AD. Listed as a national historic landmark and owned by the Town of Gila Bend, the 30-acre site has long been slated for development as an archaeological park by the town. In this photograph are re-created pit house structures. The picnic tables under the ramadas are a contemporary addition placed for visitor comfort. (Courtesy of Cyndi Eisenberger.)

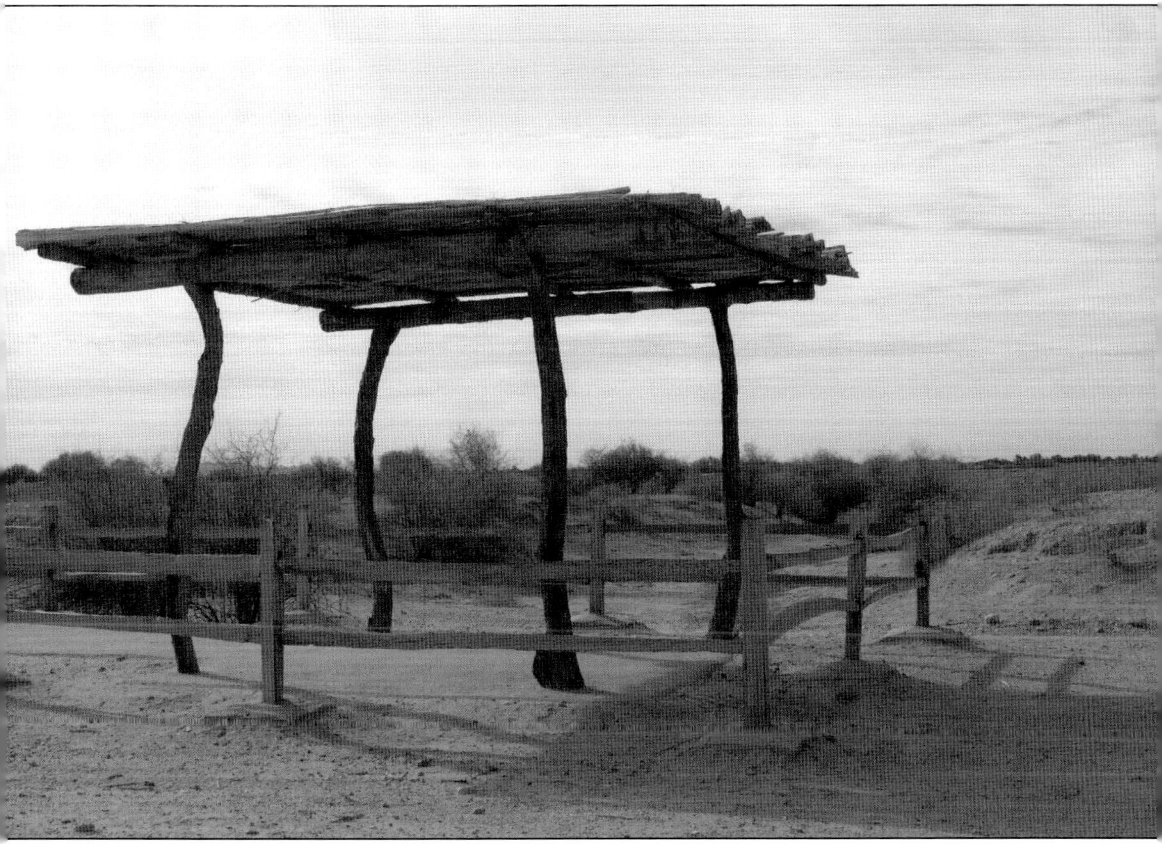

The first professional archaeological investigations conducted at the Gatlin Site were in 1958. In the early 1980s, research performed by the Museum of Northern Arizona determined the extent of the site. This enabled the development of park facilities, such as the replica ramada in this photograph, in areas devoid of archeological resources. Beyond the ramada and the fence are the remnants of an ancient irrigation canal. Canals such as this once covered much of the Phoenix metropolitan area but have since been destroyed by the onslaught of reclamation and urban development. These archaeological features are very rare and need preservation and protection, which is the function of the park. The town's plans for the park include allowing visitors to observe fieldwork and stabilization with opportunities for voluntary involvement. (Courtesy of Cyndi Eisenberger.)

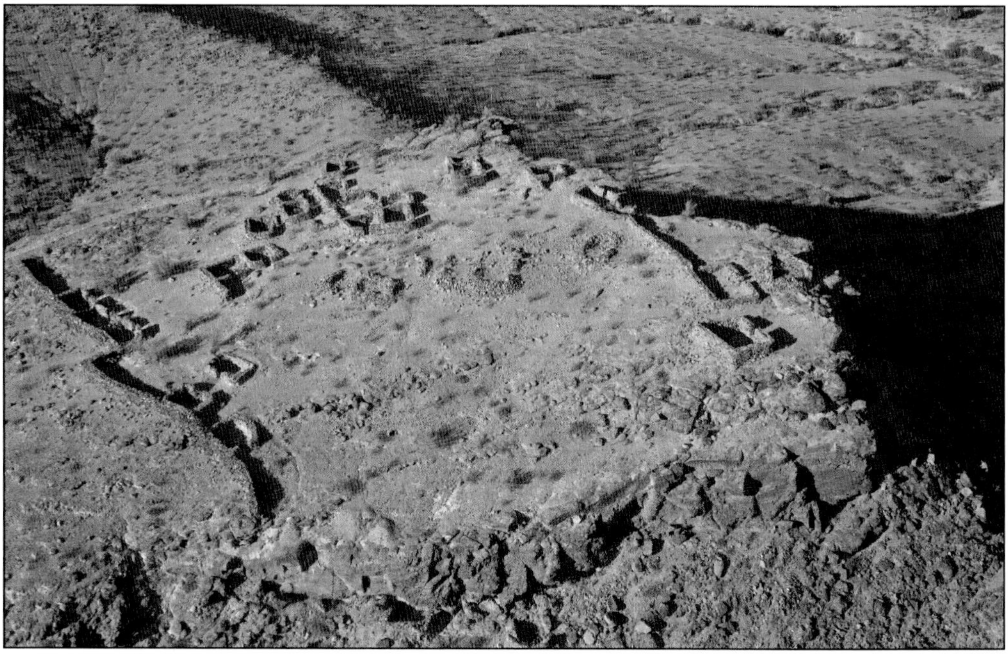

Both the agricultural fields and the trade route were undoubtedly important to the Hohokam, and they erected this hilltop stronghold, known as Fortaleza, for protection. Listed in the National Register of Historic Places, the Fortaleza site is located on the Gila Bend Indian Reservation, and access is restricted. (Courtesy of the Center for Desert Archaeology.)

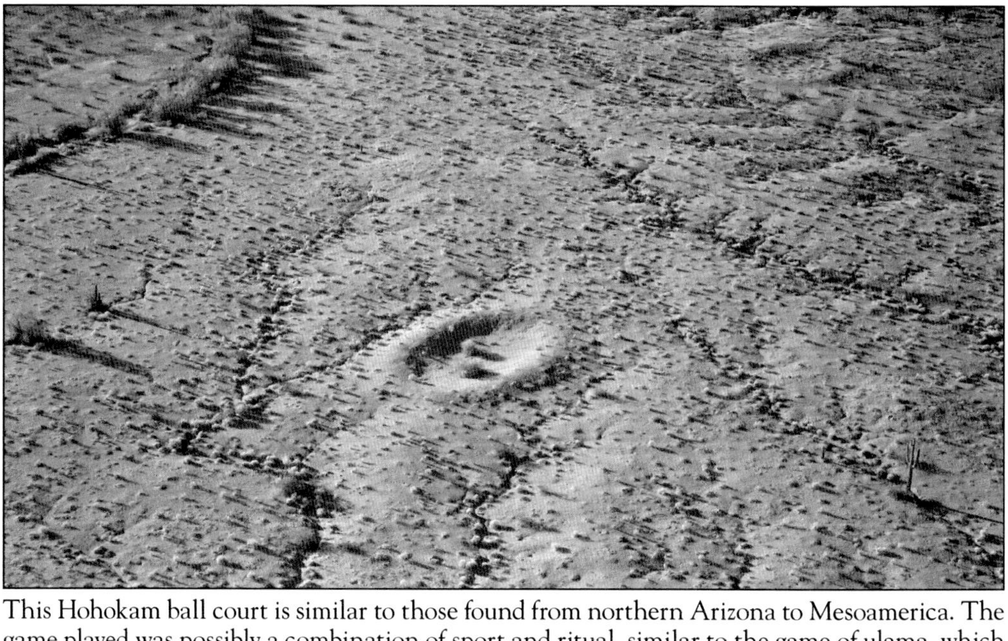

This Hohokam ball court is similar to those found from northern Arizona to Mesoamerica. The game played was possibly a combination of sport and ritual, similar to the game of ulama, which is still played in Sinaloan villages in Mexico. Agricultural development has destroyed many of the archaeological sites in the area. Those that have not been disturbed, such as this one, are usually found on public lands and are, therefore, protected by state and federal laws. (Courtesy of the Center for Desert Archaeology.)

In addition to possessing quality farmland due to the alluvium deposited by the Gila River, the bend was also on an ancient trade route that connected what is now the American Southwest with the West Coast. Besides ruins and other archeological sites along this route are petroglyphs, drawings carved into rock whose meaning is known only to their creators. Petroglyphs on public lands are protected by state and federal laws. (Courtesy of Cyndi Eisenberger.)

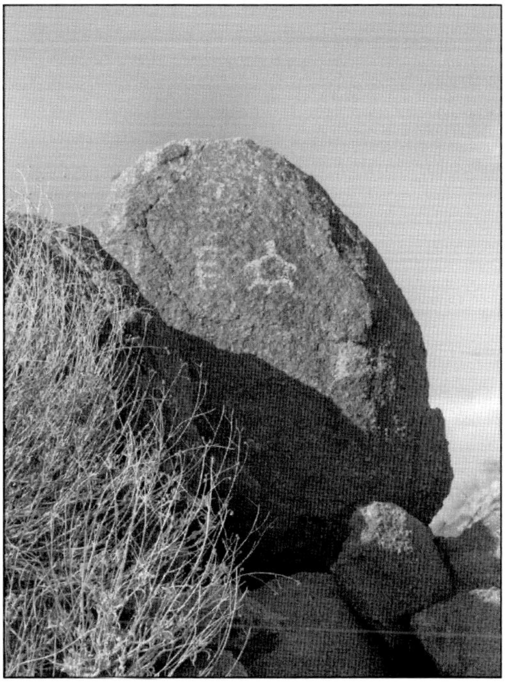

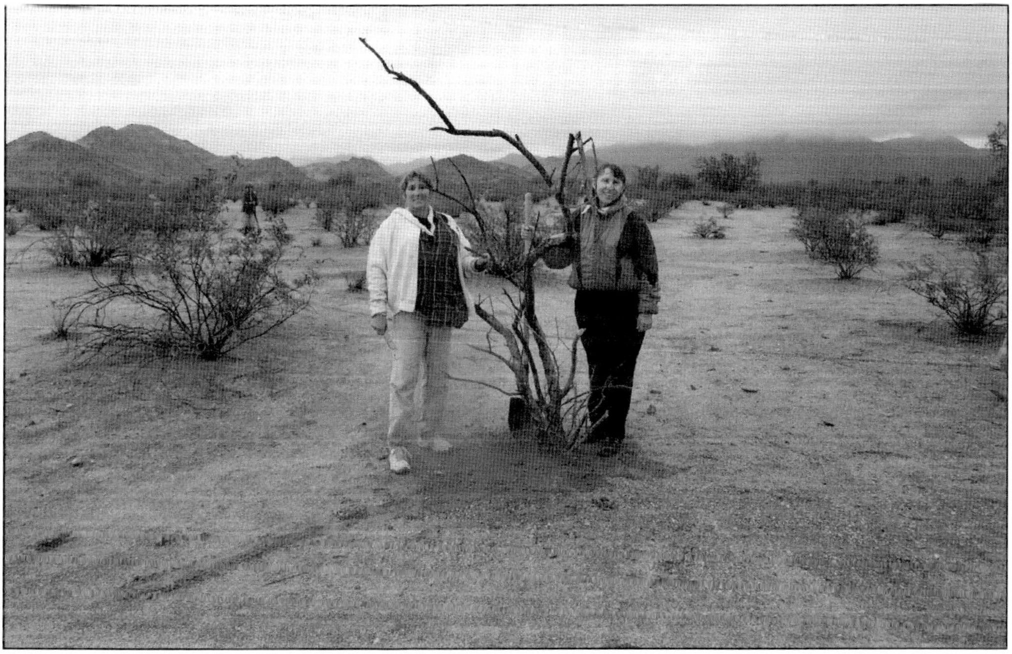

When the Anza expedition passed through the area in the 1775, there was a small Opa Indian village located on in the vicinity known as Opasoitac, translated as "the settlement of the Opas." In honor of a couple of apostles, the missionaries in the group renamed it as San Simon y Judas de Opasoitac, but it is doubtful that the ecclesiastical name caught on with the locals. Today, the Juan Bautista de Anza National Historic Trail commemorates the expedition from Mexico to San Francisco Bay. In this photograph, Gila Benders Heather Goebbels (right) and Cyndi Eisenberger work on restoration of the trail east of the city. (Courtesy of Cyndi Eisenberger.)

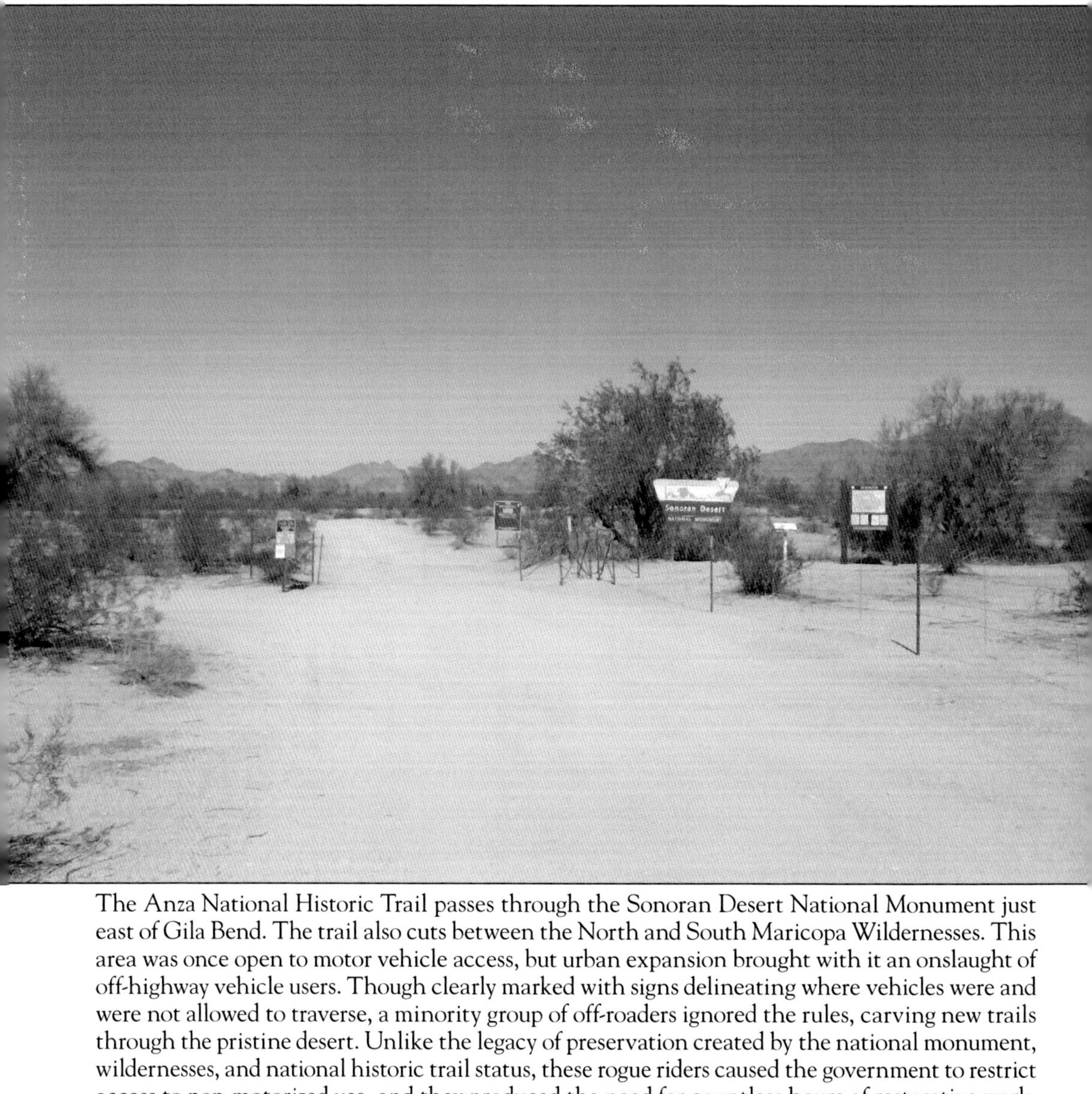

The Anza National Historic Trail passes through the Sonoran Desert National Monument just east of Gila Bend. The trail also cuts between the North and South Maricopa Wildernesses. This area was once open to motor vehicle access, but urban expansion brought with it an onslaught of off-highway vehicle users. Though clearly marked with signs delineating where vehicles were and were not allowed to traverse, a minority group of off-roaders ignored the rules, carving new trails through the pristine desert. Unlike the legacy of preservation created by the national monument, wildernesses, and national historic trail status, these rogue riders caused the government to restrict access to non-motorized use, and they produced the need for countless hours of restorative work. (Courtesy of Matt "Dragon" Murray.)

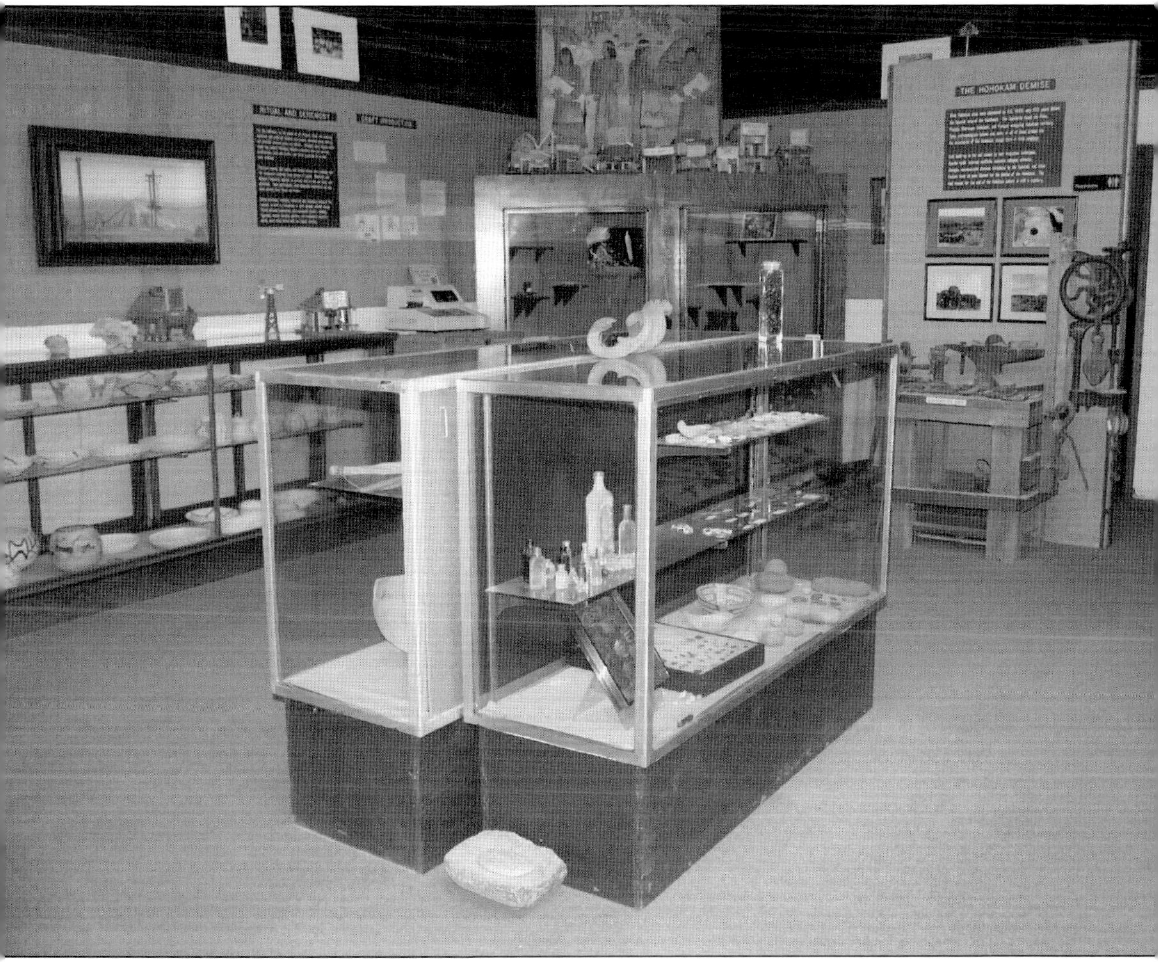

The Gila Bend Museum and Visitors Center is located at the town hall. The museum, created as a community effort, is operated by the town with volunteer staff. Exhibits with artifacts ranging from O'odham baskets to historical photographs portray the history and prehistory of the area. (Courtesy of Cyndi Eisenberger.)

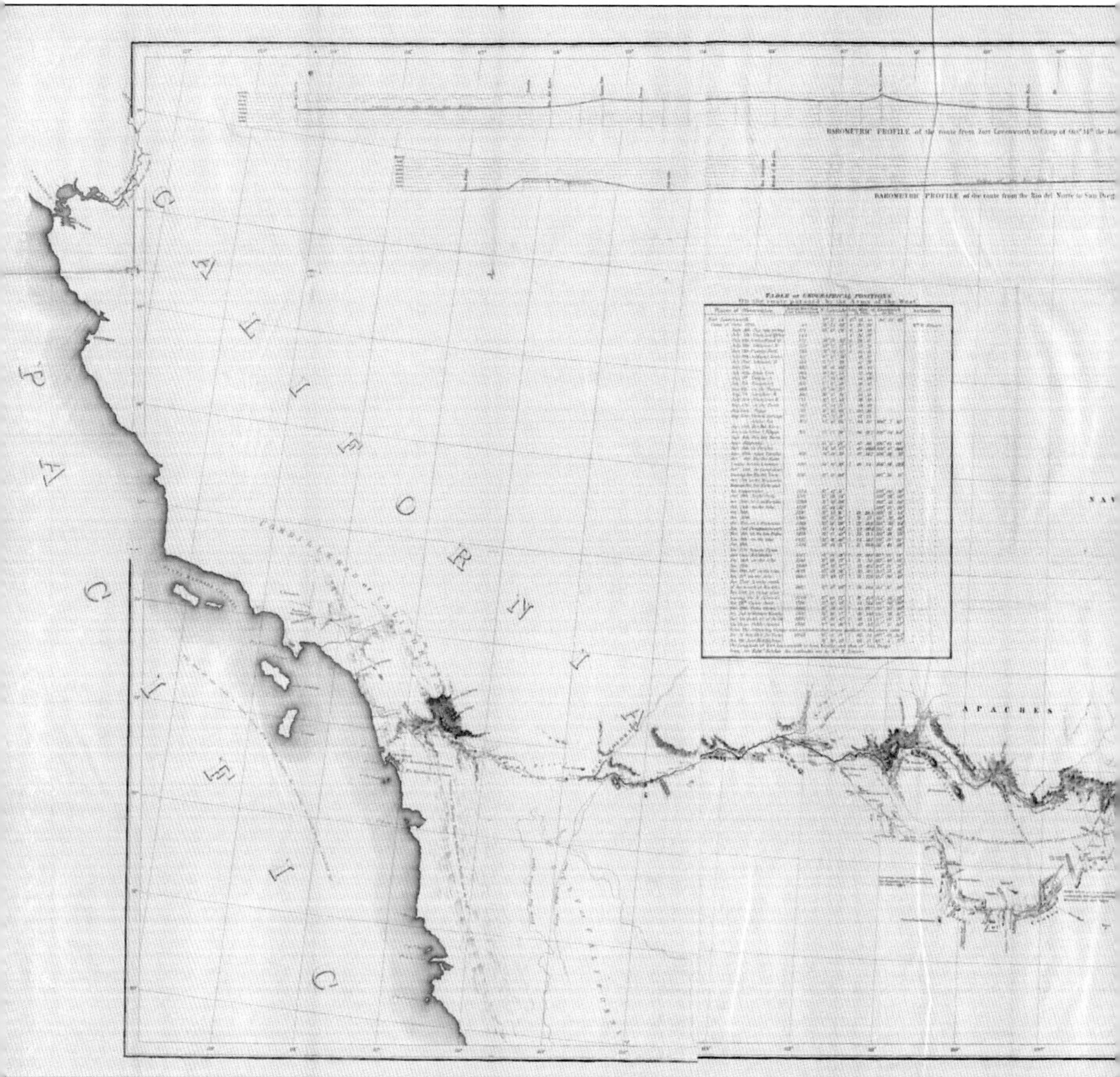

The historical record is unclear whether the Opa village disappeared or was overlooked by the vast number of gold-seekers who used the ancient route after the discovery of gold in California in 1848. Tens of thousands passed by on their way to the coast, but the 19th century argonauts typically were focused on prosperous labor positions in the nascent California mining industry and not so much on cultural tourism. Many who traversed the route used William H. Emory's

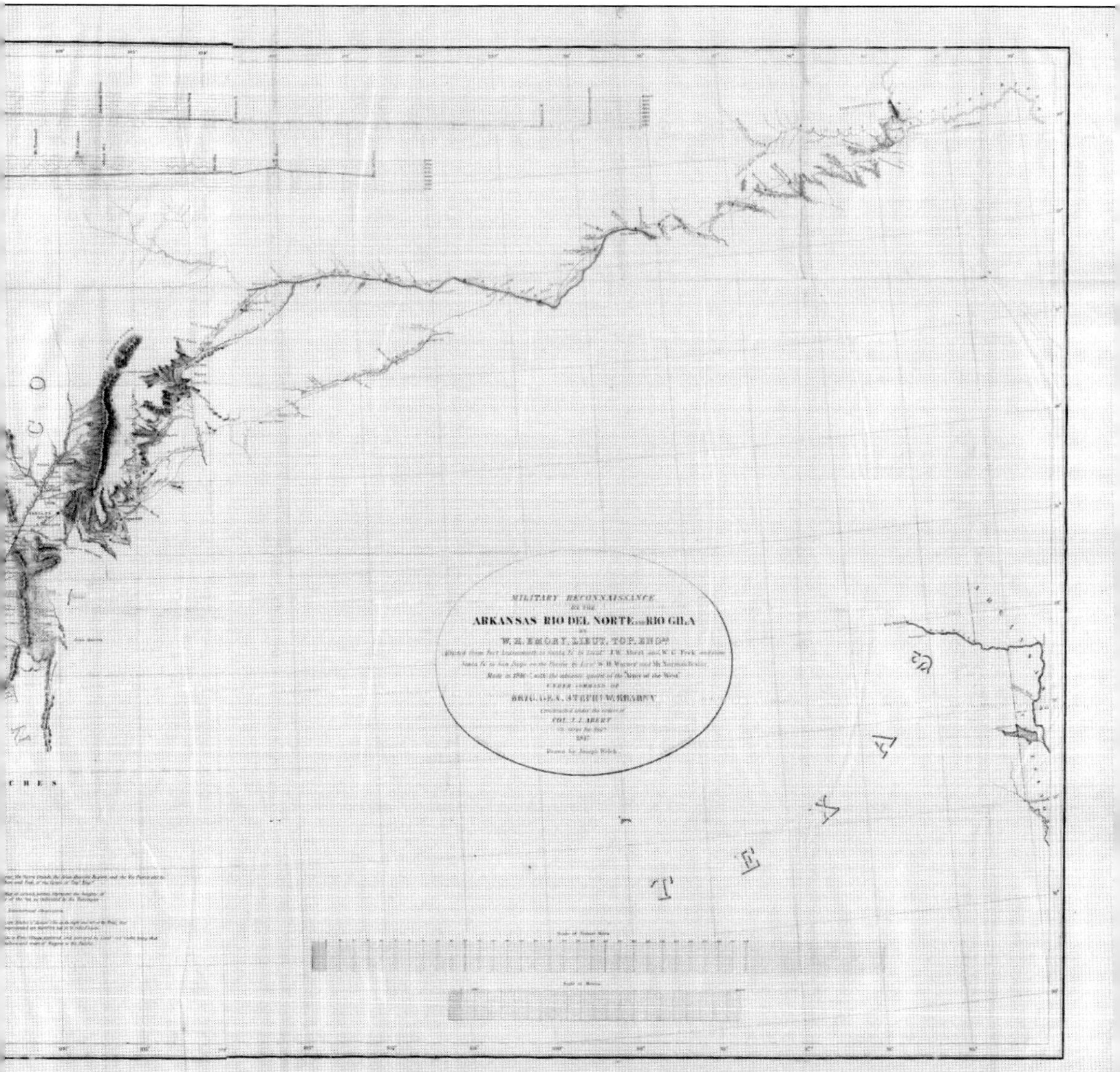

1847 *Notes of a Military Reconnoissance* [*sic*] to guide them through this area. (From *Notes of a Military Reconnoissance, From Fort Leavenworth, In Missouri, To San Diego, In California, Including Part of the Arkansas, Del Norte, and Gila Rivers* by W.H. Emory, Corps Topographical Engineers. Made in 1846–7, with the Advanced Guard of the "Army of the West." Washington: Wendell and van Benthuysen, Printers, 1848.)

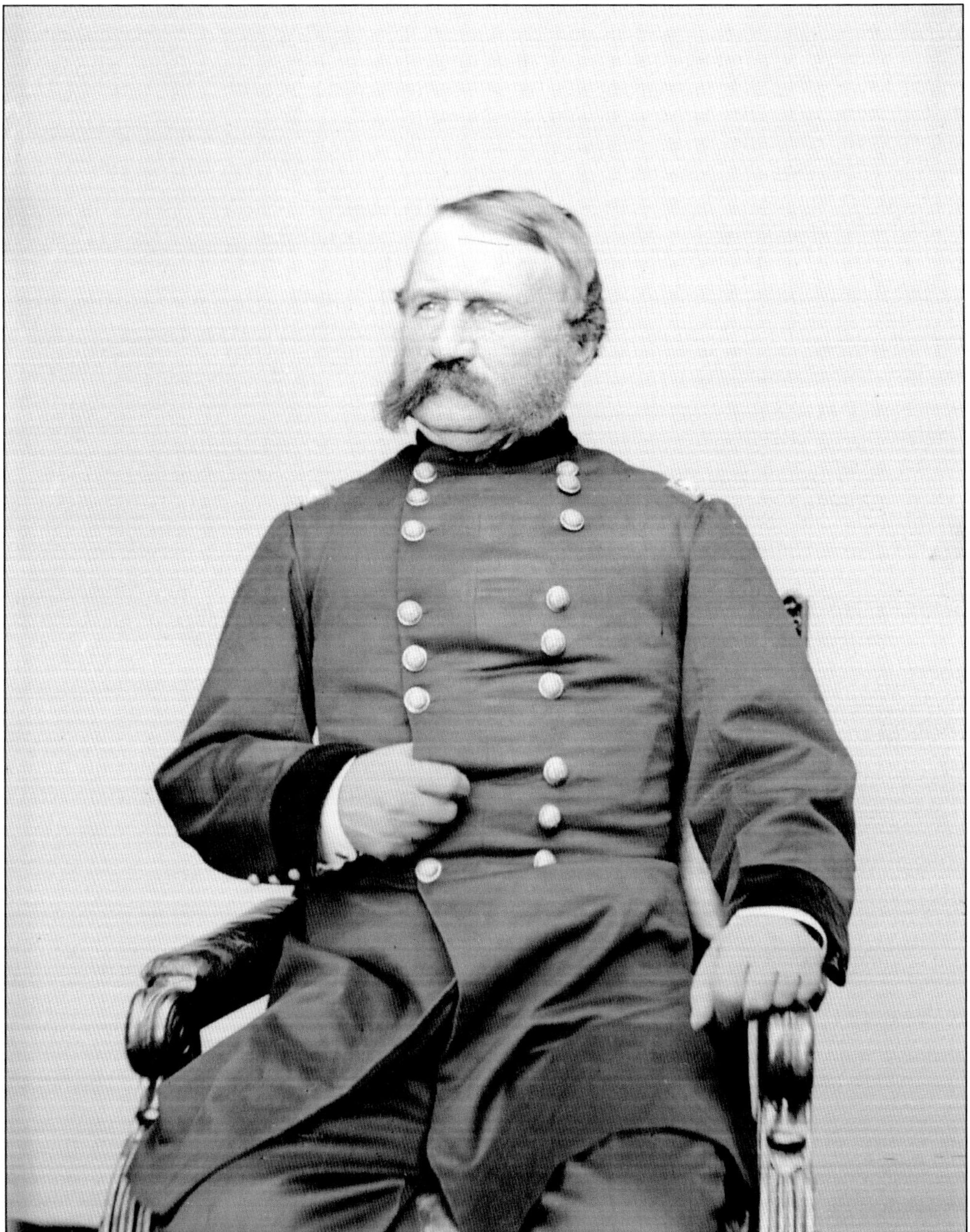

Emory was a first lieutenant in the Army of the West, which marched from to St. Louis to San Diego during the war with Mexico. In his report, which was accompanied by the map on pages 16 and 17, Emory told of ancient ditches and broken pottery, as well as modern tenements he believed might be the work of Cocomaricopa (Pee Posh) Indians. When he passed through the area in 1846, he noted that one Dr. Anderson, who had traveled the route two decades before, referred to the village at the bend as "Tezotal." He later used this name on his 1857 map of the border. This photograph of Emory was taken between 1855 and 1865. (Courtesy of the Library of Congress, Prints & Photographs Division, Reproduction LC-DIG-cwpbh-00808.)

The Pee Posh (also known as Maricopa or Cocomaricopa, as they are sometimes referred to by early diarists) lived along the lower Gila River and on the Colorado River until being displaced through intertribal warfare with other Yuma language–speaking groups. Eventually, the Pee Posh would join forces with the Akimel O'odham (Pima Indians) upstream in what is now the Gila River Indian Reservation. Being adjacent to their neighbors, they shared many of their traditions, such as the harvesting of saguaro fruit as seen in this 1907 photograph. (Courtesy of the Library of Congress, Prints & Photographs Division, Edward S. Curtis Collection, LC-USZ62-106799.)

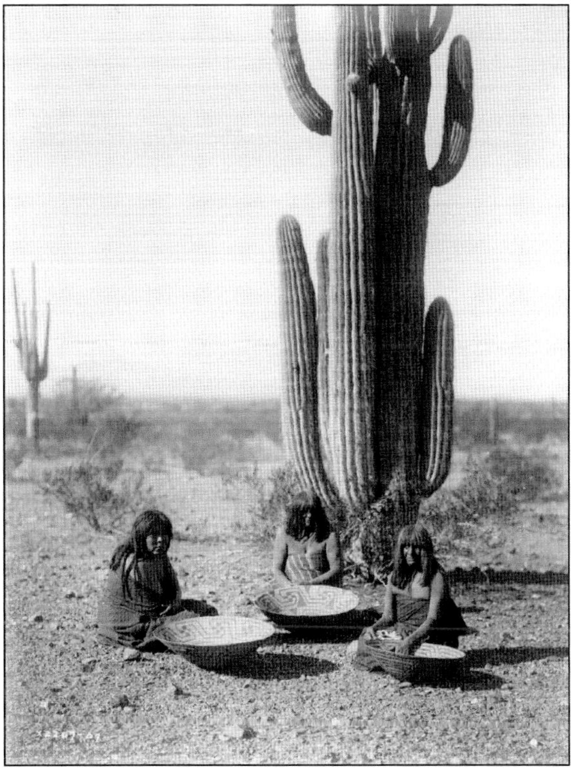

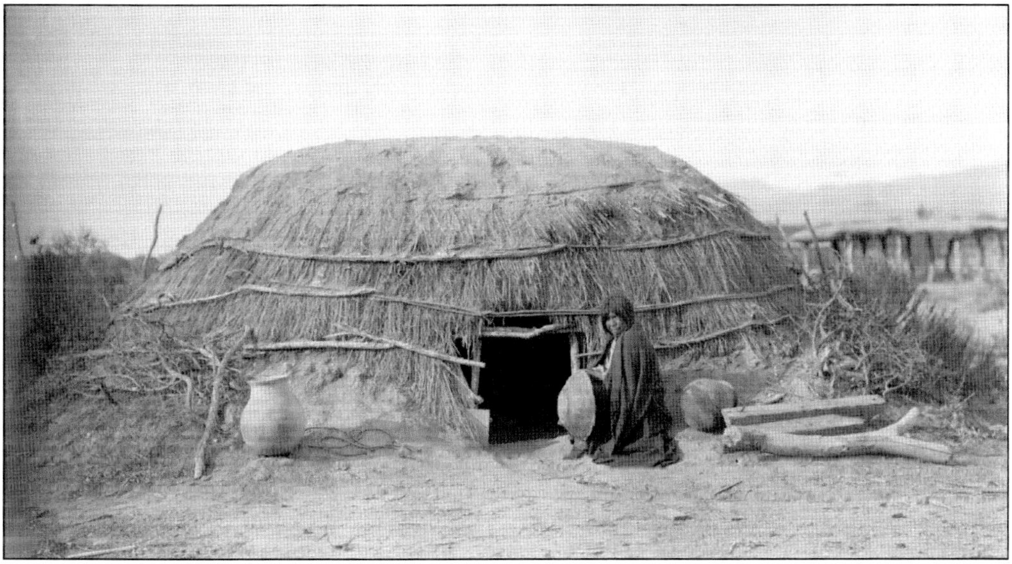

Up to and through the 19th century, the Pee Posh and Akimel O'odham lived in houses very similar to the pit houses of the Hohokam. These houses, as shown in the photograph, were called *ki*—the O'odham word for house or home—and were constructed of reeds, branches, or other local resources, supported by wood beams, and sometimes covered in a caliche stucco. Well insulated, the ki provided protection from the elements. The structure in this 1907 photograph is made of arrow weed, a plant that grows in the sandy washes of the American Southwest. (Courtesy of the Library of Congress, Prints & Photographs Division, Edward S. Curtis Collection, LC-USZ62-106799.)

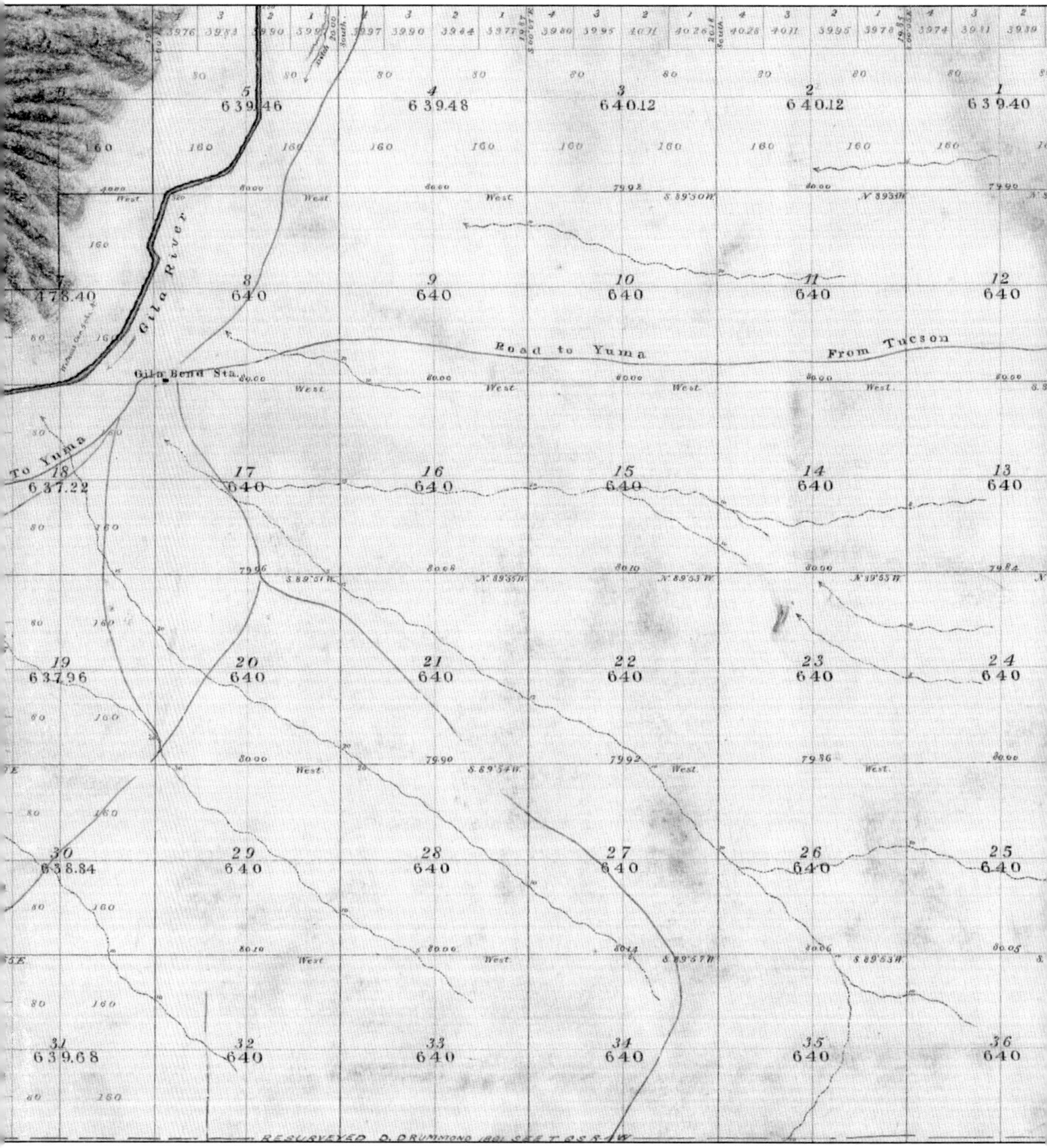

In the summer of 1858, the Butterfield Overland Mail Company, under contract to provide mail service, built a station called Gila Ranch near a Pee Posh Indian village at the big bend. A freight road between El Paso and Fort Yuma was contracted with James Leach at the same time and intercepted the Butterfield route at the Gila River Indian villages about 50 miles east of the station. Between the villages and the station was a 40-mile expanse of rugged and mostly waterless desert. Though the mail and stage line ceased with the outbreak of the Civil War, the road was the best southern route through the American Southwest. After the war, Albert Decker and Thomas Childs opened a ditch and grew grain near the bend, making a handsome profit from freighters. (Courtesy of the Bureau of Land Management.)

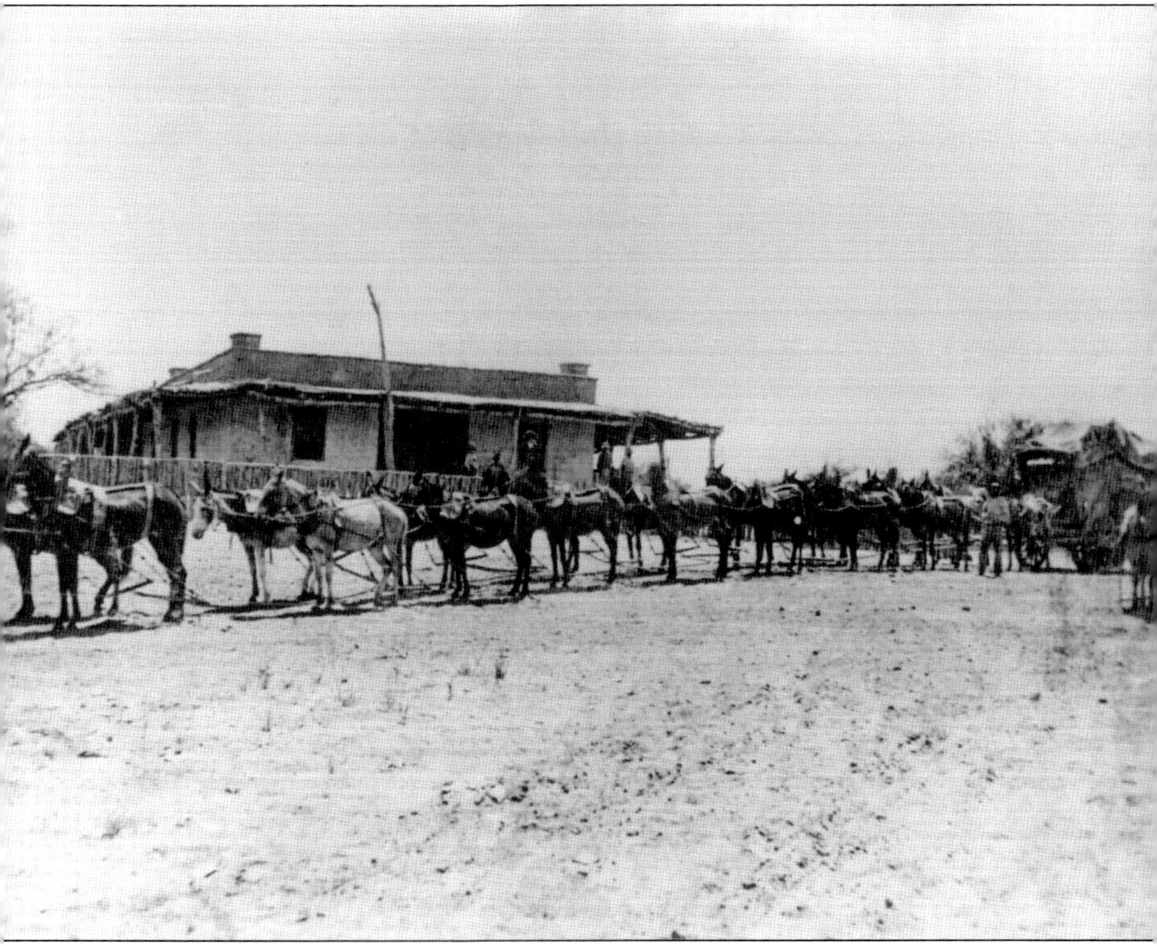

Decker became the agent for the new Gila Bend station. When a post office was established in 1871, he became its first postmaster. Early American conservationist Josephine Clifford dedicated an entire chapter of her 1877 book *Overland Tales* to a romance at the station, reflecting, "How charming the grove of trees looks, when you draw up under their shadow at Gila Bend, after days of travel over tedious sand-plains and through wildernesses of greasewood and cactus." (Courtesy of Arizona State Libraries, Archives, and Public Records, 97-0734.)

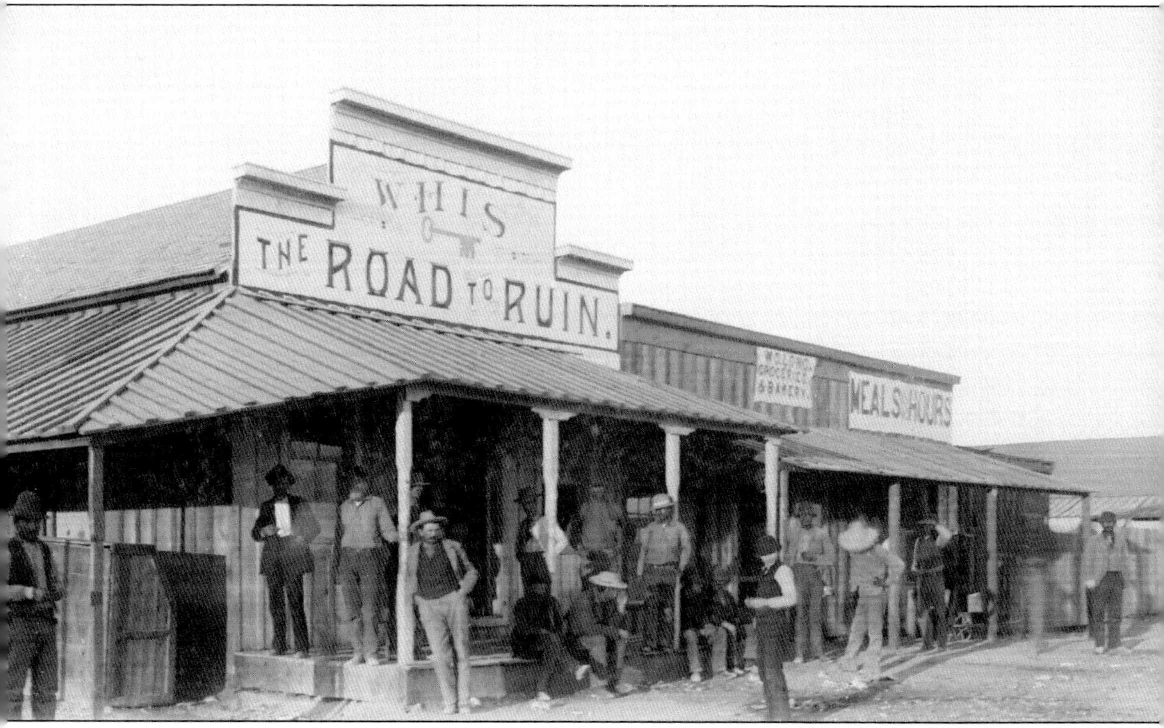

According to the Arizona State Archives, this saloon, with the colorful moniker Whis "key," the Road to Ruin was a regular hangout for Arizona ranger Harry Wheeler. This is doubtful, as the photograph was taken in the 1880s, when Wheeler was between 5 and 15 years old. However, the name proved popular, and more than one drinking establishment has adopted it. A replica of the saloon was built in the Pioneer Village north of Phoenix, but the name was removed when the building was converted into a more family-friendly gift shop. (Courtesy of Arizona State Libraries, Archives, and Public Records, 98-0582.)

Two

TRAINS, PLANES, AND DOODLE BUGS

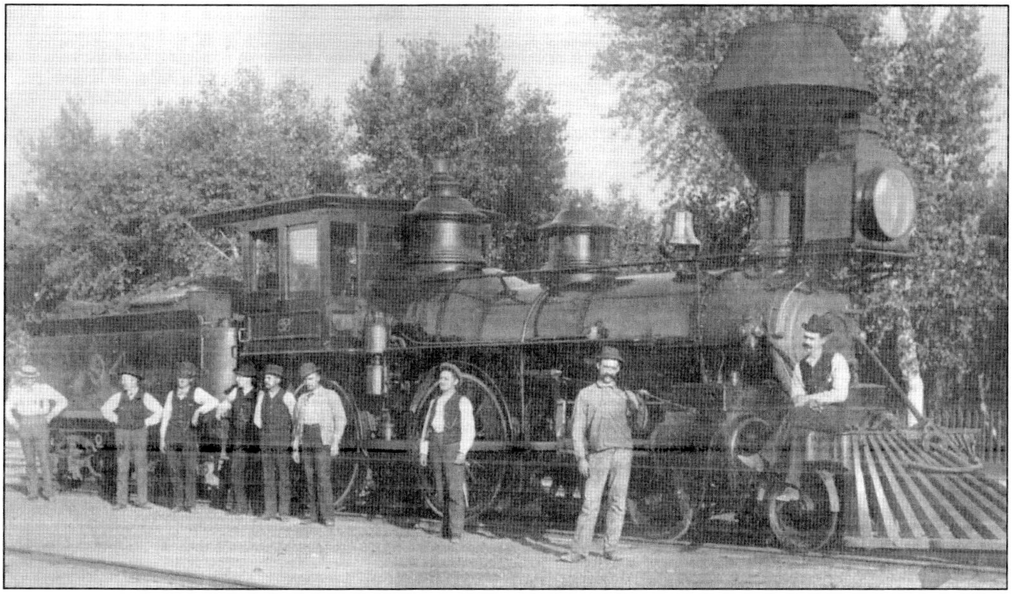

Under the banner of the Southern Pacific, the transcontinental railroad arrived at Gila Bend in 1879 on its way to eventually connect the West Coast with Texas and points east. At the time, the number of people living at the stage-stop community had to be small; federal census records show only 40 people living in the area, and that included the community of Agua Caliente 35 miles to the west. The rail line was three miles south of the station, and the town slowly gravitated towards the tracks. (Courtesy of the Gila Bend Museum.)

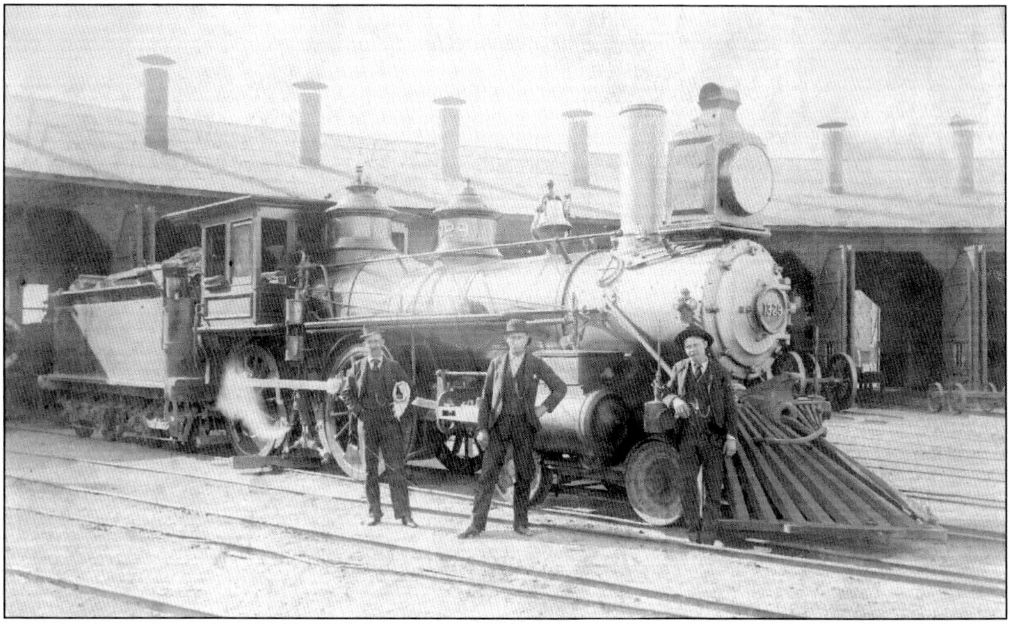

The Southern Pacific needed facilities for supplying coal and water for steam engines and for the changing crews and machinery; Gila Bend was a perfect candidate. The station, called Gila, was an ideal location for railroad facilities between Tucson and Yuma, and in 1885, the federal government granted land to the railroad company for its use. The railroad constructed a bunkhouse, depot and section house, roundhouse, coal shed, and water tank. As the railroad property continued to develop, more settlers moved away from the old station to the new location. (Courtesy of Edward Stout.)

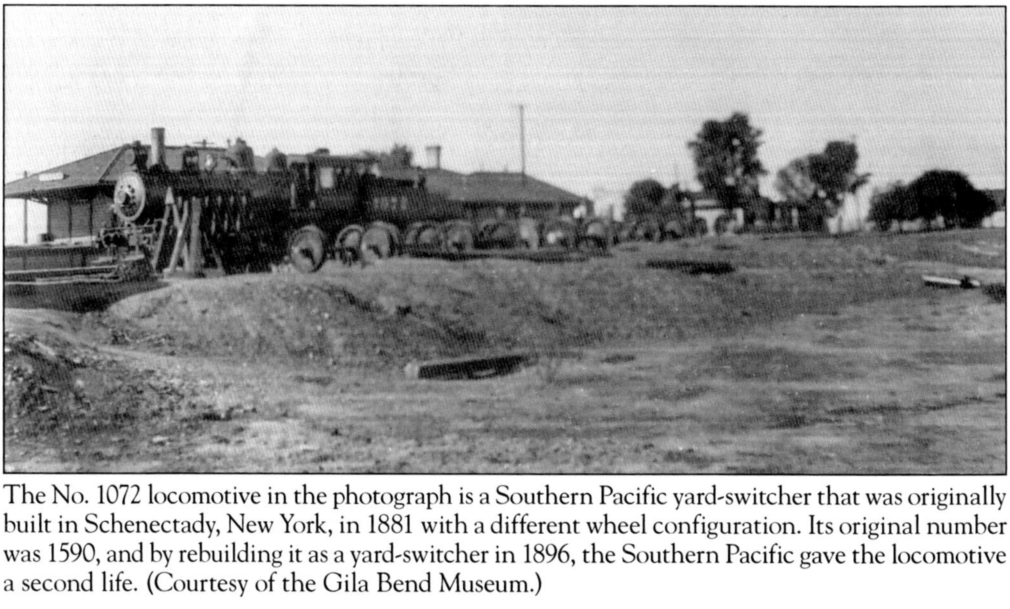

The No. 1072 locomotive in the photograph is a Southern Pacific yard-switcher that was originally built in Schenectady, New York, in 1881 with a different wheel configuration. Its original number was 1590, and by rebuilding it as a yard-switcher in 1896, the Southern Pacific gave the locomotive a second life. (Courtesy of the Gila Bend Museum.)

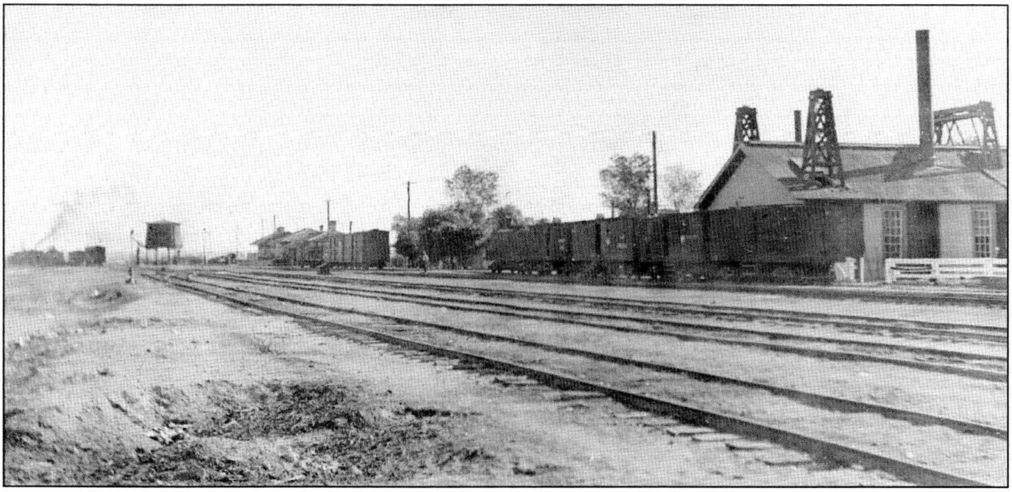

Railroad cars are waiting to be loaded at what appears to be a combination power plant and icehouse in this photograph. Operating an ice plant in conjunction with an electrical power plant was quite common. While providing electricity for day-to-day operation of the railroad yard, the Southern Pacific also provided ice for shipping produce to points east and west. (Courtesy of the Gila Bend Museum.)

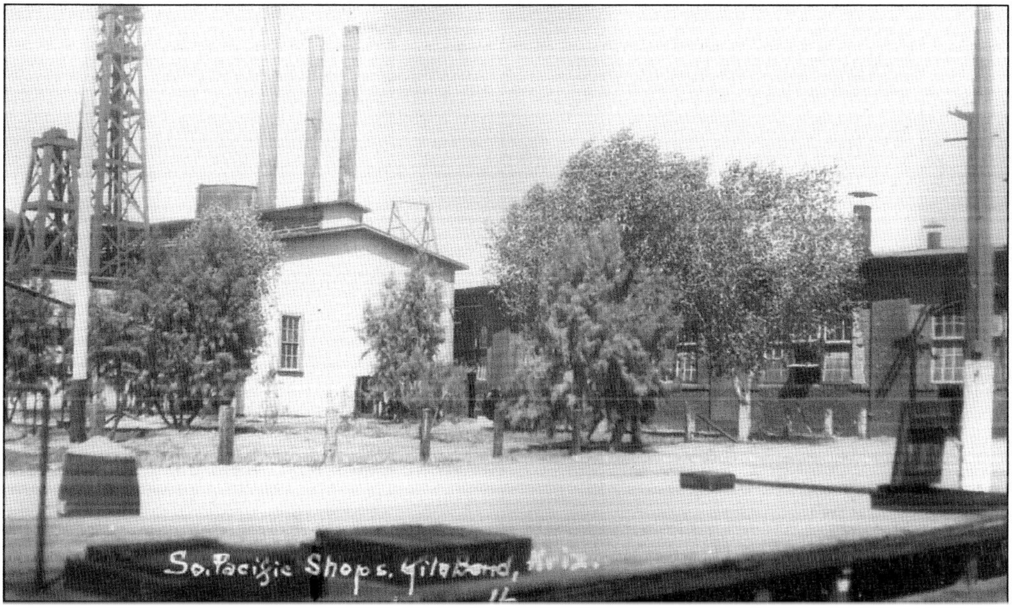

The Southern Pacific had a complex of support buildings including the powerhouse on the left and the roundhouse on the right. These buildings were collectively referred to as "the shops." (Courtesy of the Gila Bend Museum.)

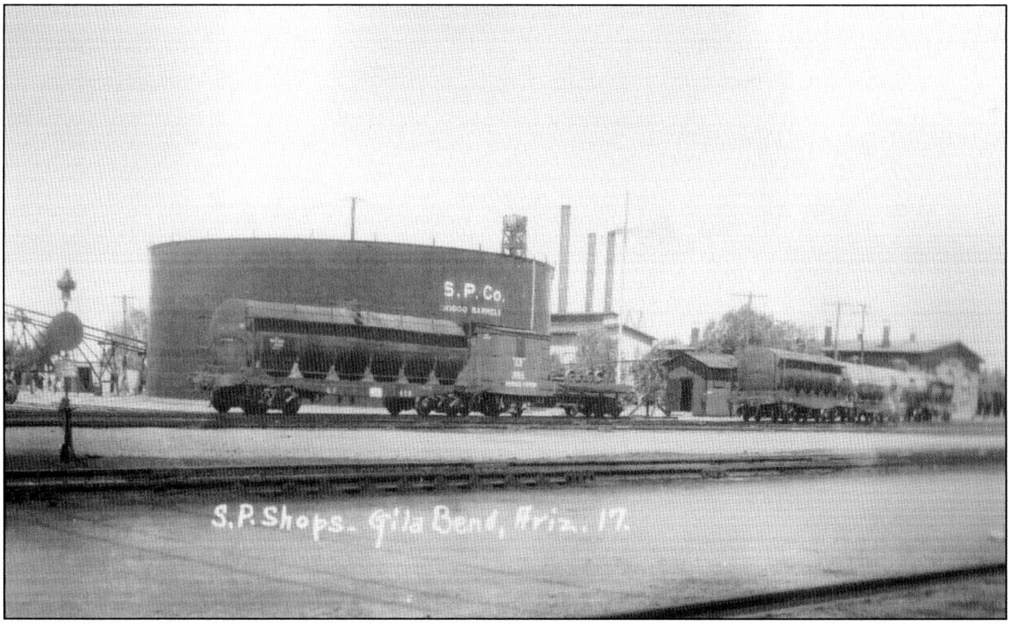

West of the shops was an immense tank capable of holding 30,000 gallons of fuel. Also in this photograph is the derrick tender, which was used for clearing and repairing track. (Courtesy of the Gila Bend Museum.)

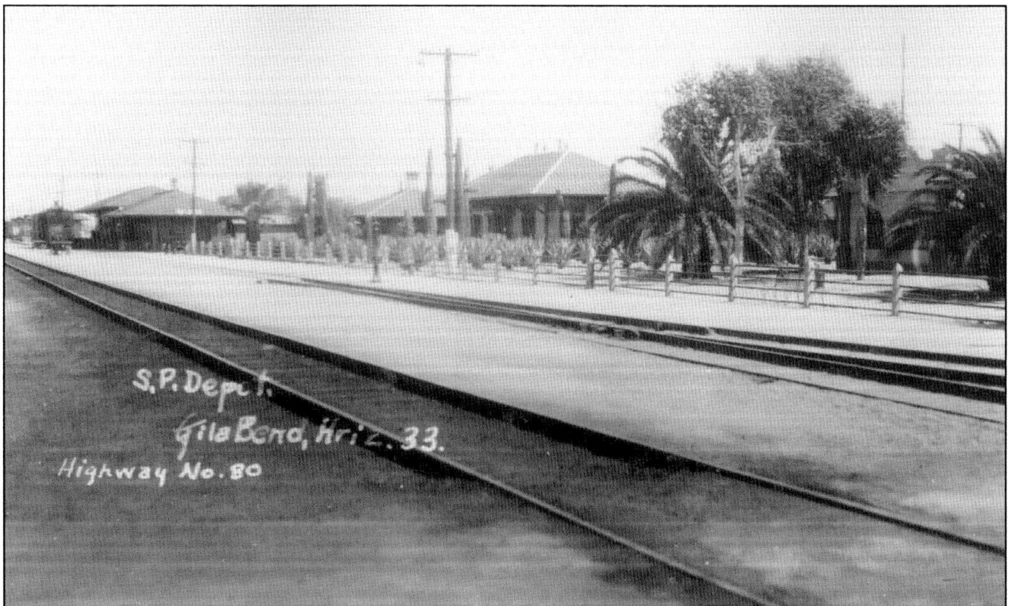

This view of the Southern Pacific railroad yards shows, from left to right, the depot, superintendent's residence, hospital, and clubhouse. (Courtesy of the Gila Bend Museum.)

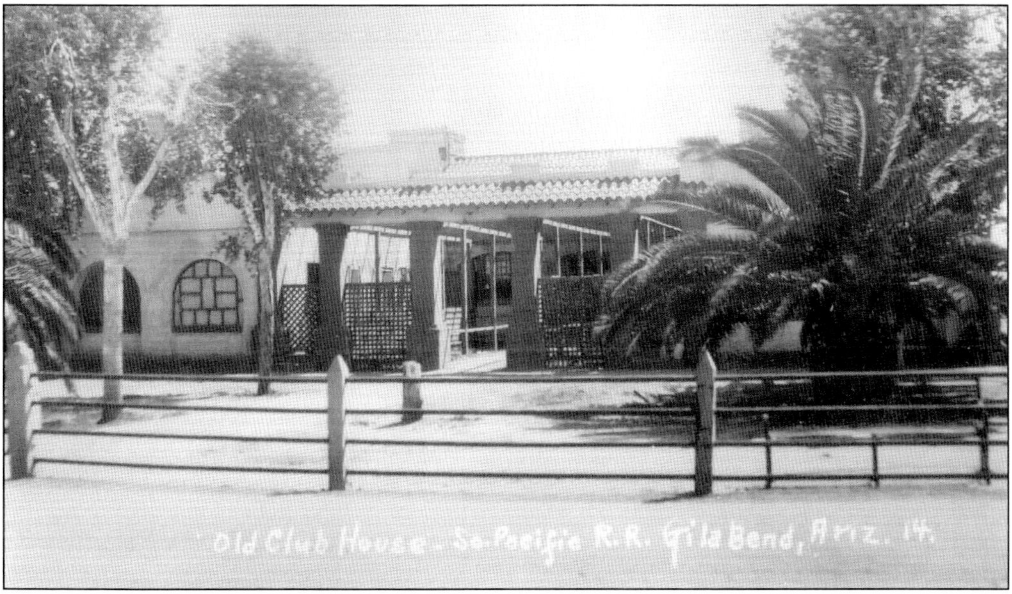

The clubhouse is an unusual structure with an arbor entry. In this photograph, it is already considered old. (Courtesy of Johnny Laird.)

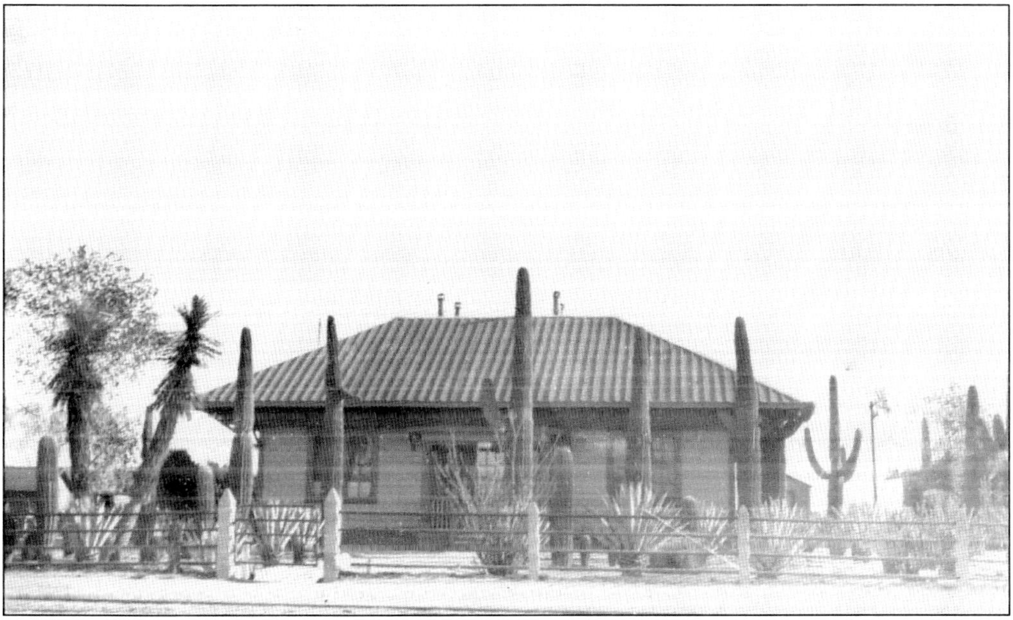

The hospital was built around 1912, and the grounds were decorated with saguaro cactus and agave plants. (Courtesy of the Gila Bend Museum.)

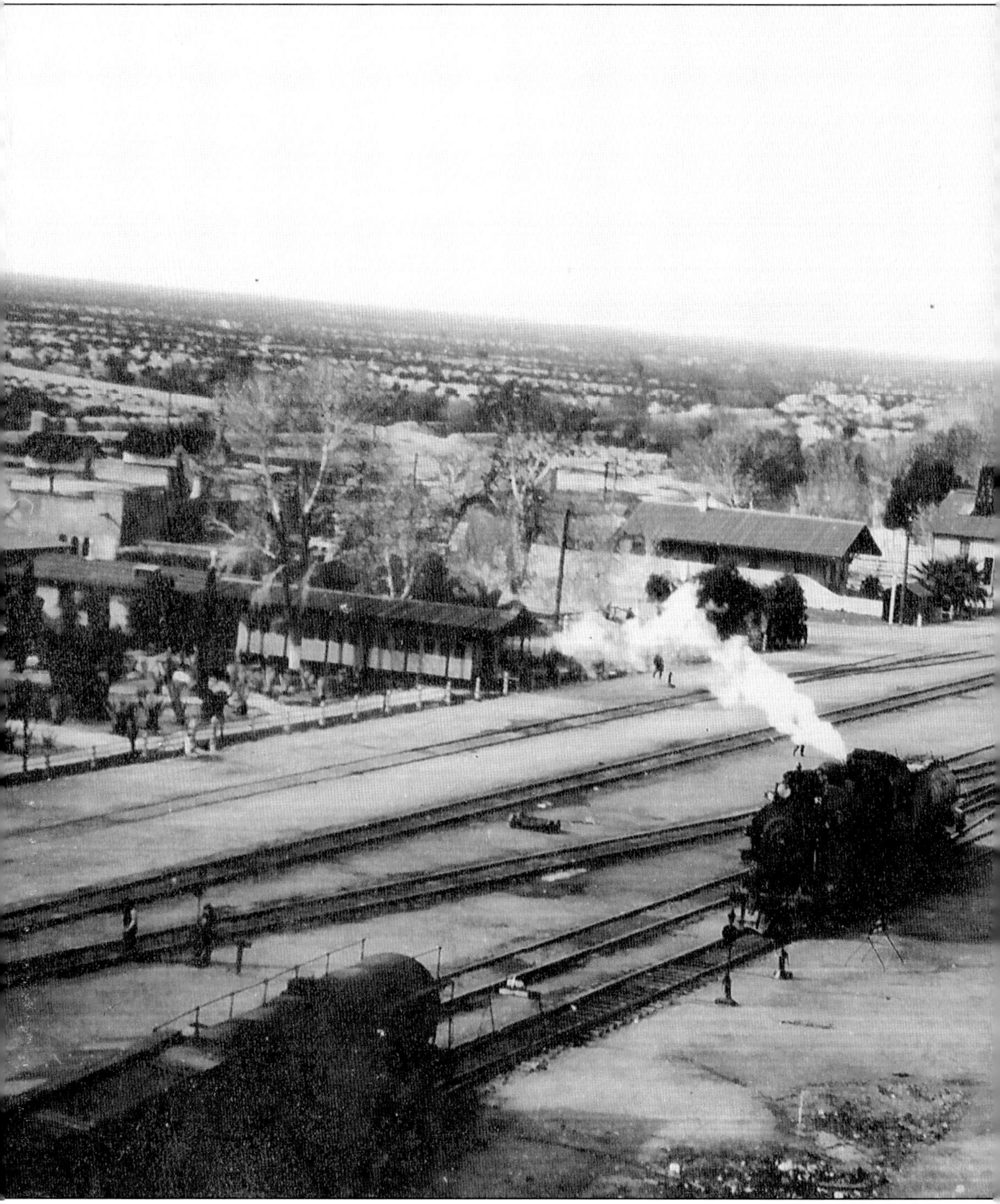

This photograph was possibly taken from the roof of the water tank. The buildings on the left (south) of the tracks are, from left to right, the bunkhouse, a residence, the powerhouse, icehouse,

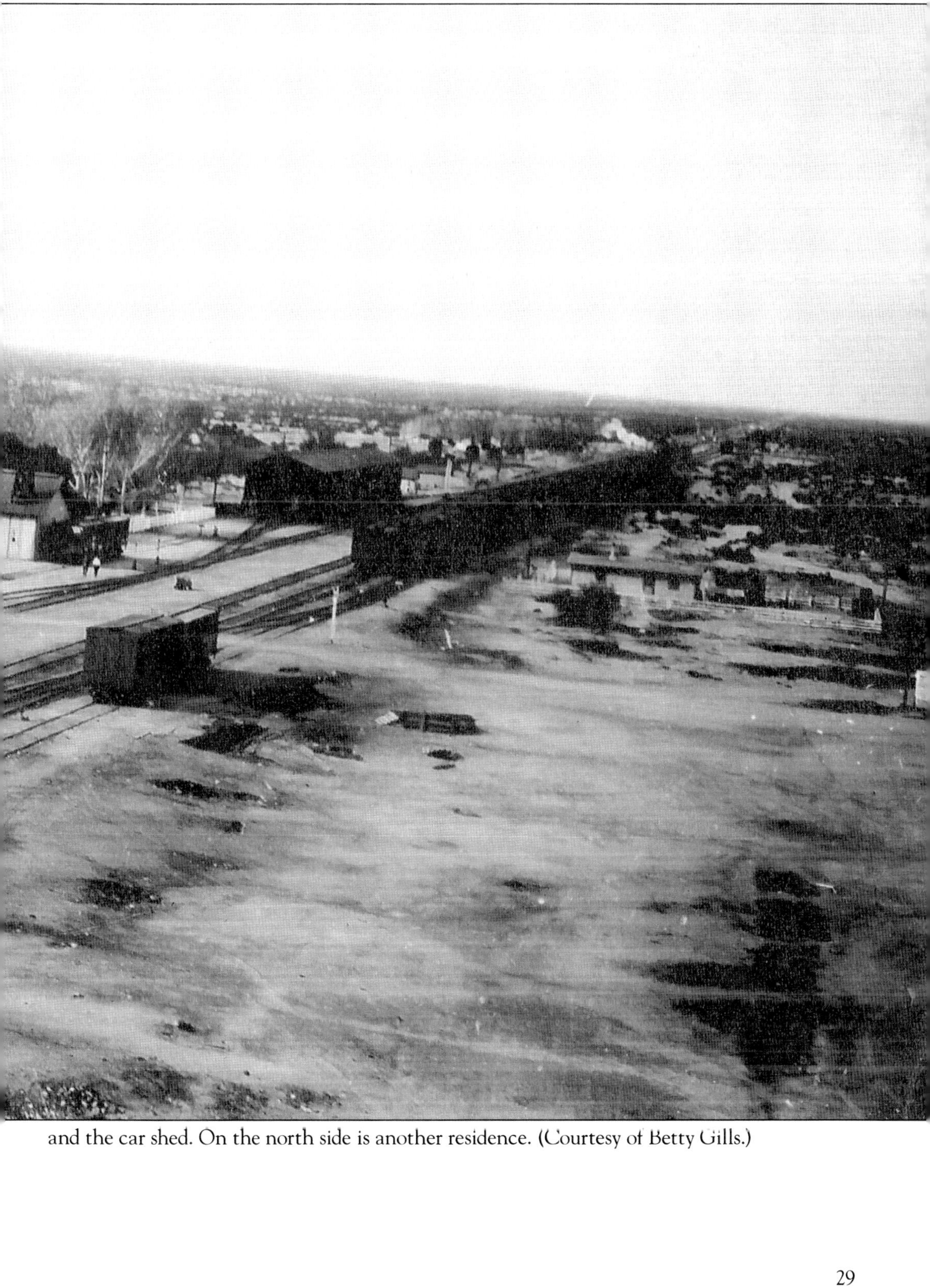

and the car shed. On the north side is another residence. (Courtesy of Betty Gills.)

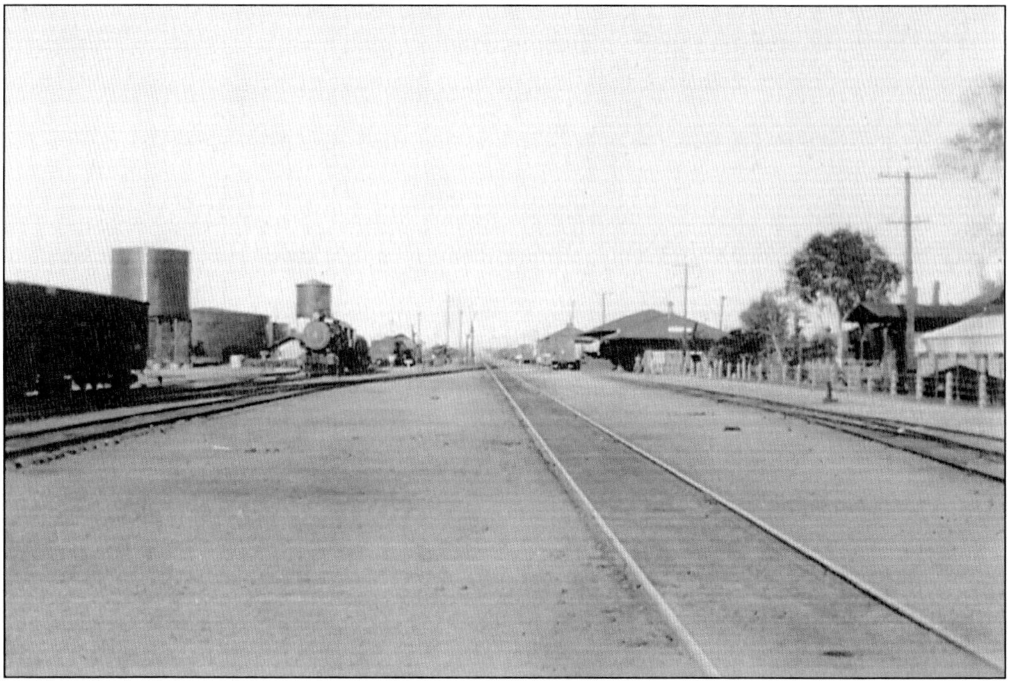

This photograph, originally identified as "Main Street in 1930–1934," is actually looking eastward along the tracks. Main Street is further to the south (left) on the other side of the Southern Pacific buildings. (Courtesy of the Gila Bend Museum.)

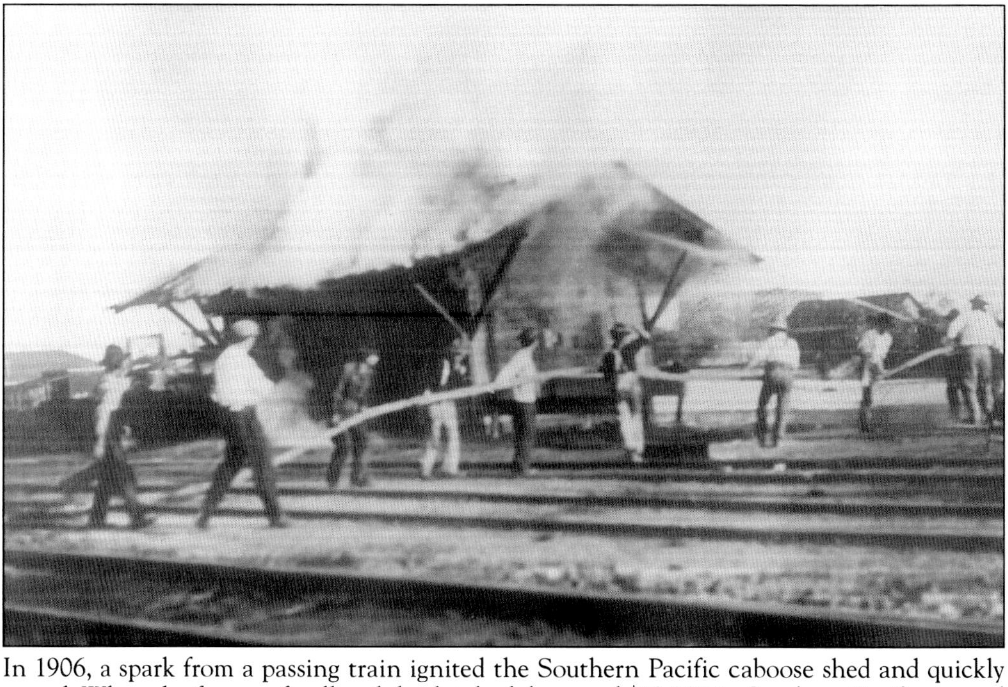

In 1906, a spark from a passing train ignited the Southern Pacific caboose shed and quickly spread. When the fire was finally subdued, it had destroyed $10,000 in Southern Pacific–owned buildings. Another blaze in 1912 destroyed the foreman's office and toolshed despite the efforts to extinguish it, as shown in the photograph. (Courtesy of the Gila Bend Museum.)

On an inaugural flight from Santa Barbara to Washington, DC, this twin-engine Loughead (Lockheed) F-1A—a land version of the F-1 seaplane—experienced trouble and landed in Gila Bend in November 1918, with the whole town turning out to watch. (Courtesy of the Gila Bend Museum.)

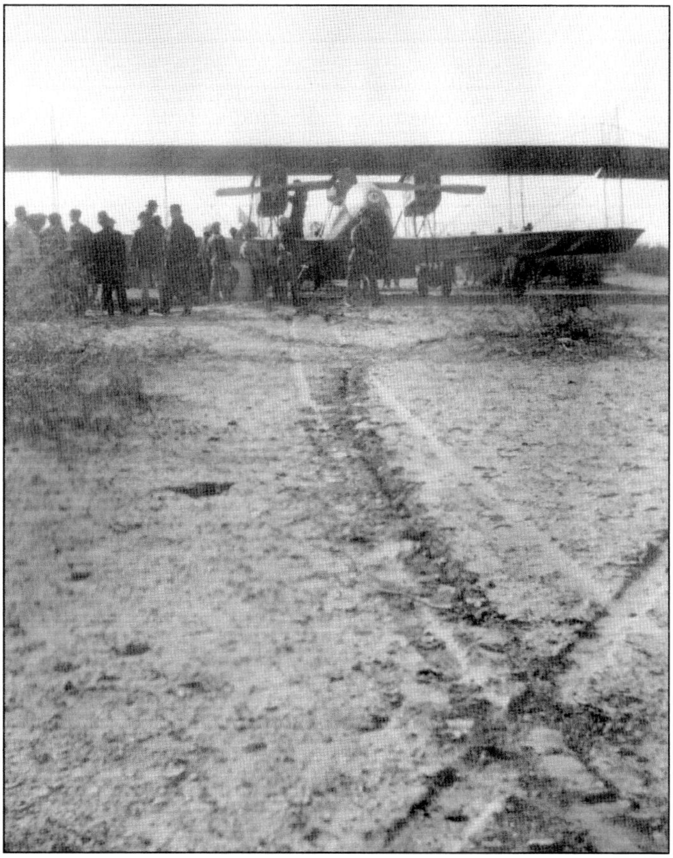

On the first attempt to take off from an improvised airfield near town, the plane blew a tire trying to outmaneuver one of the locals who tried racing the plane in his Ford. (Courtesy of the Gila Bend Museum.)

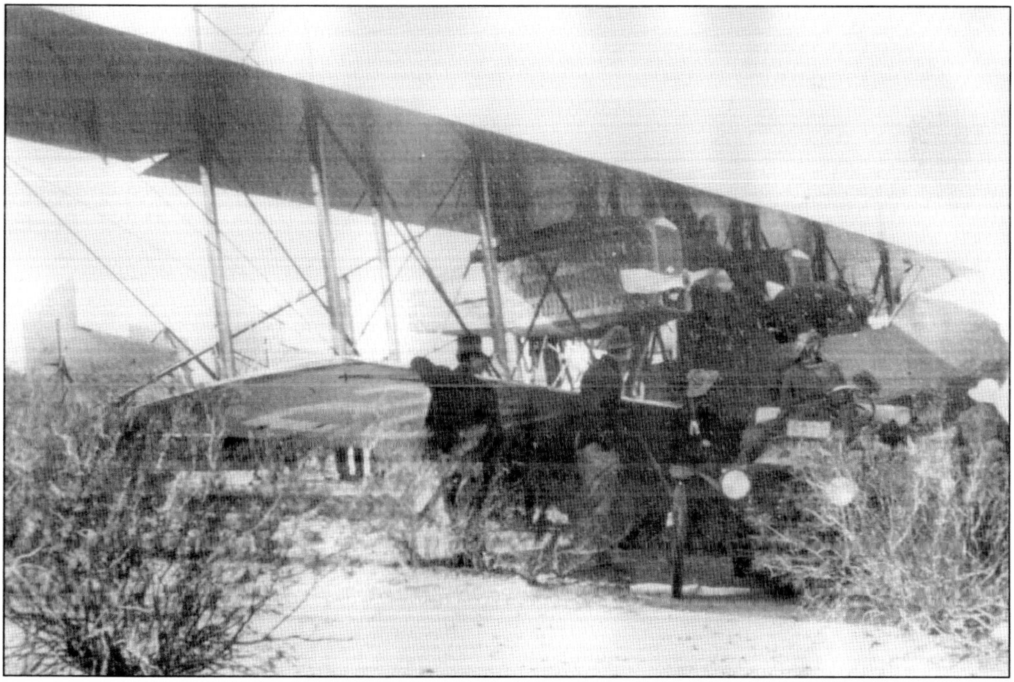

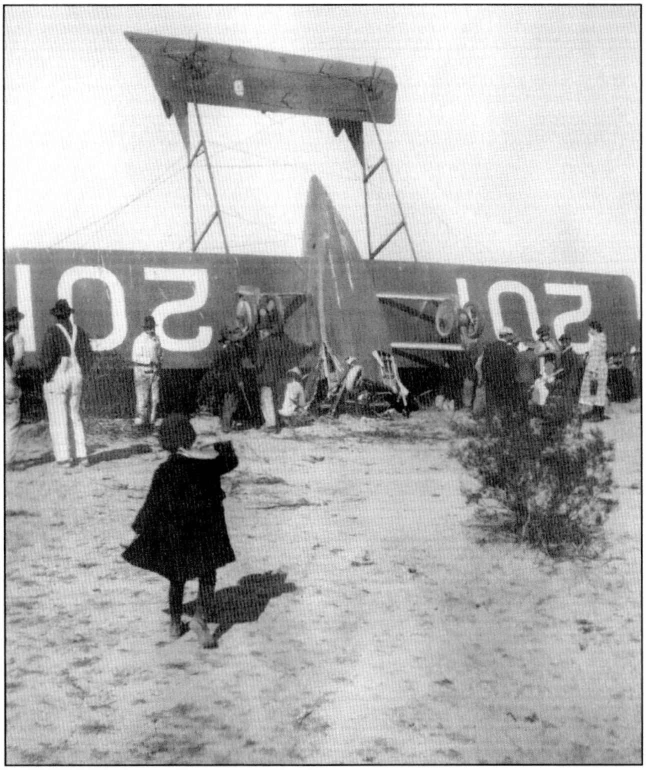

On the second attempt, the left engine stopped, and the plane nosed into the ground, pinning the crewmen beneath. The crash ended the Loughead F-1A's one and only attempt at a transcontinental flight. (Courtesy of the Gila Bend Museum.)

Pilot Bob Ferneau was unhurt, but crewmen Leo Flint and Swede Meyerhoffer were badly injured. The plane also did not fare well, and since parts were rare, difficult to acquire, or nonexistent, the flight was cancelled. (Courtesy of the Gila Bend Museum.)

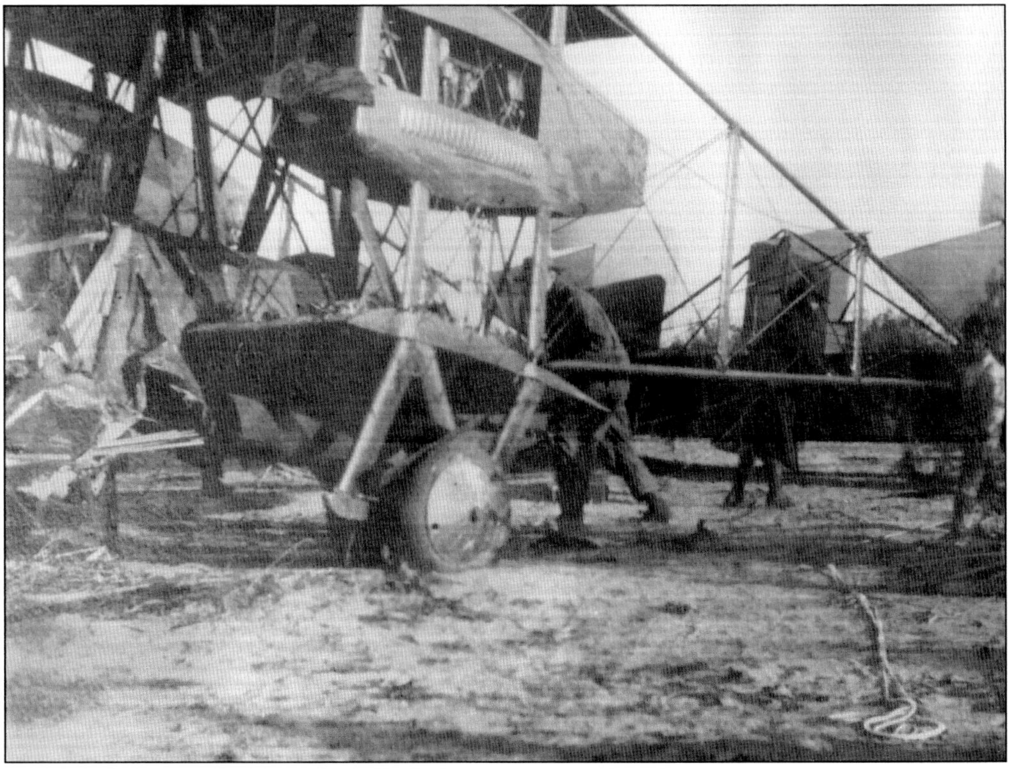

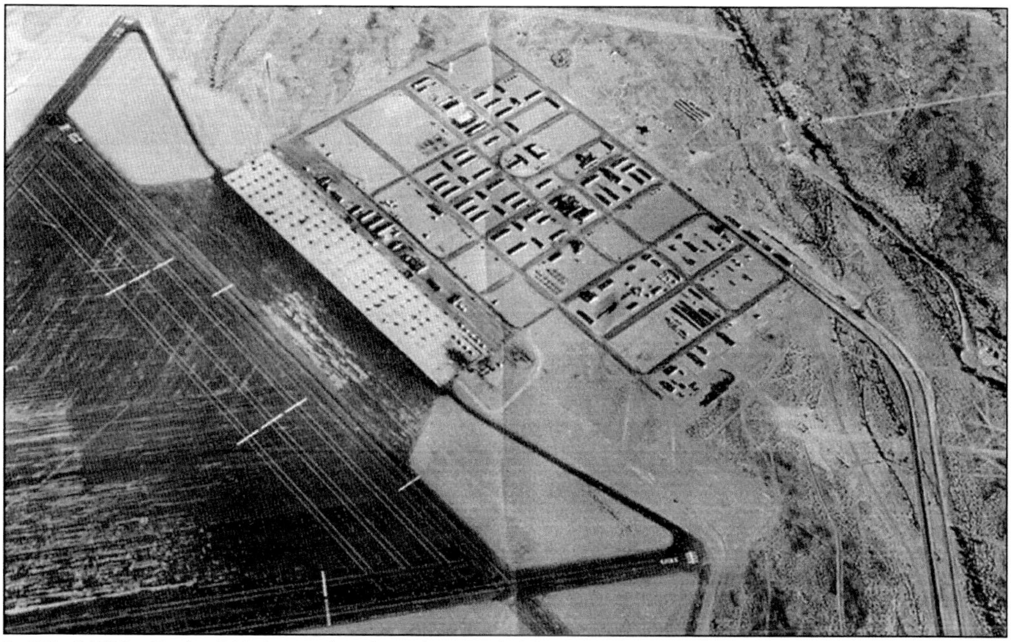

In World War II, the US Army developed an airfield in conjunction with Gila Bend Bombing and Gunnery Range. Located six miles from Gila Bend's downtown, the field (shown here in an aerial from 1943) consisted of three runways running north-south, east-west, and northeast-southwest. The first was 150 feet wide and 6,200 feet in length, while the other two were 150 feet by 5,200 feet. Additionally, three smaller fields were part of the auxiliary complex. Each of those fields was on 640 acres of land and were accompanied by three 150-by-3,654-foot runways. (Courtesy of the US Air Force 442nd Fighter Wing.)

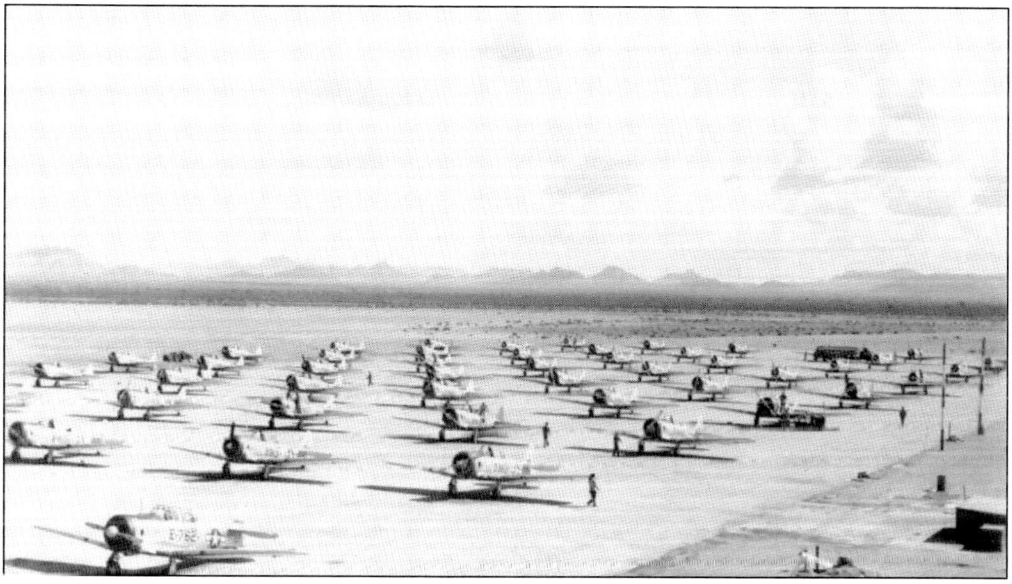

The preferred aircraft for training was the AT-6 Texan, a single-engine advanced trainer. Developed by North American Aviation, over 1,800 Texans were built for training during the war. The plane came with a 600-horsepower Pratt & Whitney engine and a removable wing center-section fuel tank. (Courtesy of the Air Force Historical Research Agency.)

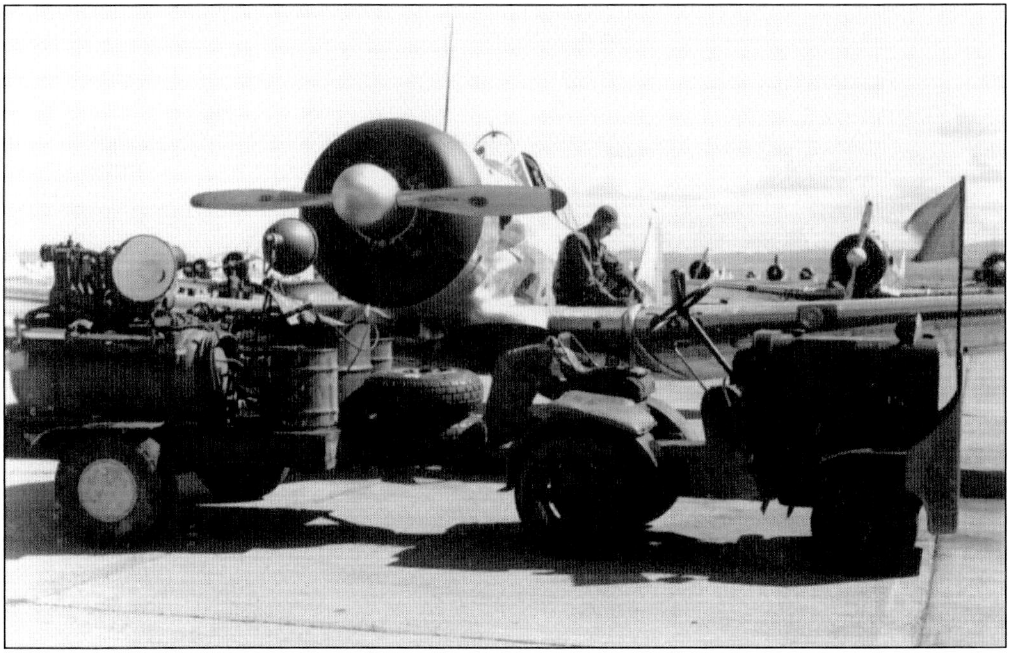

When properly maintained, the AT-6 had a range of 629 miles and a cruise speed of 145 miles per hour. Considered one of the most widely used planes in aviation history, the AT-6 was used as a trainer until fairly recently and was employed for both training and aerial combat in dozens of countries. (Courtesy of the Air Force Historical Research Agency.)

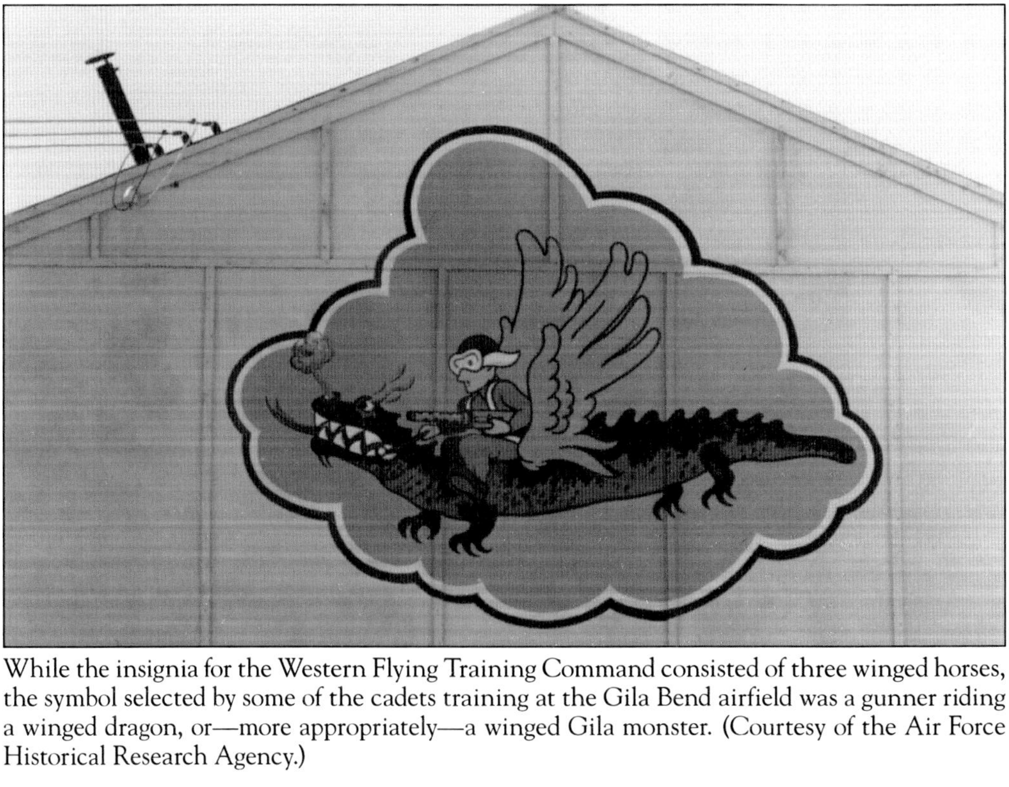

While the insignia for the Western Flying Training Command consisted of three winged horses, the symbol selected by some of the cadets training at the Gila Bend airfield was a gunner riding a winged dragon, or—more appropriately—a winged Gila monster. (Courtesy of the Air Force Historical Research Agency.)

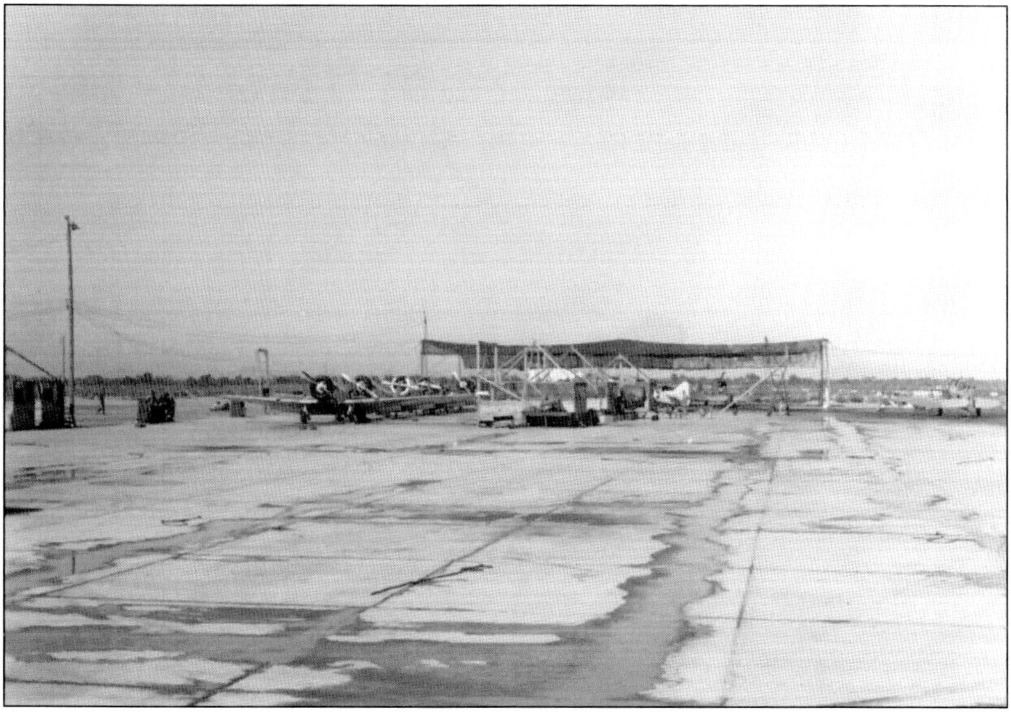

Early buildings at the Gila Bend training base were rudimentary, consisting of wood-framed, pyramid-roofed structures covered by tent canvas. (Courtesy of the Air Force Historical Research Agency.)

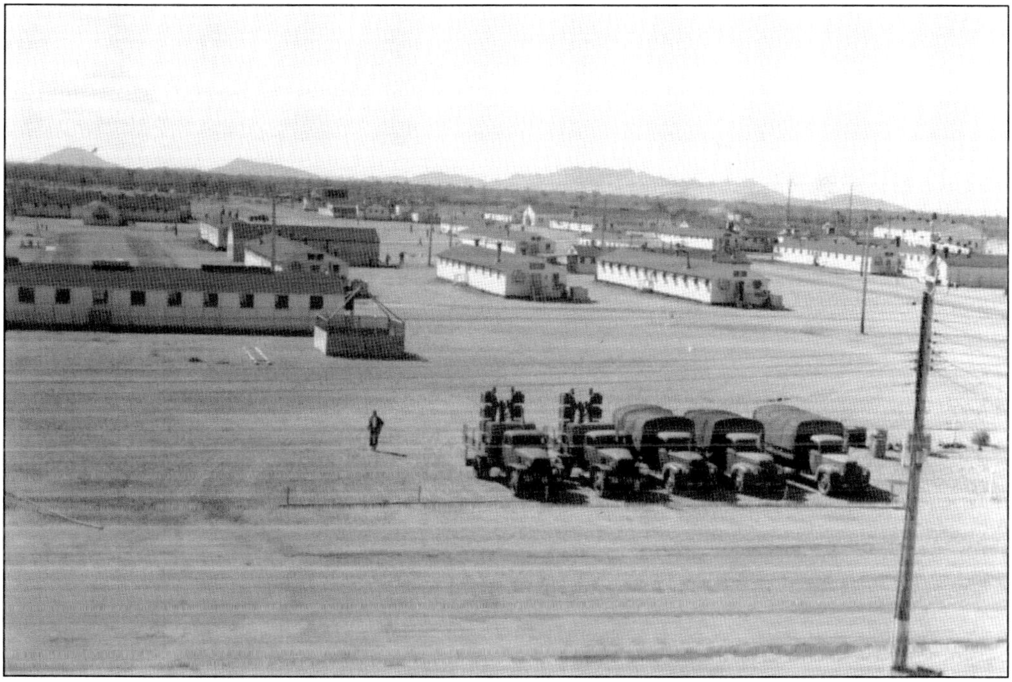

Within a short time, the complex was quite substantial. The tent houses gave way to large barrack-like structures. (Courtesy of the Air Force Historical Research Agency.)

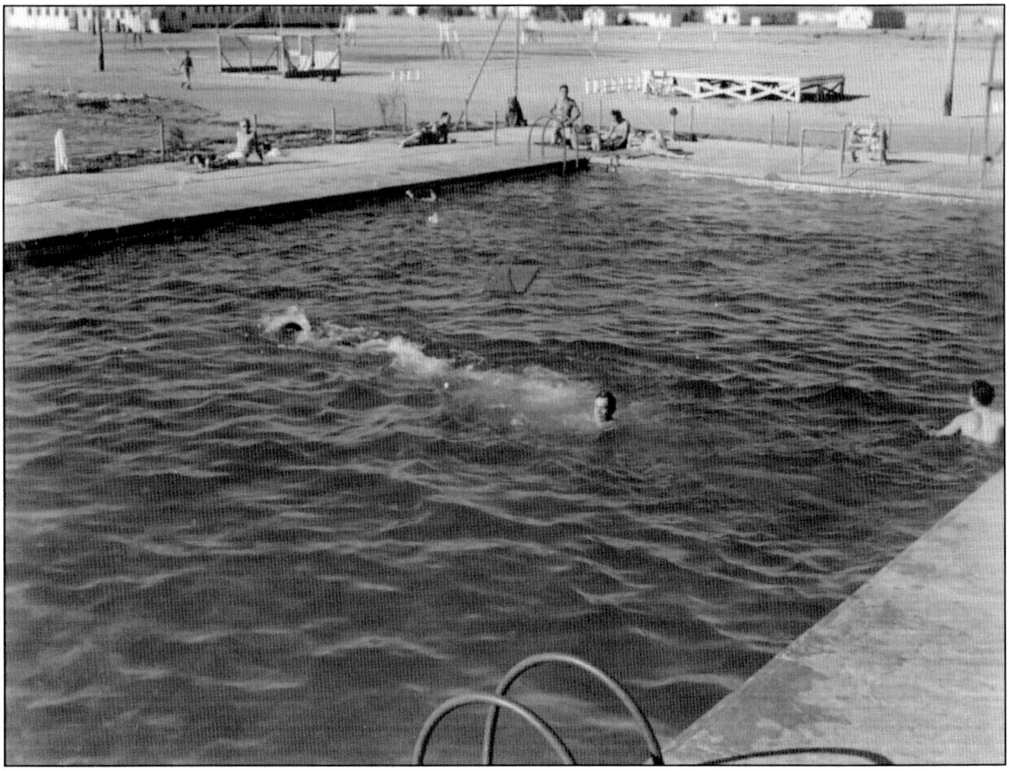

As anyone arriving at Phoenix's Sky Harbor Airport in the summer can attest, the large tarmac necessary for the runways creates stifling heat. Gila Bend's army airfield was no different, so a large swimming pool was built to provide a modicum of relief in the days before air-conditioning. (Courtesy of the Air Force Historical Research Agency.)

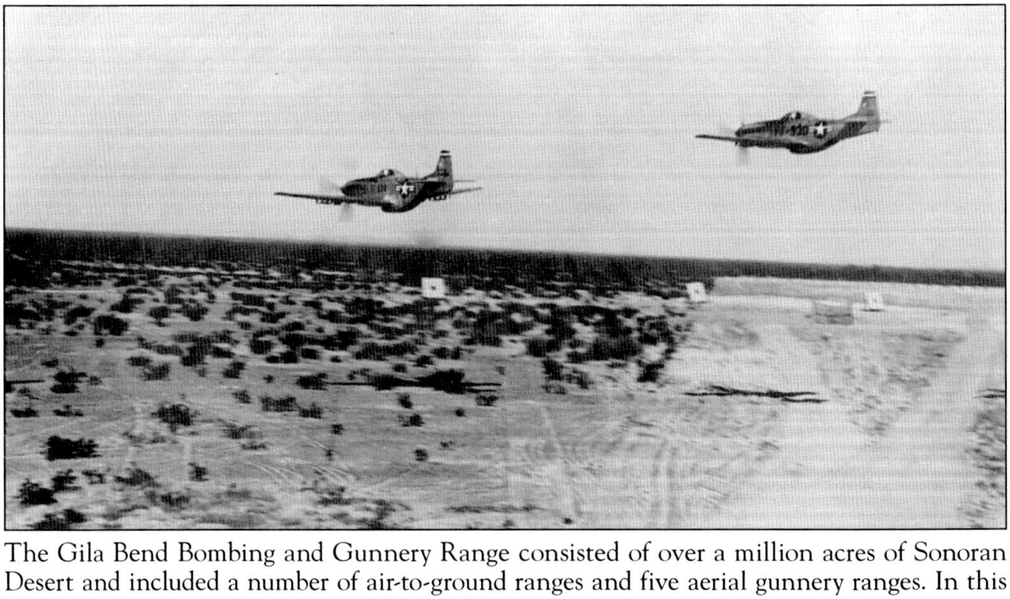

The Gila Bend Bombing and Gunnery Range consisted of over a million acres of Sonoran Desert and included a number of air-to-ground ranges and five aerial gunnery ranges. In this photograph, P-51 Mustangs are conducting low-strafing passes. (Courtesy of the US Air Force 442nd Fighter Wing.)

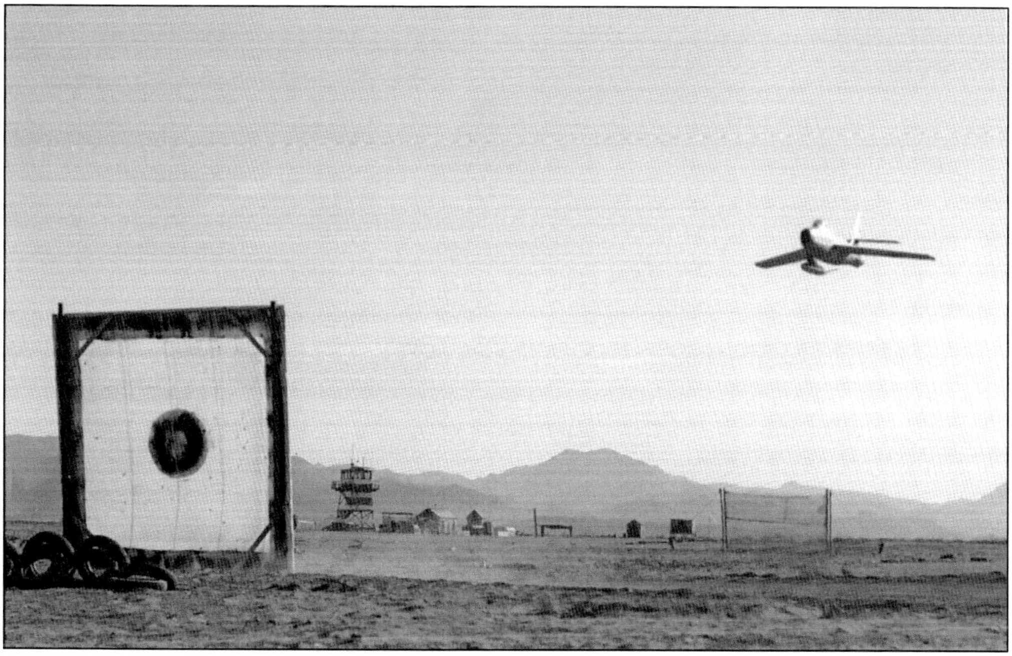

In this photograph taken during the 1950s, F-86 Sabres are also practice strafing at the range, which is now known as the Barry M. Goldwater Range and encompasses 2.7 million acres. The Gila Bend Air Force Auxiliary Field is still in operation. (Courtesy of the US Air Force 442nd Fighter Wing.)

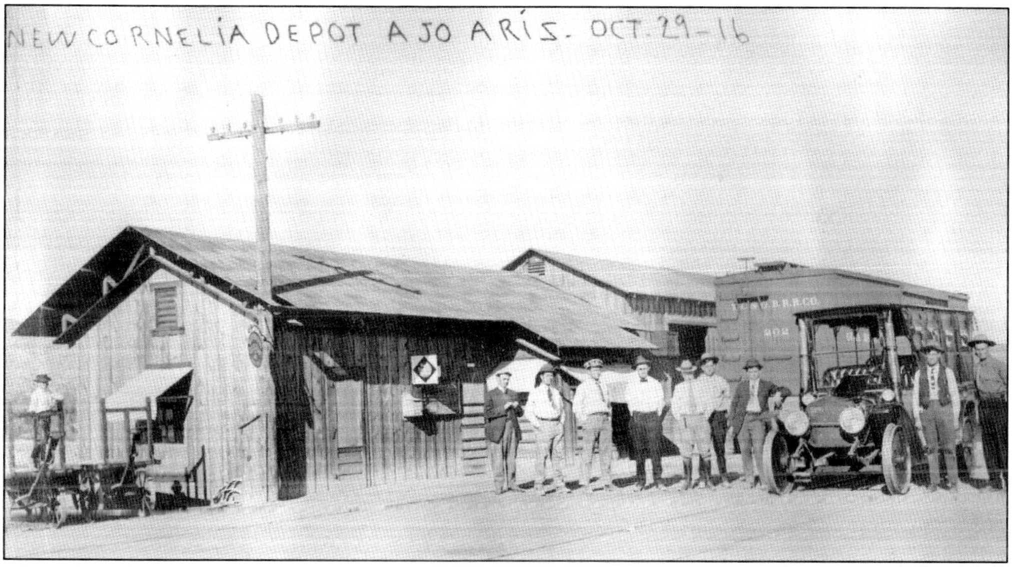

The New Cornelia Copper Company opened a large copper-mining operation in 1912 in the town of Ajo, located 40 miles south of Gila Bend. The Southern Pacific at Gila Bend was the closest rail connection, so the mining company developed the Tucson, Cornelia & Gila Bend Railroad Company (TC&GB) to connect to Gila Bend to the north and, later, Tucson to the east. However, the Tucson section was never built, so Gila Bend became the transfer station for supplies and products to and from Ajo. The TC&GB built its own facilities, including the depot shown, and began service in 1916. (Courtesy of the Gila Bend Museum.)

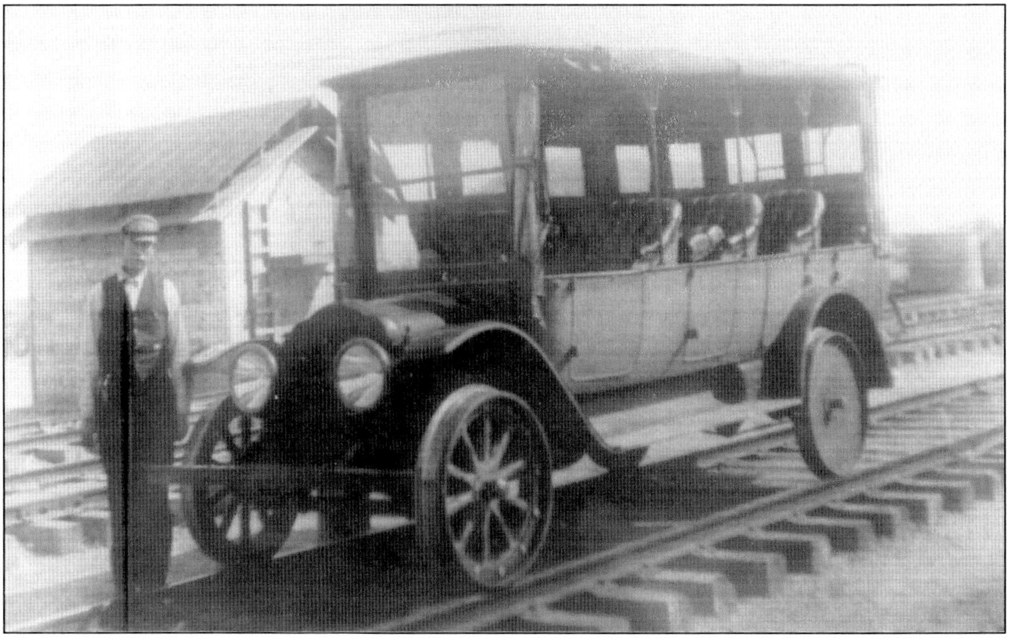

Most of the passenger transportation between Ajo and Gila Bend was via a motorcar. It was quite common for small, short-line railroads like the TC&GB to adapt highway vehicles for rail use as an alternative to running a locomotive and passenger car. The railroads used everything from an automobile to a bus to a pickup truck. In most instances, the small railroads built these contraptions in their shops. In this case, it was a White Motors with roll-down curtains. This motorcar, No.7, started service with Daniel Noonan Jr. as its driver in 1916. (Courtesy of the Gila Bend Museum.)

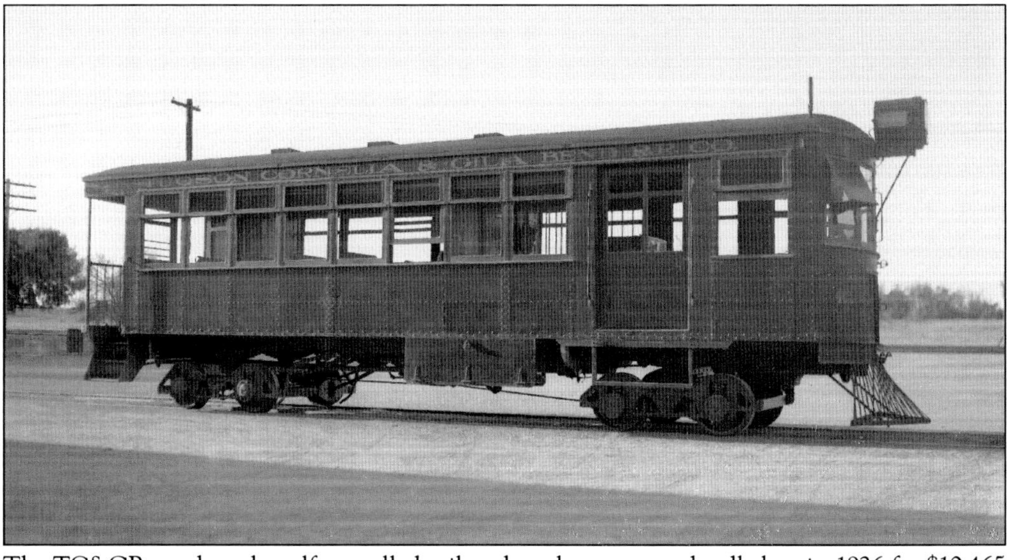

The TC&GB purchased a self-propelled railroad car known as a doodle bug in 1926 for $10,465 from the Edwards Railway Motor Car Company of Sanford, North Carolina. During the first part of the 20th century, several railroads, mostly small regional and local networks, provided their main passenger and mail services through doodle bugs in a cost-cutting effort. (Courtesy of the California State Railroad Museum.)

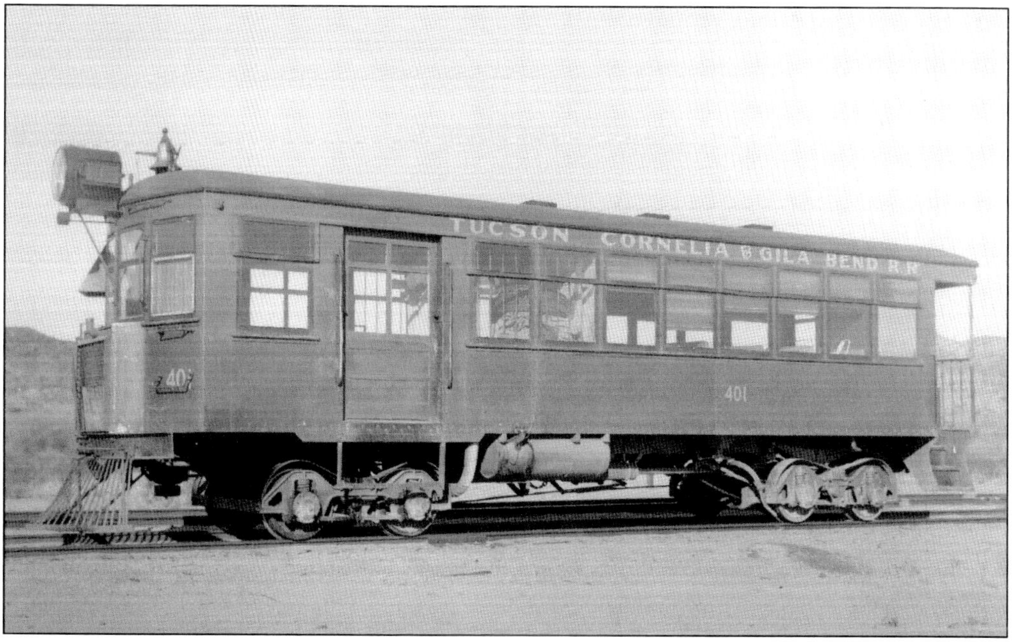

Car 401 is shown here in 1943 right after the railroad replaced the original four-cylinder Continental gas engine with a larger six-cylinder White gas engine, moving the radiator forward in the process. The car operated until December 1947 when it was taken out of service after traveling more than 783,000 miles. It was retired in the early 1950s and donated to the Travel Town Museum in Los Angeles. (Courtesy of the California State Railroad Museum.)

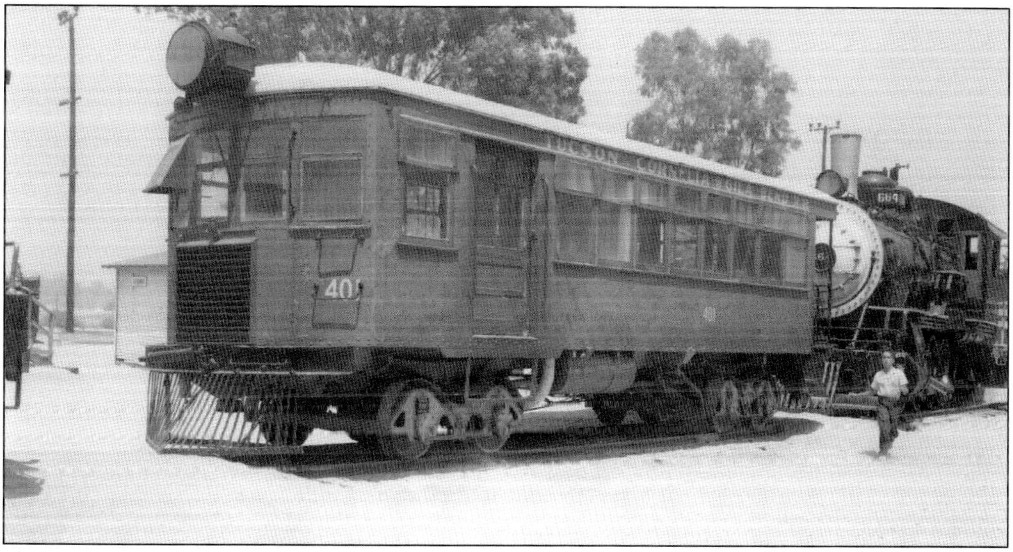

Photographed in 1961 by Wendell Huffman, Car 401 was traded to a private owner in 1963 for two Los Angeles trolley cars. It was then acquired by Short Line industries in 1975. The doodle bug was restored, repainted, relettered, and operated on a tourist railroad in Virginia City, Nevada, under the name *Washoe Zephyr No. 50*. (Courtesy of Wendell Huffman, Nevada State Railroad Museum.)

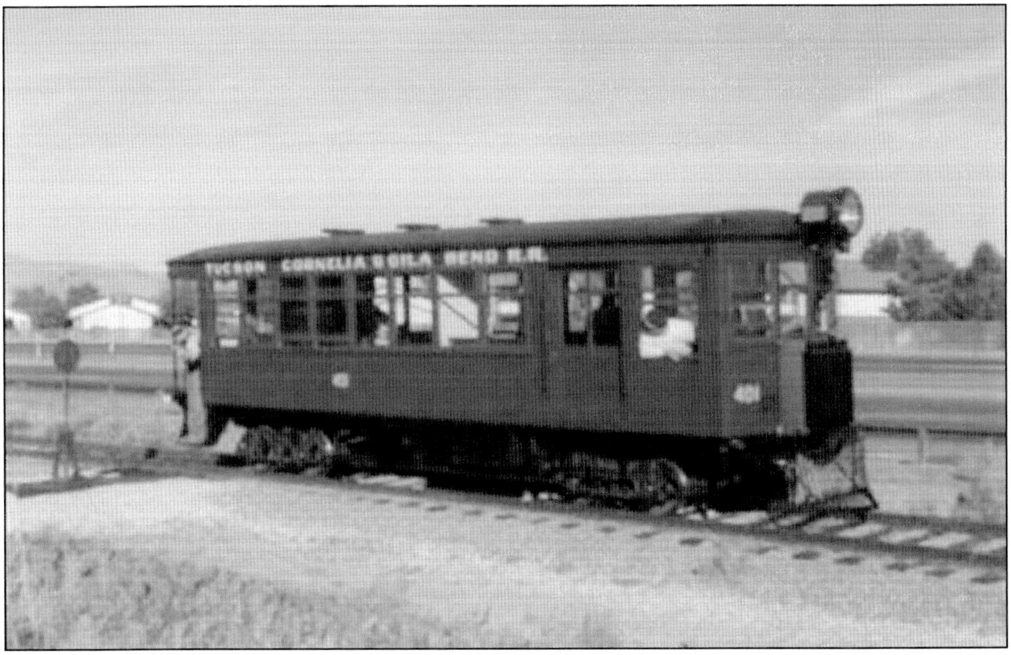

The Nevada State Railroad Museum in Carson City acquired Car 401 in 1988. While restoring it to its original appearance in 1999, the museum updated the 1943 White engine to a more efficient diesel with a hydraulic drive. The Tucson, Cornelia & Gila Bend Car 401 now operates every weekend at the museum from May to September. (Courtesy of the Nevada State Railroad Museum.)

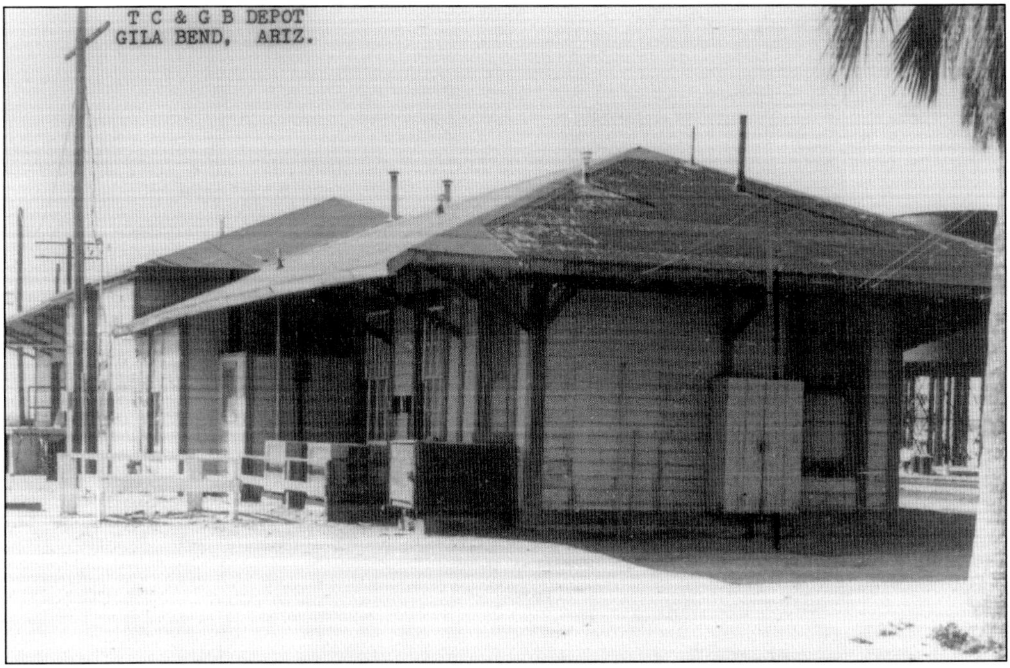

When the regular travel to Gila Bend stopped in 1989, the Tucson, Cornelia, & Gila Bend station was no longer needed. Like many railroad-related buildings in Gila Bend, the TC&GB depot was eventually demolished. (Courtesy of Ron Henry.)

Three

Gila Bourgeois

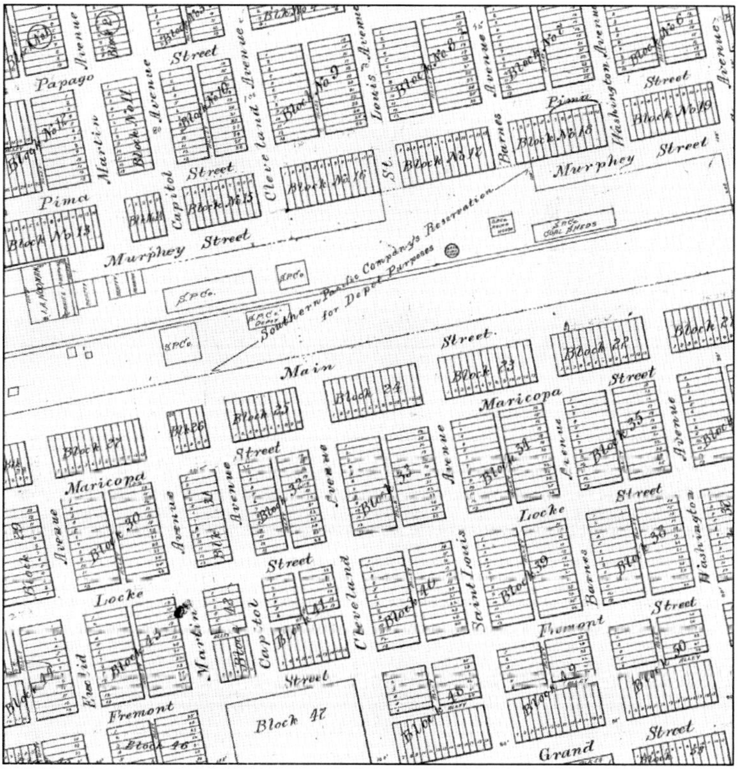

By 1887, plans were in the works by land speculators to develop a townsite in proximity to the railroad and replacing the community that evolved at the stage station. The following year, John H. Martin and Morris R. Locke filed the plat of the town of Gila Bend with the Maricopa County recorder, and people immediately began buying up lots. The layout aligned to the rail line, with Main Street south of the Southern and Pacific property and Murphey Street [*sic*] on the north. (Courtesy of the Maricopa County Recorder's Office.)

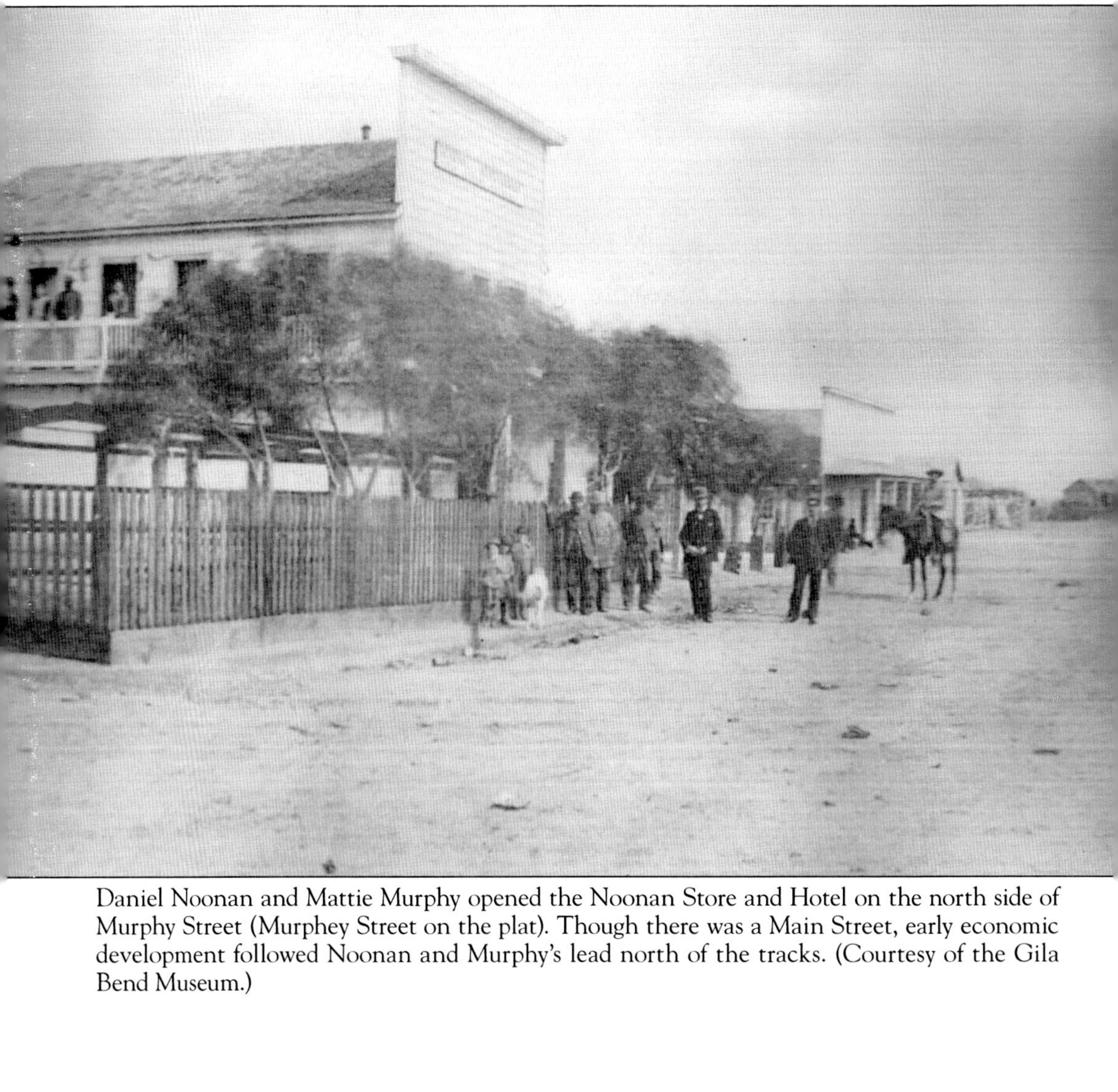

Daniel Noonan and Mattie Murphy opened the Noonan Store and Hotel on the north side of Murphy Street (Murphey Street on the plat). Though there was a Main Street, early economic development followed Noonan and Murphy's lead north of the tracks. (Courtesy of the Gila Bend Museum.)

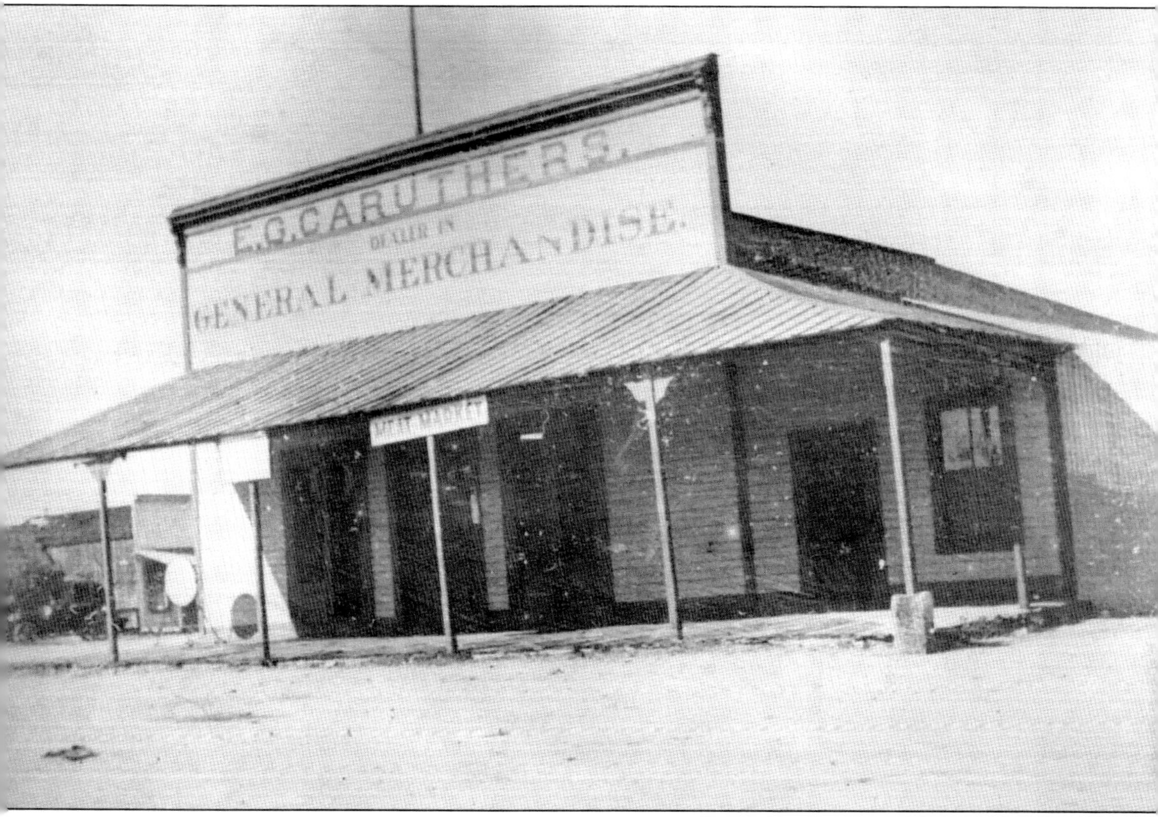

In 1887, Yuma merchant Eugene F. Sanguetti and partner John Gandolfo opened a general store on Pima Street. The duo only operated the store for a couple years before selling the entire operation to E.G. Caruthers and returning to Yuma. Caruthers also moved to Yuma in 1907, leaving the store to be locally managed. (Courtesy of the Gila Bend Museum.)

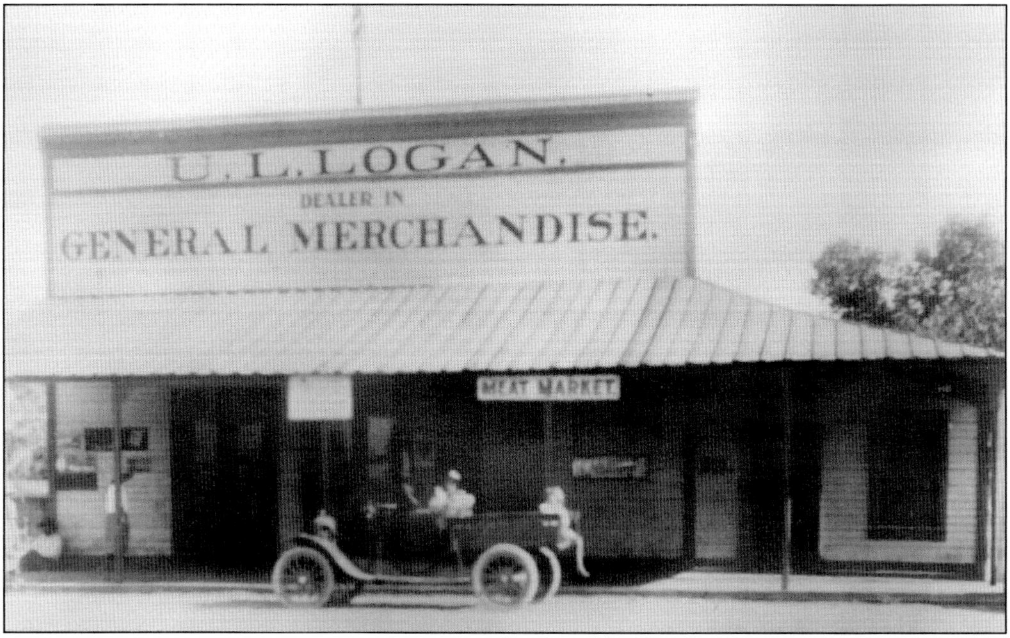

U.L. Logan bought Caruthers's store in 1911 and operated it until he died in 1925. His wife, Louise, managed the store until 1932 when she turned the company over to her son, U.L. Jr., who ran the store with his sister, who was also named Louise. (Courtesy of the Gila Bend Museum.)

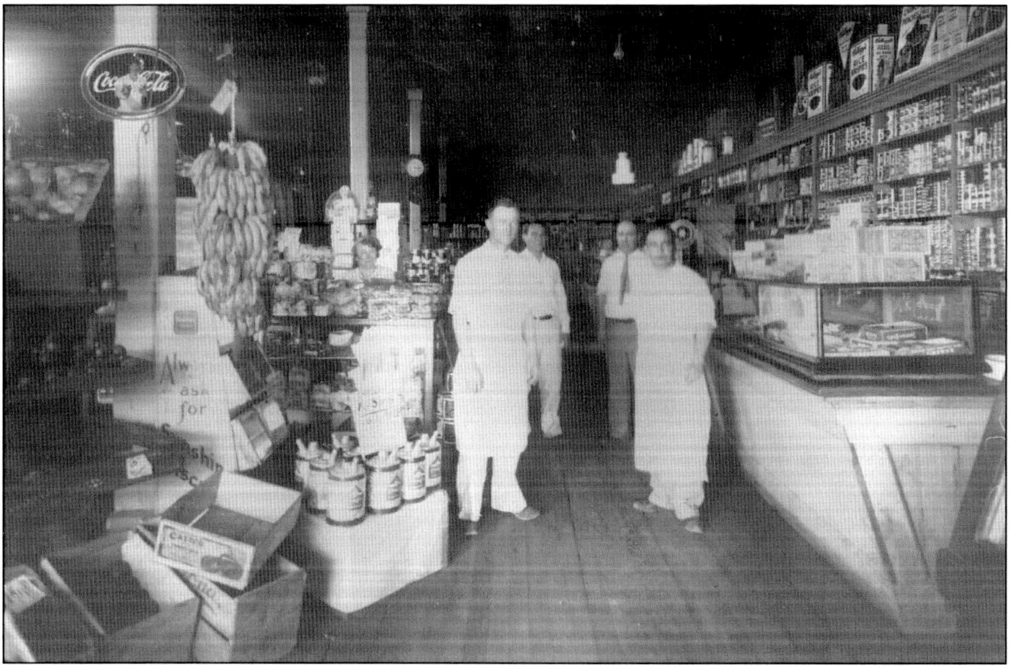

U.L. Logan purchased the store with $30,000 worth of merchandise for $7,000 down. Advice came with the purchase. According to an interview with Louise Logan almost 50 years later, Caruthers told the Logans that previous store owners came when the economy was good and left when it was bad and that was something the Logans should not do. They followed his advice, and the Logan store was a fixture in Gila Bend until the 1960s. (Courtesy of the Gila Bend Museum.)

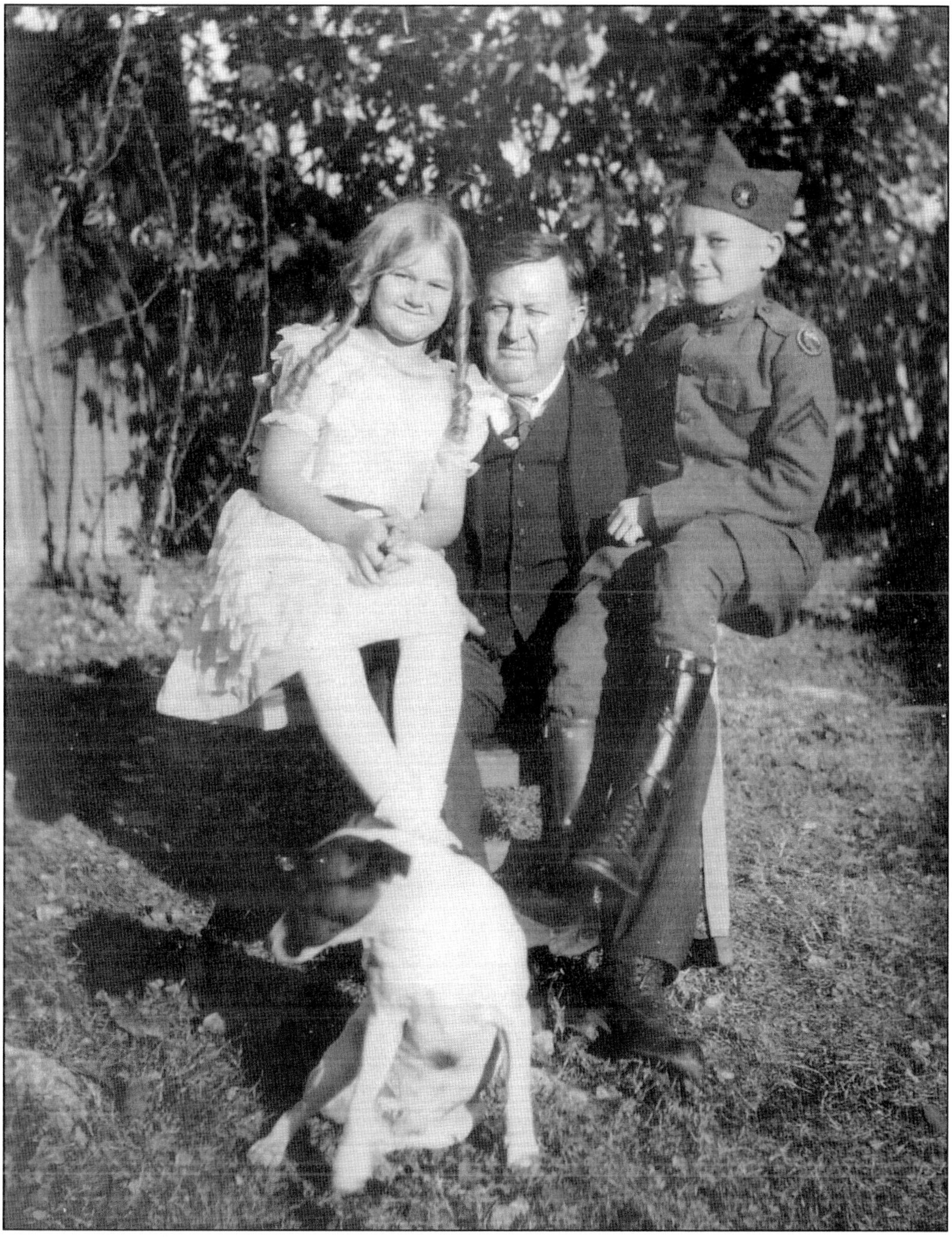

U.L. Logan was born on the ranch owned by his father, Trank, in Bosque County, Texas. When Trank Logan's son was born, he named him after a wrangler named U.L. Livingston, who had taken care of him on a trail drive from Texas to Kansas. U.L.'s mother thought the name "U.L. Livingston Logan" was too long, so she dropped the "Livingston." U.L. came to Arizona in 1900 and worked as a bookkeeper and storekeeper for the Arizona Copper Company in Greenlee County. When the mines closed, the Logan family, seeking a healthy environment for U.L. Jr., eventually made their way to Gila Bend. In this photograph are U.L. Sr. with children Louise (left, and named after her mother) and U.L. Jr. on his knees. (Courtesy of the Gila Bend Museum.)

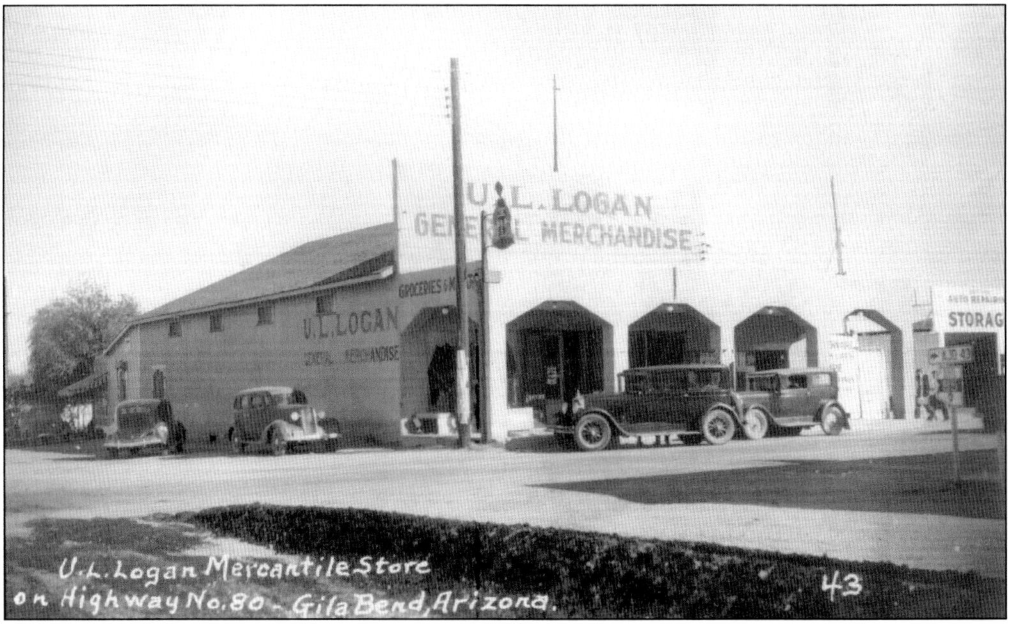

In 1926, after Louise (Mrs. U.L.) Logan discovered the highway was coming through town, she refurbished the front porch, adding the canopy. The Logan family lived in the residence to the rear of the store. Scotty's auto repair was located next door. (Courtesy of the Gila Bend Museum.)

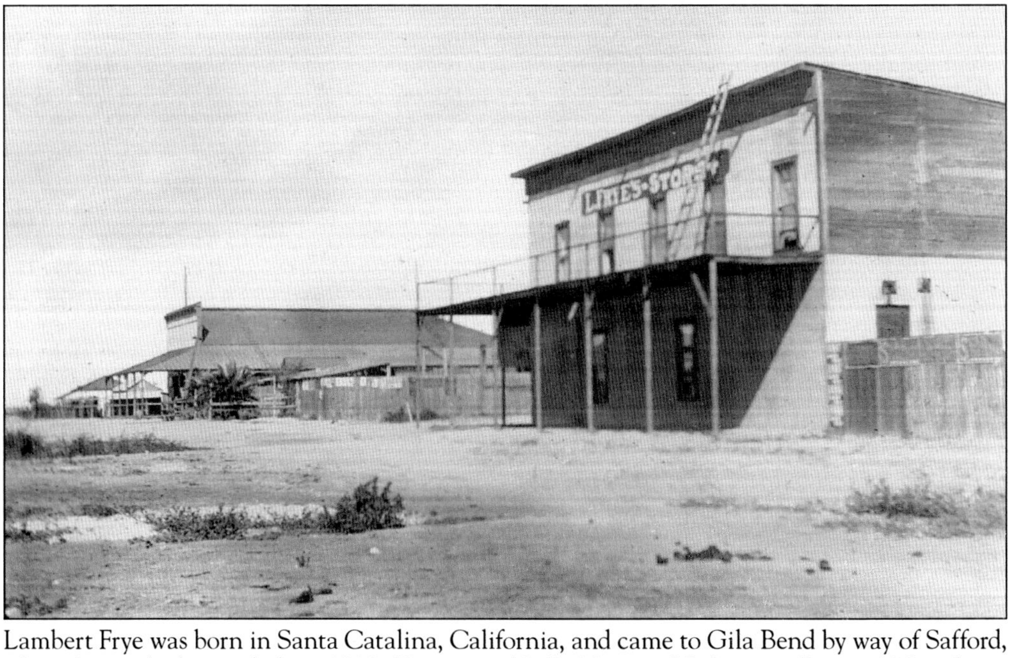

Lambert Frye was born in Santa Catalina, California, and came to Gila Bend by way of Safford, where he worked as a clerk in 1880. He married Lilly Neece of Solomonville in 1886 and was active in the Populist Party in Graham County during the 1890s. Frye leased the Hotel Kendall in Gila Bend from W.A. Blinn in 1909. He opened his store, seen here, just down the street from Caruthers's. In 1909, he partnered with Caruthers and others in asphalt mining claims. Blinn sold the building in 1912, and Frye closed the store, but he continued to mine in the area until at least 1915. By 1920, the Frye family had moved on to Chandler. (Courtesy of Johnny Laird.)

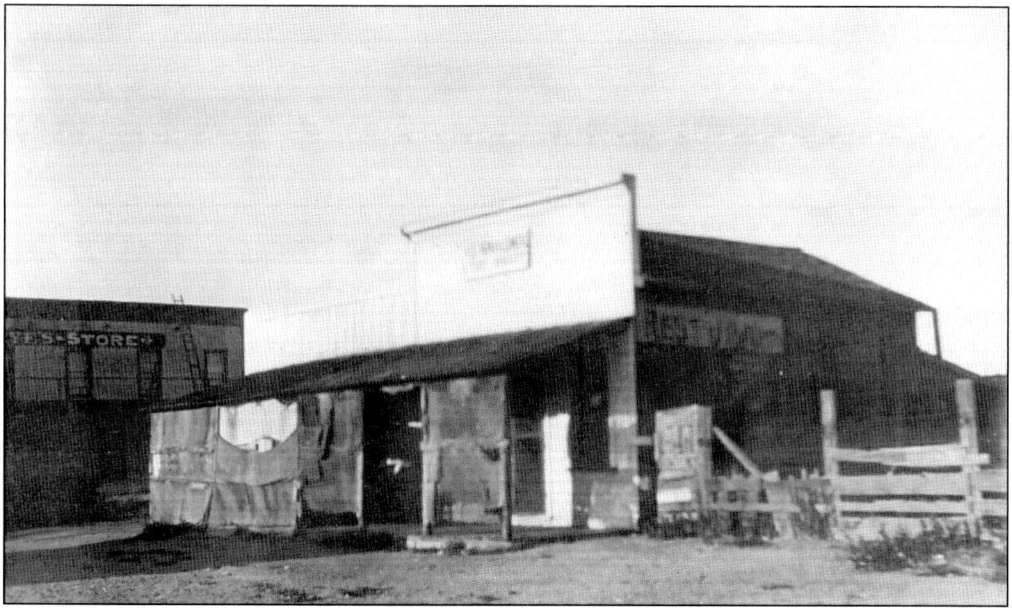

This establishment may have been a restaurant and store operated by Chinese merchants Lum Tom and Sing Lee, immigrants to the United States during the 1880s. According to the 1910 census, there were five Chinese immigrants living in Gila Bend. (Courtesy of Johnny Laird.)

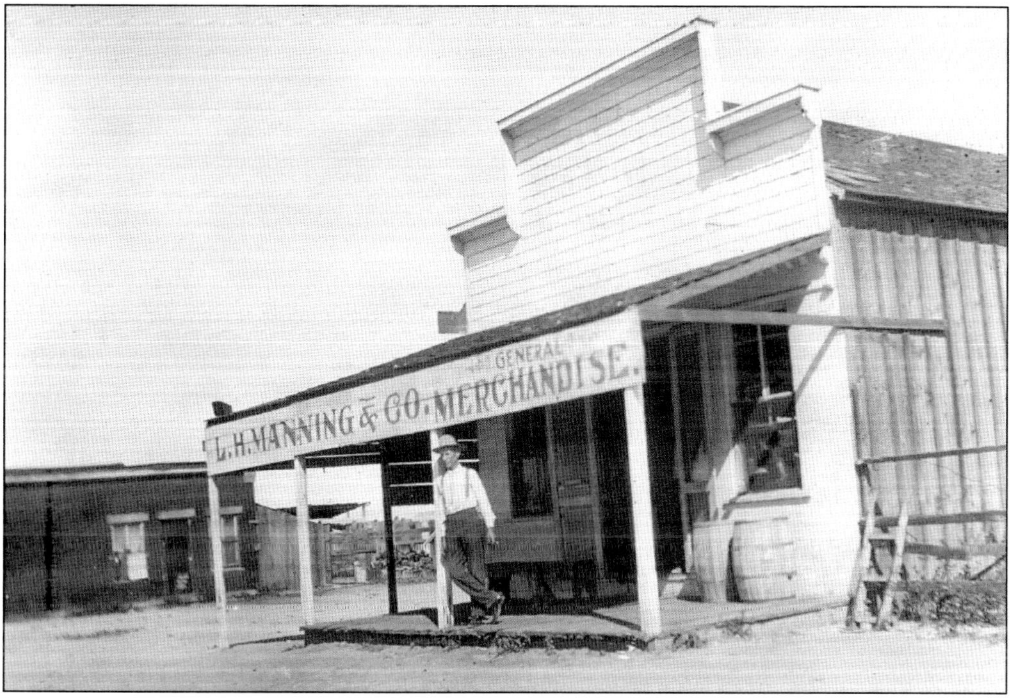

Located on Pima Street, the L.H. Manning and Company Store was one of many ventures pursued by "General" Levi Howell Manning. Manning arrived in Tucson in 1884 and worked briefly as a reporter. He eventually worked his way into the position of general manager of the Tucson Ice and Electric Company and amassed a large fortune. Manning was territorial surveyor general and the mayor of Tucson. He sold the property to L.H. Richards in 1922. (Courtesy of Johnny Laird.)

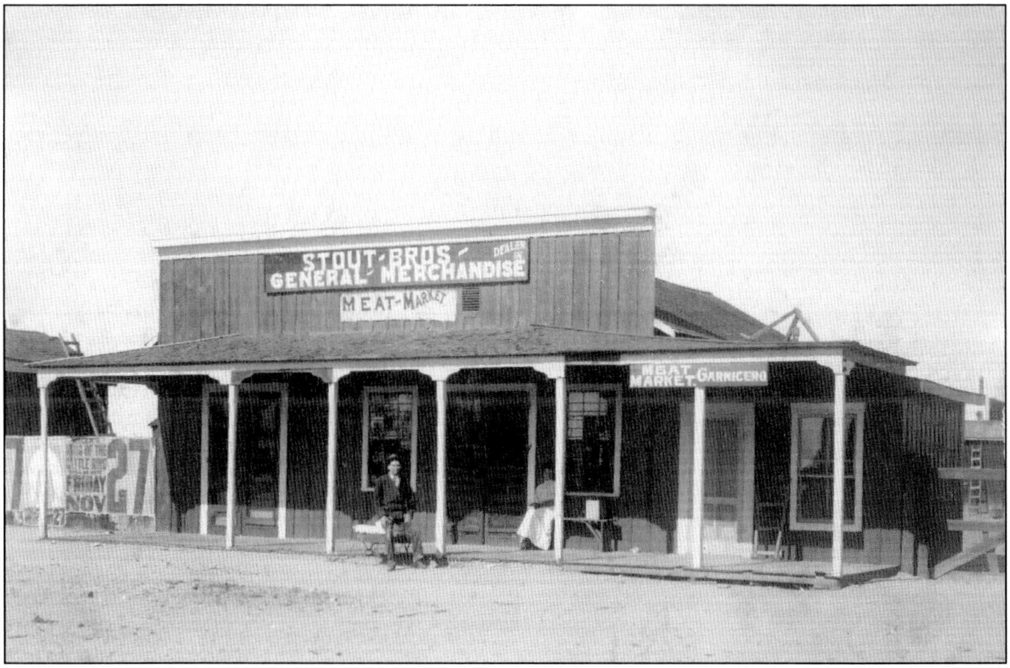

In 1895, brothers Albert and Charles Stout opened a store on Murphy Street on property their father Edward had purchased in 1892. The senior Stout had come to Arizona during the silver boom in Tombstone and gone to work for the Southern Pacific as an engineer when the railroad came through. (Courtesy of Edward Stout.)

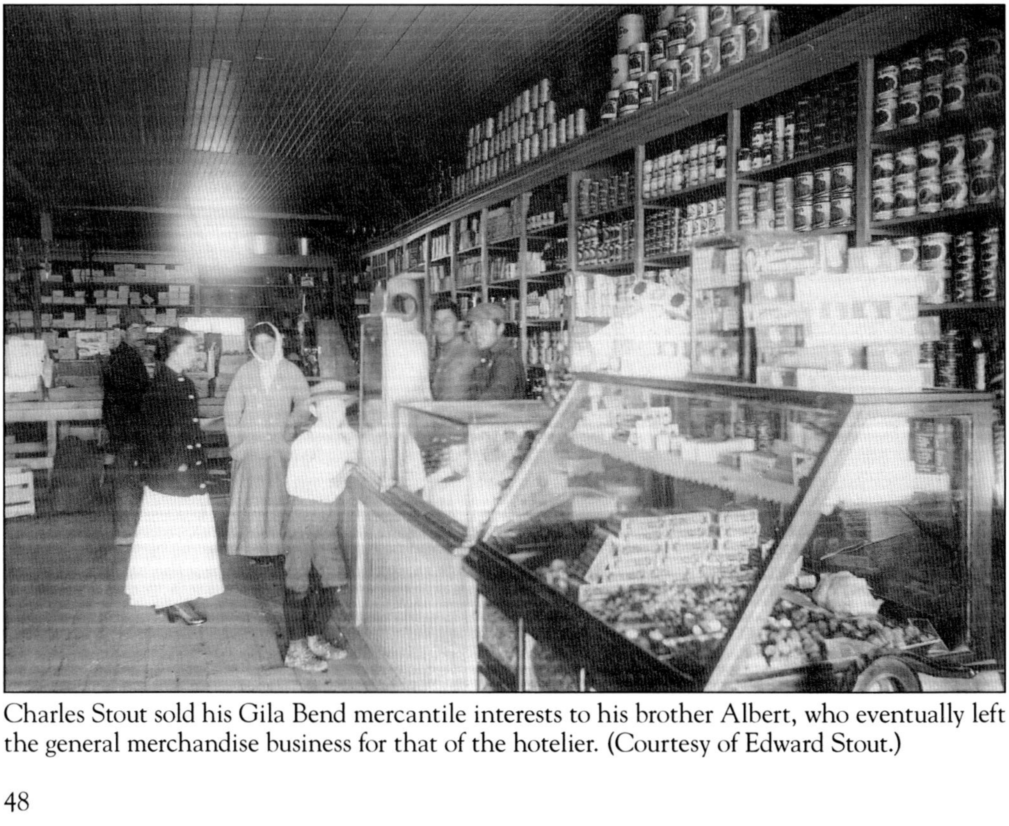

Charles Stout sold his Gila Bend mercantile interests to his brother Albert, who eventually left the general merchandise business for that of the hotelier. (Courtesy of Edward Stout.)

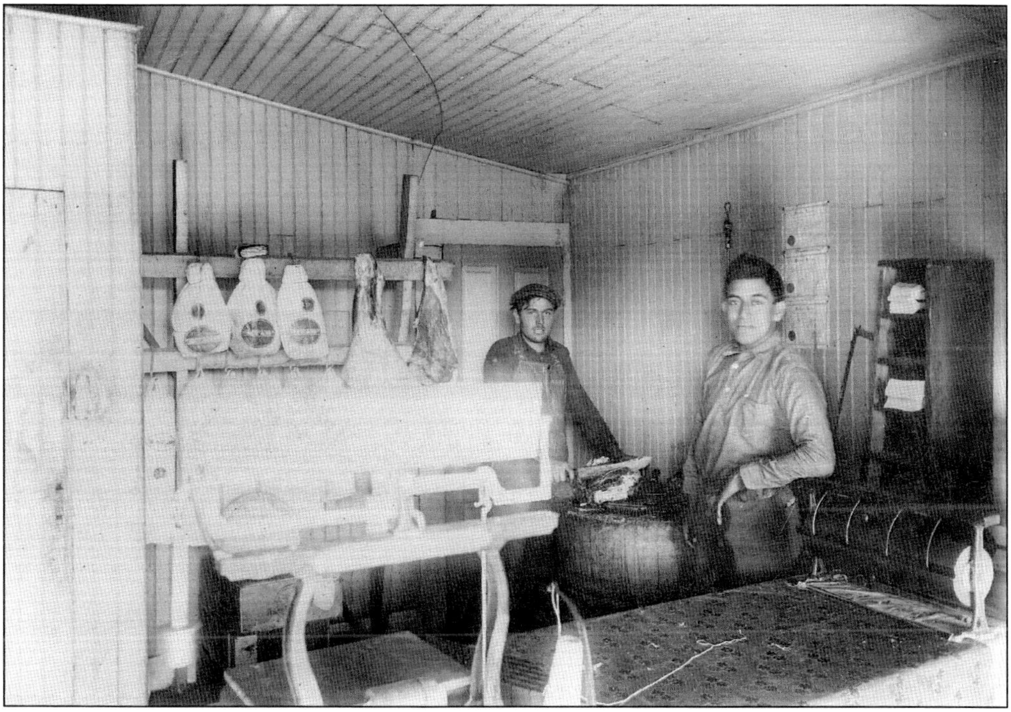

The Stouts and other local general store owners could rely on a supply of perishable supplies such as milk and produce from local farms and ranches. Other goods could be obtained via the railroad. For meat, the Stouts' store had access to the family's ranch just outside of town. (Courtesy of Edward Stout.)

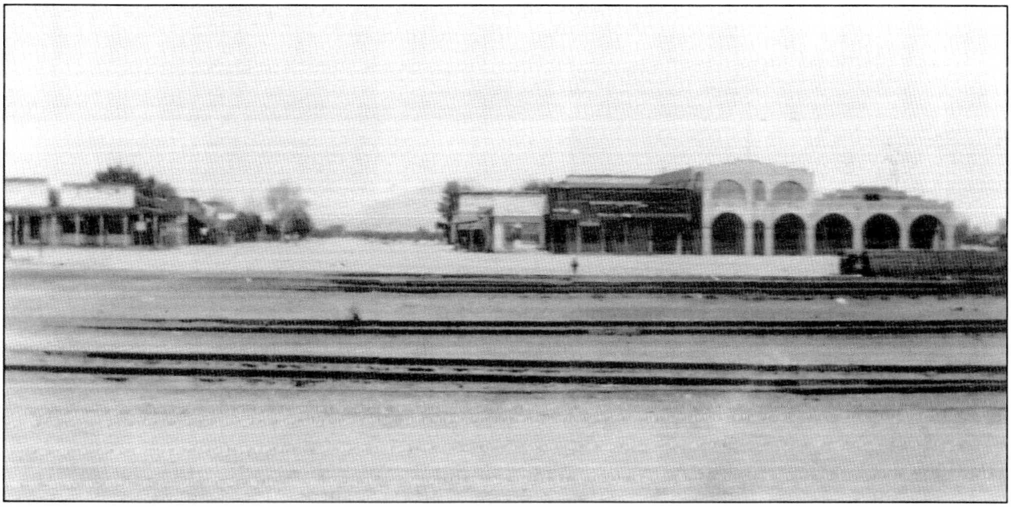

New businesses opened along Murphy Street to accommodate the economic expansion, while outside of town, farms and ranches prospered from supplying both the town and the ability to ship and receive products via the railroad. Albert Stout built a hotel on the street in 1906. It burned down in 1908. After the owner recovered from the loss of the first hotel, the Stout Hotel (on the far right) was rebuilt in 1911 and quickly became the most prominent structure on Murphy Street, as is apparent in this 1912 photograph looking north on Martin Avenue. (Courtesy of the Gila Bend Museum.)

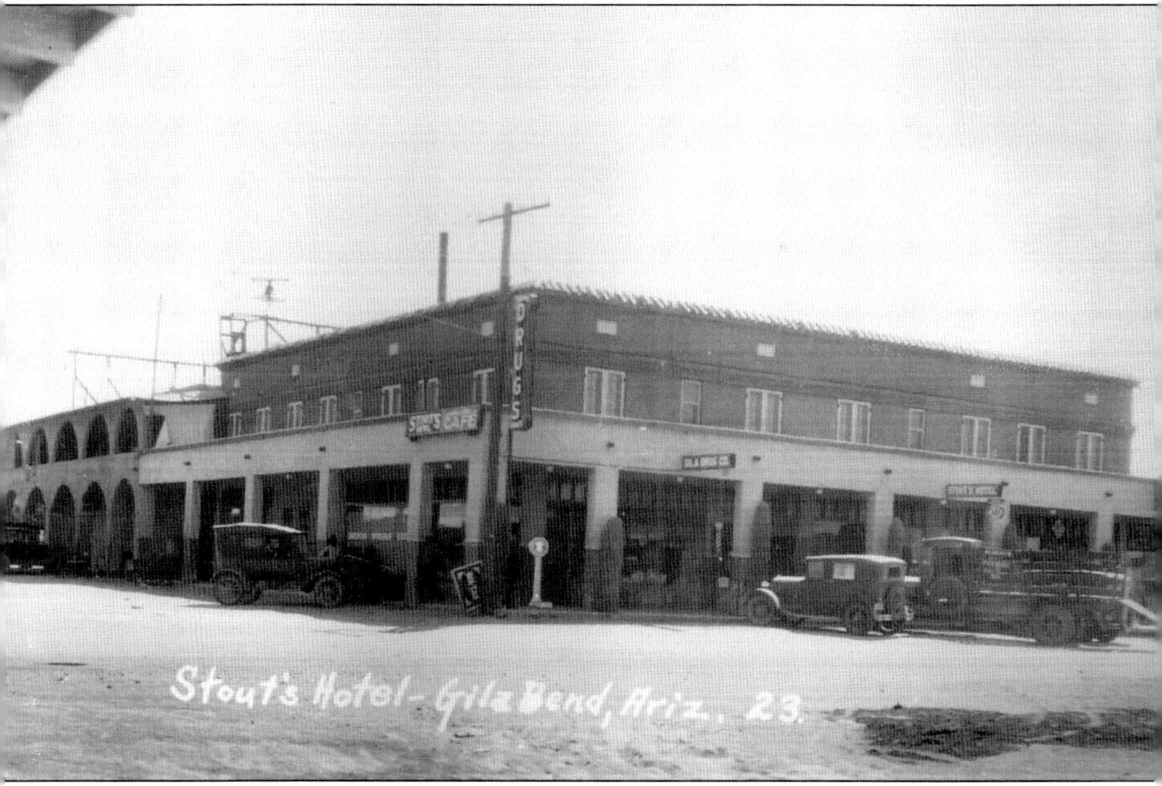

Albert Stout made the decision to have an addition built on to the rear of the original hotel. This became the new front of the hotel, facing Pima Street, which was on the new highway. Built in 1923, the addition was state of the art, with all then modern conveniences such as private, electric lighting, showers and tub baths, running water in every room, and cool, screened sleeping porches upstairs. (Courtesy of the Gila Bend Museum.)

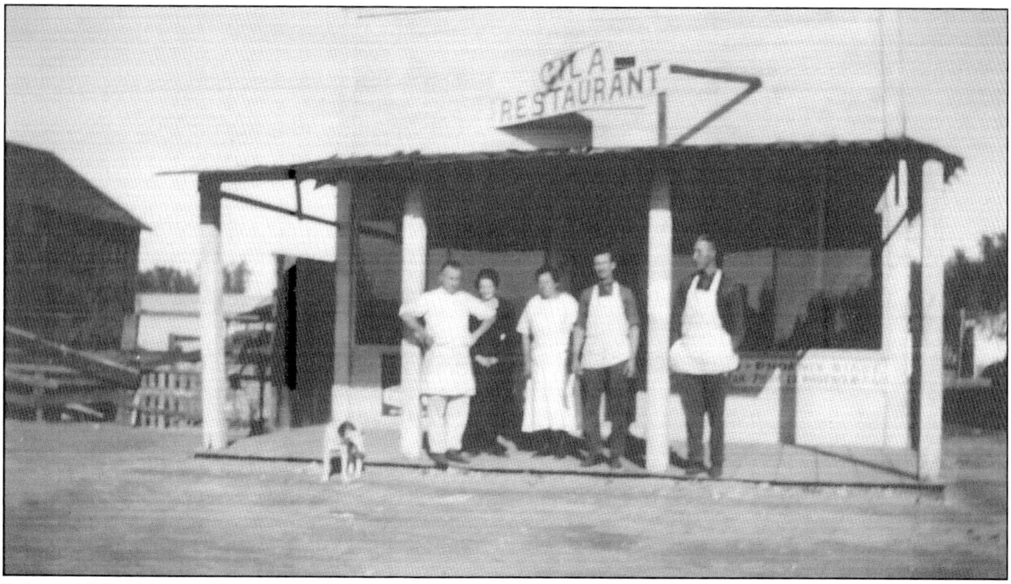

Jake and Esther Miller opened the Gila Restaurant on Murphy Street, across from the depot. The Millers were immigrants; Jake was from Poland, and Esther was from Sweden. They came to the United States in the 1890s. By the 1920s, they had gained possession of the entire block. (Courtesy of Ron Henry.)

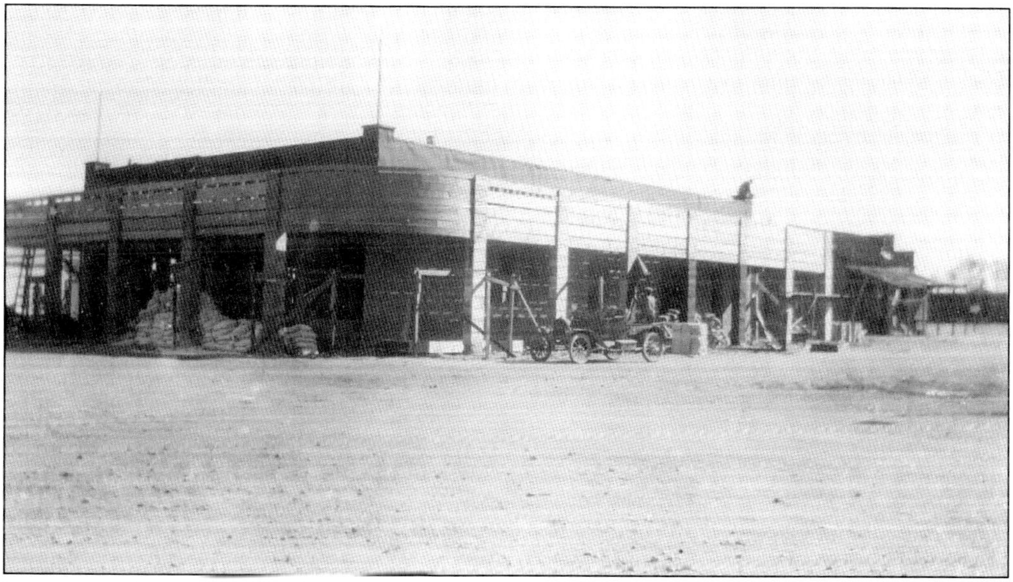

Following a late-1910-to-early-1920s trend, the Millers constructed a new building on Lot 15, facing Pima Street. According to Sanborn Fire Insurance Maps, the building was constructed of adobe, but in this photograph, it appears there was a substantial amount of concrete. (Courtesy of the Gila Bend Museum.)

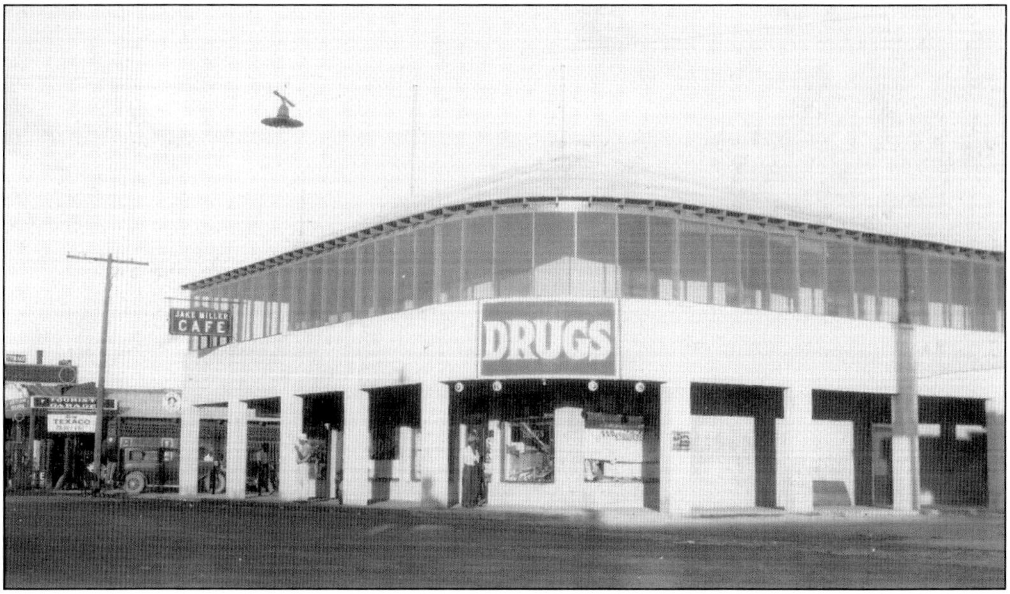

When it was completed, the new building had a corner drugstore, Jake Miller Cafe, on its east end. Later, the second floor became a hotel, and a sleeping porch was added. Miller partnered with Joe and Grace Beauchamp in the Desert Pharmacy. (Courtesy of the Gila Bend Museum.)

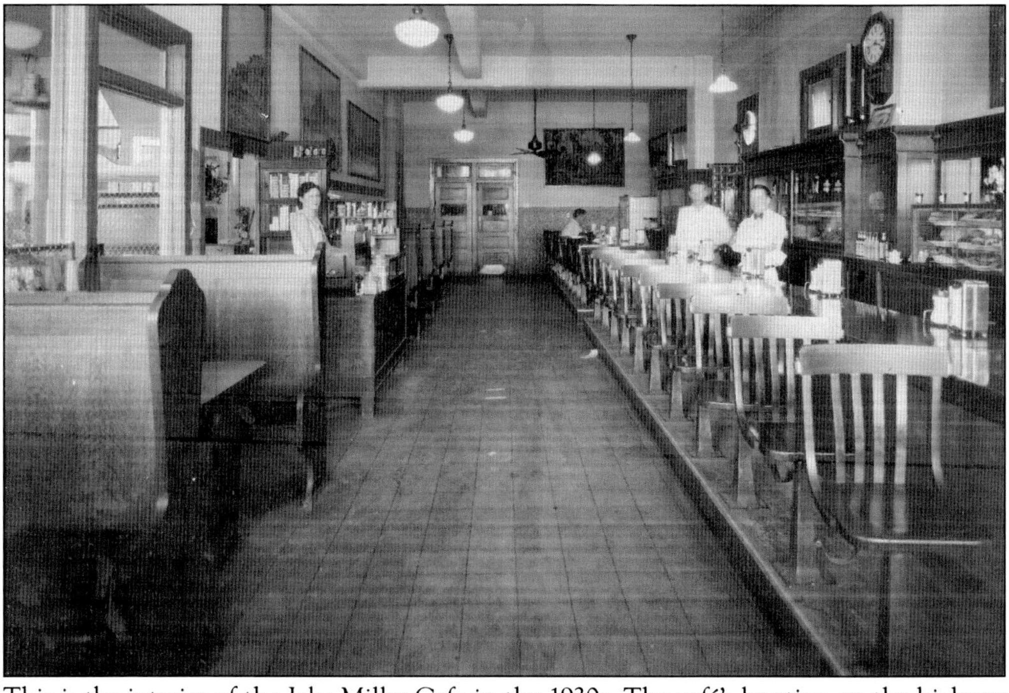

This is the interior of the Jake Miller Cafe in the 1930s. The café's location on the highway brought a lot of cross-country travelers, as well as local business, to the Miller's establishment. (Courtesy of the Gila Bend Museum.)

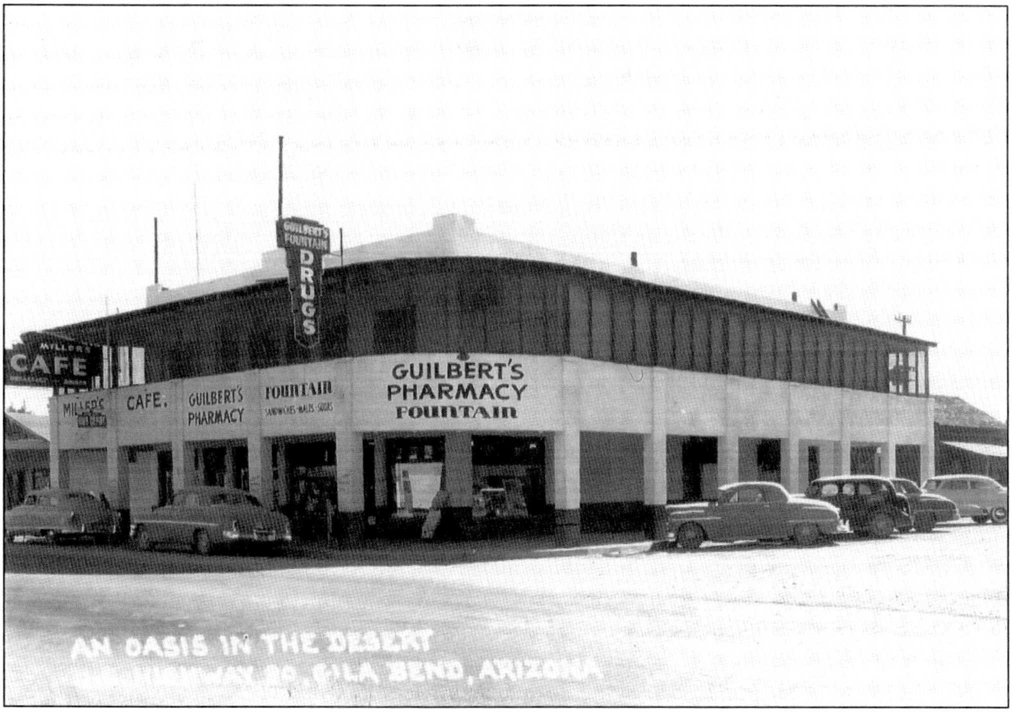

Guilbert's Pharmacy and its requisite soda fountain occupied the Miller Building beginning in the late 1930s and remained there for decades. Like most of the old structures on the highway, the Miller Building has long since been demolished. (Courtesy of Betty Gills.)

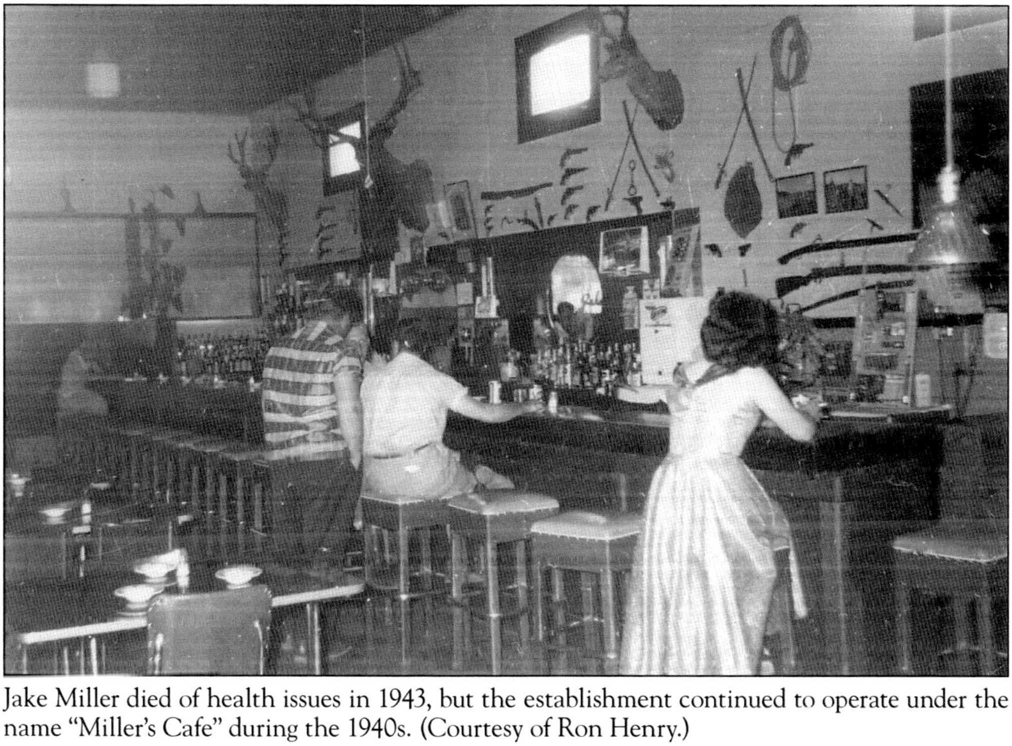

Jake Miller died of health issues in 1943, but the establishment continued to operate under the name "Miller's Cafe" during the 1940s. (Courtesy of Ron Henry.)

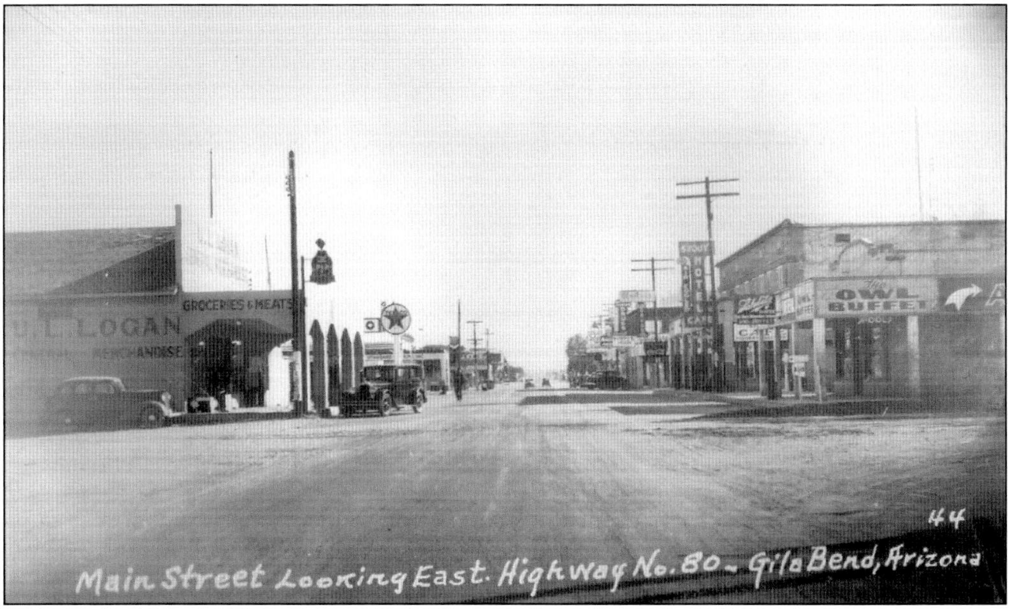

The Owl Buffet, seen on the far right of this late 1920s photograph, was one of the town's most well-known drinking establishments. (Courtesy of the Gila Bend Museum.)

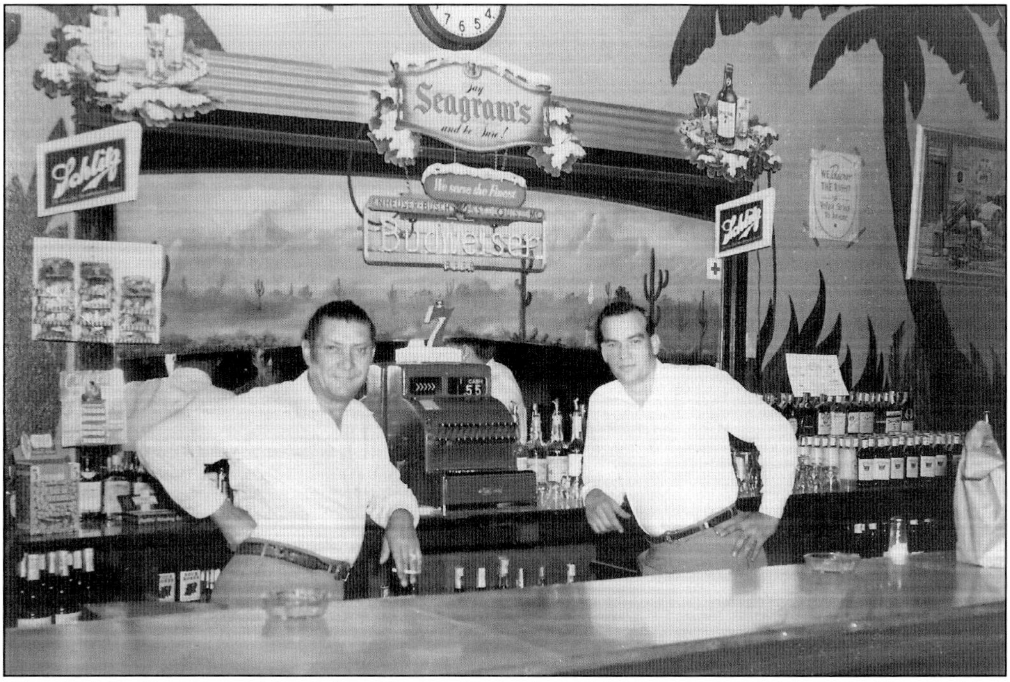

The Owl Buffet, opened by Bill and Louis Bentel in 1934, was one of the most popular bars in town. Bill Bentel (left) and Jack Neal are shown behind the bar in this 1947 photograph. (Courtesy of Betty Gills.)

Four

On the Dam Highway

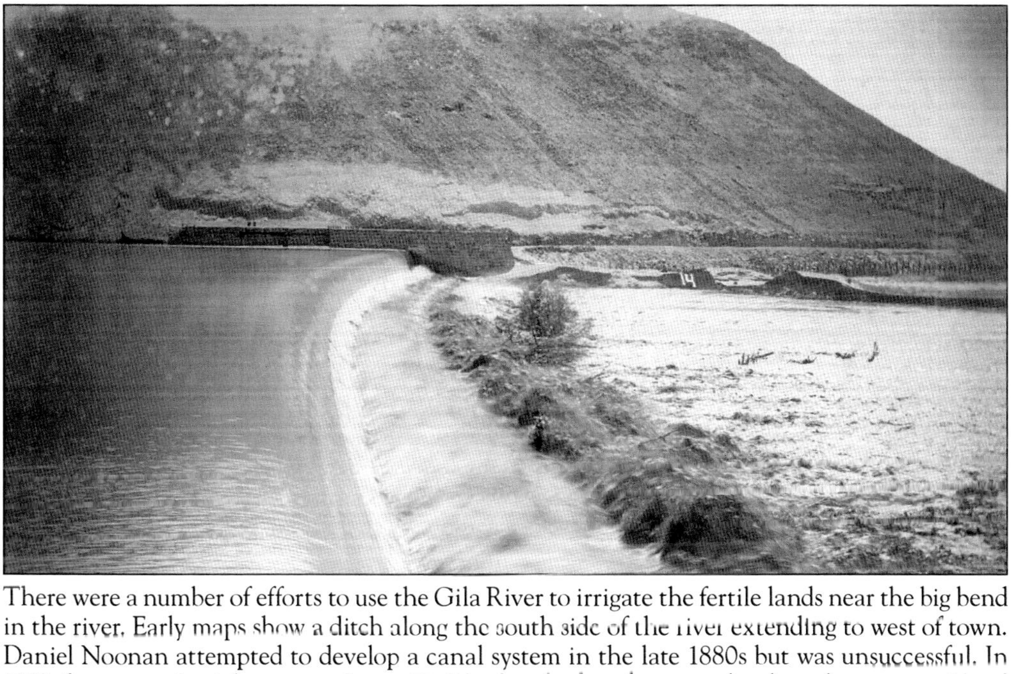

There were a number of efforts to use the Gila River to irrigate the fertile lands near the big bend in the river. Early maps show a ditch along the south side of the river extending to west of town. Daniel Noonan attempted to develop a canal system in the late 1880s but was unsuccessful. In 1891, former territorial governor Lewis Wolfley hatched a scheme to develop a large tract of land near Gila Bend through a dam and canal irrigation system upstream. The photograph is of the weir from the west. (Courtesy of Edward Stout.)

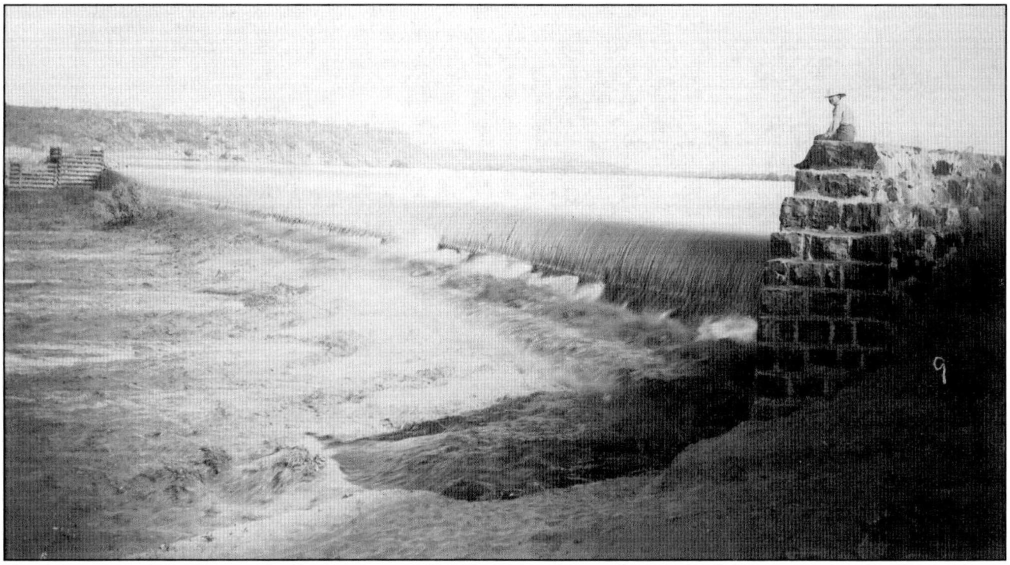

The dam was located on the Gila River at a location where the river is squeezed between two hills 23 miles north of Gila Bend. The weir, a dam designed to raise the river level to divert water, was a reinforced earthen berm similar to a dam in use on the Salt River above Phoenix. (Courtesy of Edward Stout.)

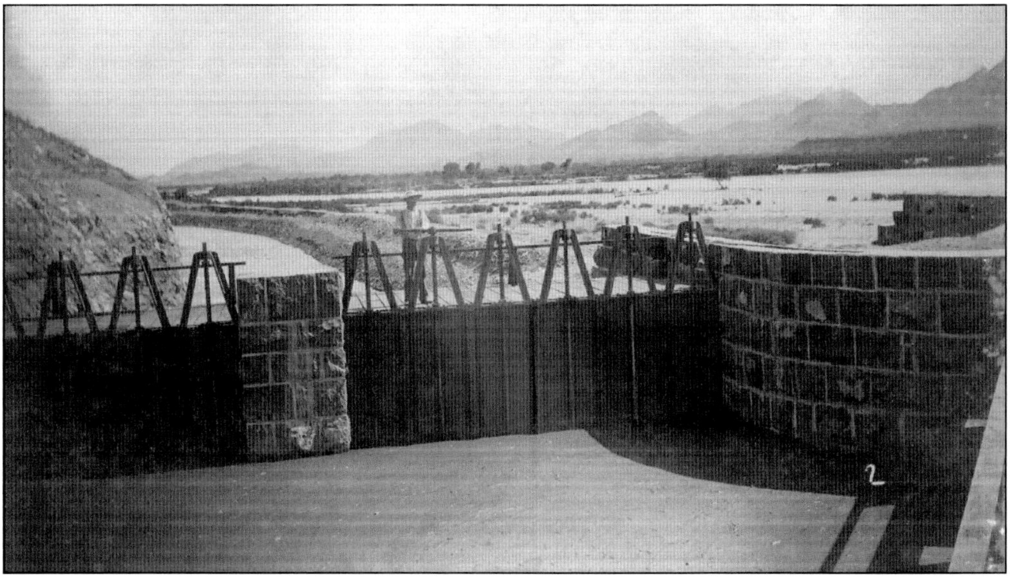

When the water would rise to the proper height, the gates of the weir would open to release the waters into the canal, controlling the flow of the water. The system was very similar to what was being used to irrigate the crops in Phoenix, Mesa, and other towns in the Salt River Valley. (Courtesy of Edward Stout.)

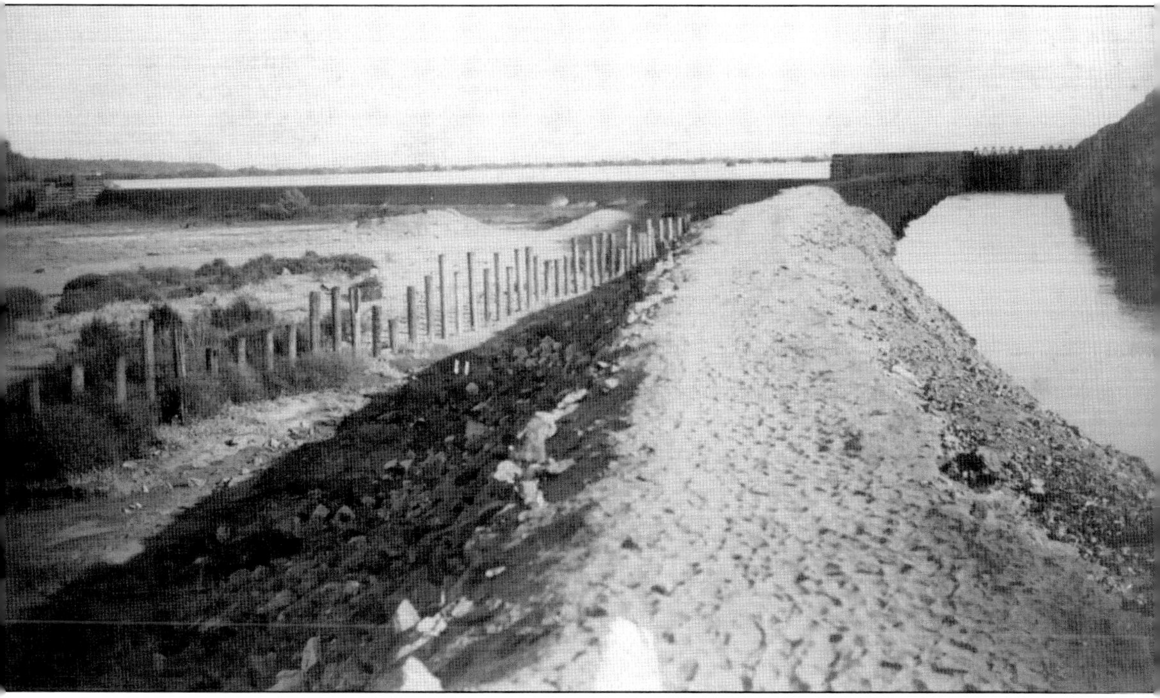

Though he had been the territorial governor, Wolfley worked in his post-political position as a civil engineer and surveyed the lands upstream and around the bend of the Gila River. With an earthen berm weir upstream and miles of canals, Wolfley expected to irrigate thousands of acres near Gila Bend. Over $750,000 was expended before a flood wiped out the dam. Wolfley's plans succumbed to legal problems, which seemed emblematic of all irrigation endeavors. Pictured above are the Wolfley Weir (facing upstream) and Gila Bend Canal before a deluge wiped out the dam. (Courtesy of Edward Stout.)

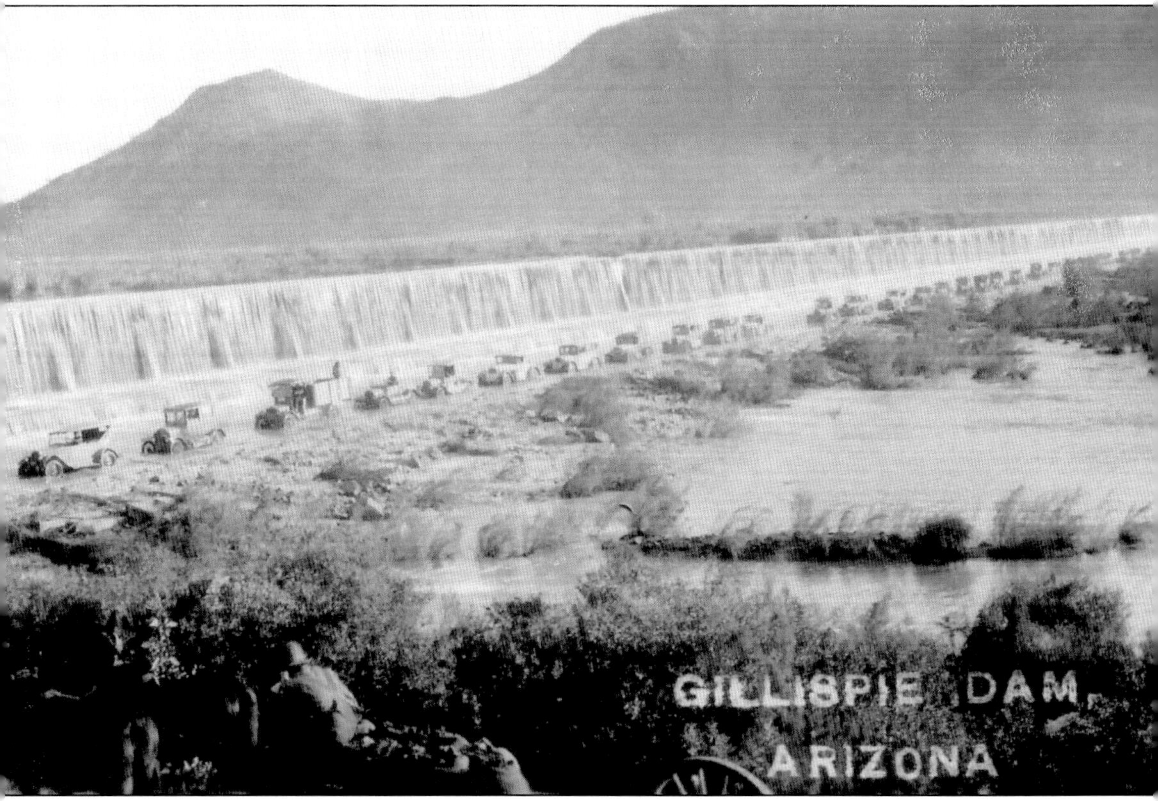

World War I had created a huge demand for cotton, and Frank A. Gillespie arrived on the scene ready to capitalize on that need. He also had enough money to make Wolfley's folly an economic reality. Creating the Gila Water Company, Gillespie funded a dam below the north bend of the river where Wolfley's dam had failed. Built between 1919 and 1921 for $1.6 million, the Gillespie Dam opened up thousands of acres near Gila Bend for agricultural development. The dam created a new market for the town. Though Gila Bend was on the highway between Tucson and Yuma and San Diego, traffic from Phoenix passed to the north, crossing the Gila River by ferry near Agua Caliente. The dam changed all that because in addition to being part of one the largest privately owned irrigation projects in the United States, it had an apron that could be used for automobile traffic to cross the river. In conjunction with federal funds for road construction, the dam allowed the new highway US 80 to be directed through Gila Bend. (Courtesy of Gary Miller.)

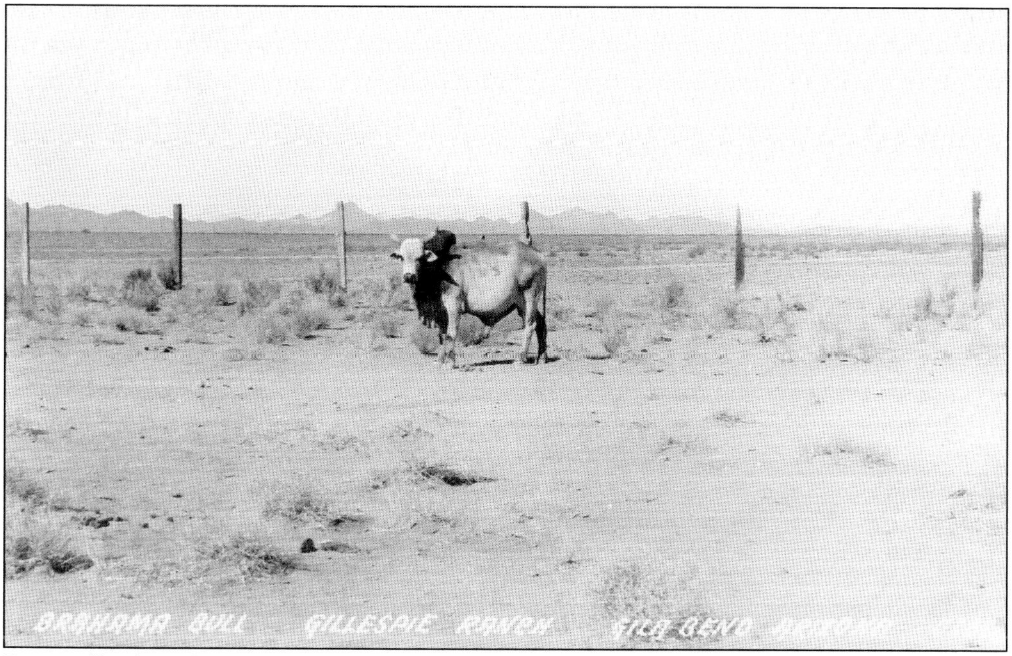

Eventually, the Gillespie Ranch reached 85,000 acres. In addition to raising cotton and other cash crops, it was a cattle farm and experimented with Brahman cattle. The Brahman has a higher tolerance to heat than other breeds, so it was ideal for the high summer temperatures experienced in Gila Bend. (Courtesy of Gary Miller.)

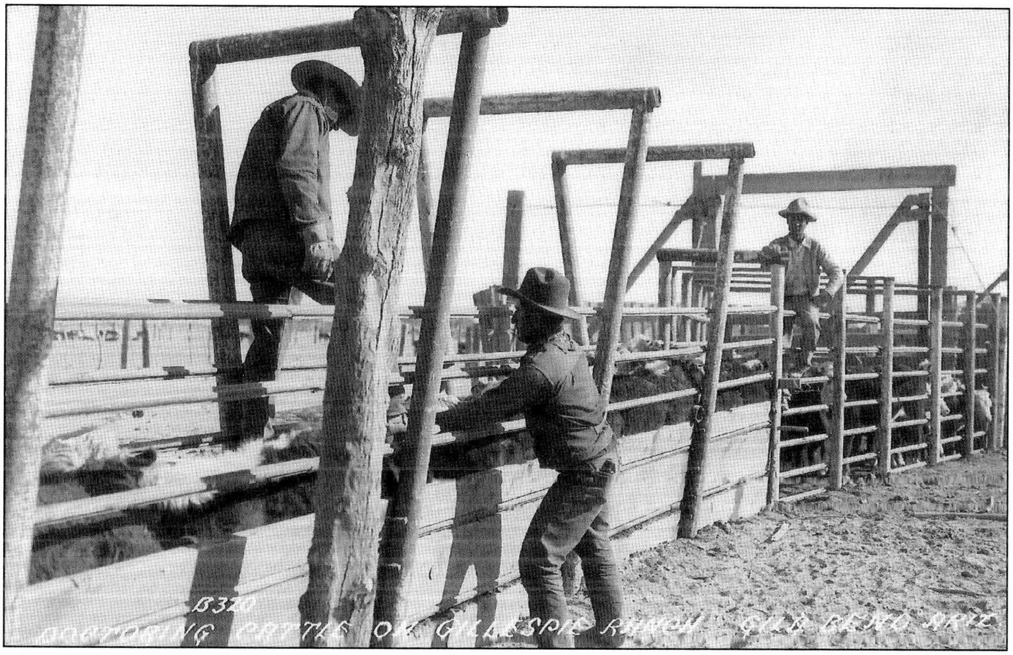

Naturally, Gila Bend reaped the profits of Gillepsie's endeavor. The ranch employed a large workforce of agricultural workers, and Gillespie developed the south side of town to accommodate his employees. In this photograph, Gillespie Ranch cowboys vaccinate a herd of cattle. (Courtesy of Gary Miller.)

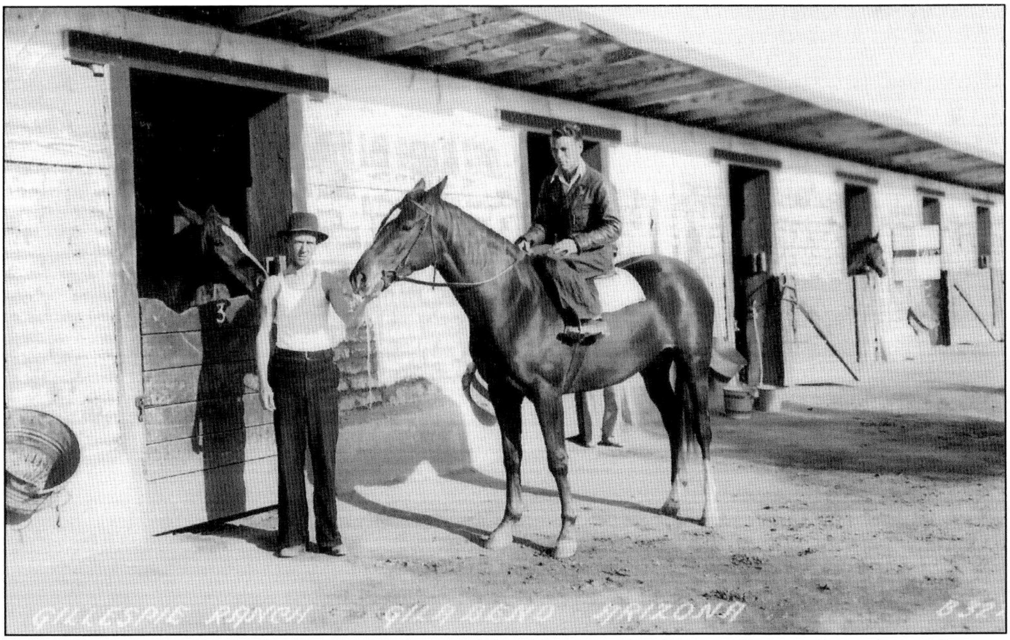

The Gillespie Ranch was known for its thoroughbred horses. Frank's son, Bernard, employed famous jockeys such as Frank Sorci to break the colts and then race them at places like Sportsman's Park in Phoenix. (Courtesy of the Gary Miller.)

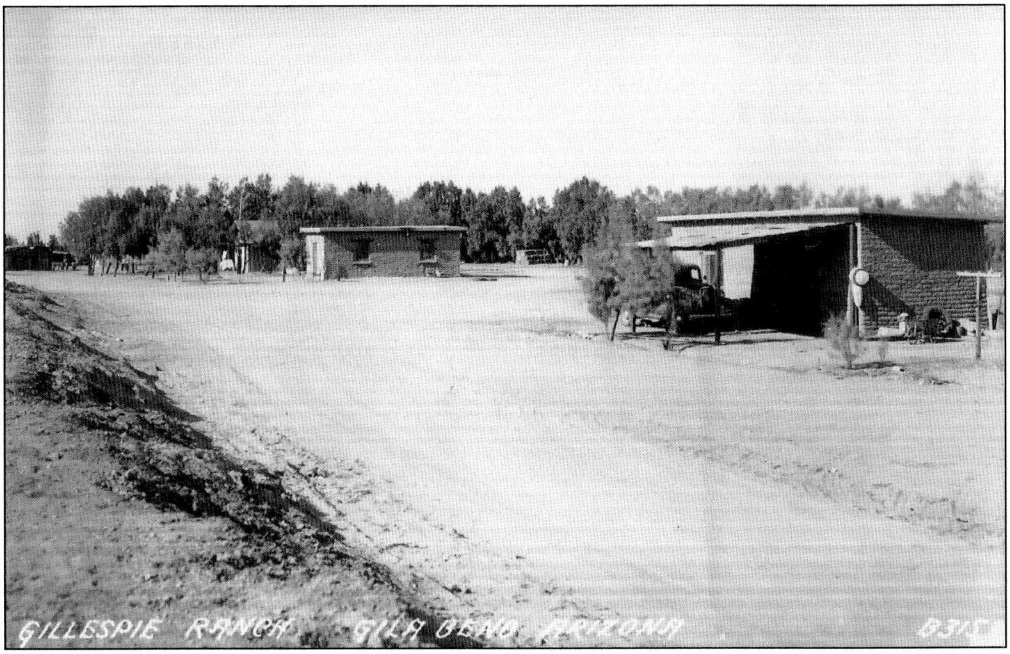

Housing for employees living on the Gillespie Ranch consisted of small adobe houses. In the days before air-conditioning, the insulation factor provided by the adobe allowed the homes to be a little cooler in the summer months and warmer in the winter than a typical frame house. (Courtesy of the Gary Miller.)

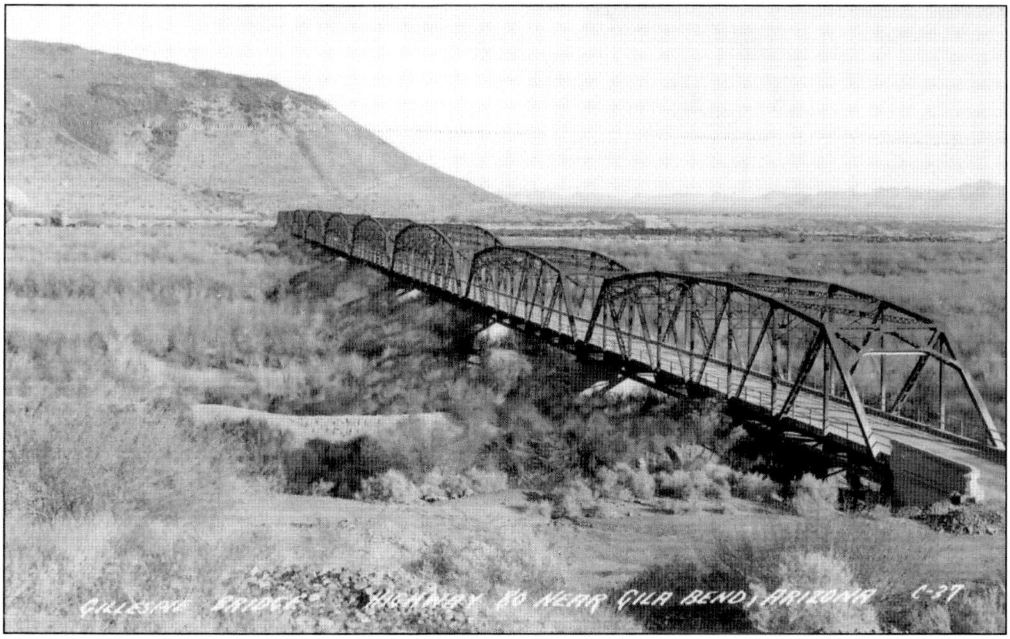

Increased prosperity brought more investment. A new school was funded by bonds in 1925, and a new bridge was completed, replacing the dam apron in 1927. As a vital component on US 80, the bridge assured Gila Bend's position at the crossroads of routes between Phoenix, Tucson, and San Diego. (Courtesy of the Gary Miller.)

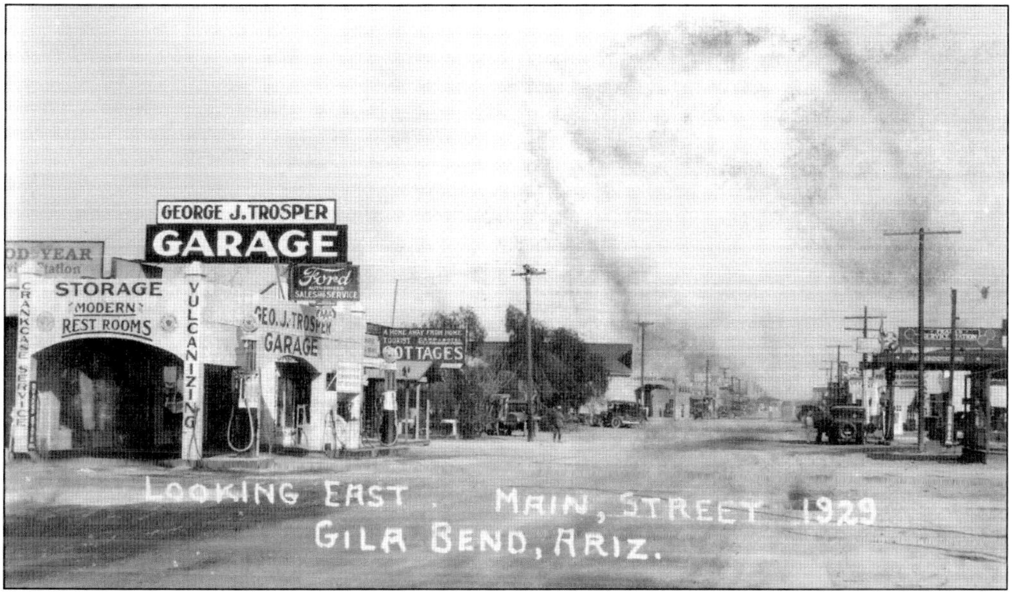

US 80 had an almost immediate impact on Gila Bend, physically and economically. The commercial route through town moved to Pima Street, and automobile-related businesses began to thrive. Brothers George and Homer Trosper were among the first entrepreneurs to take advantage of the town's new prosperity. They developed a service station and sizable automobile camp. The Trospers' operation was also the first business encountered when entering the town from the west. (Courtesy of Daisy Bean Policy.)

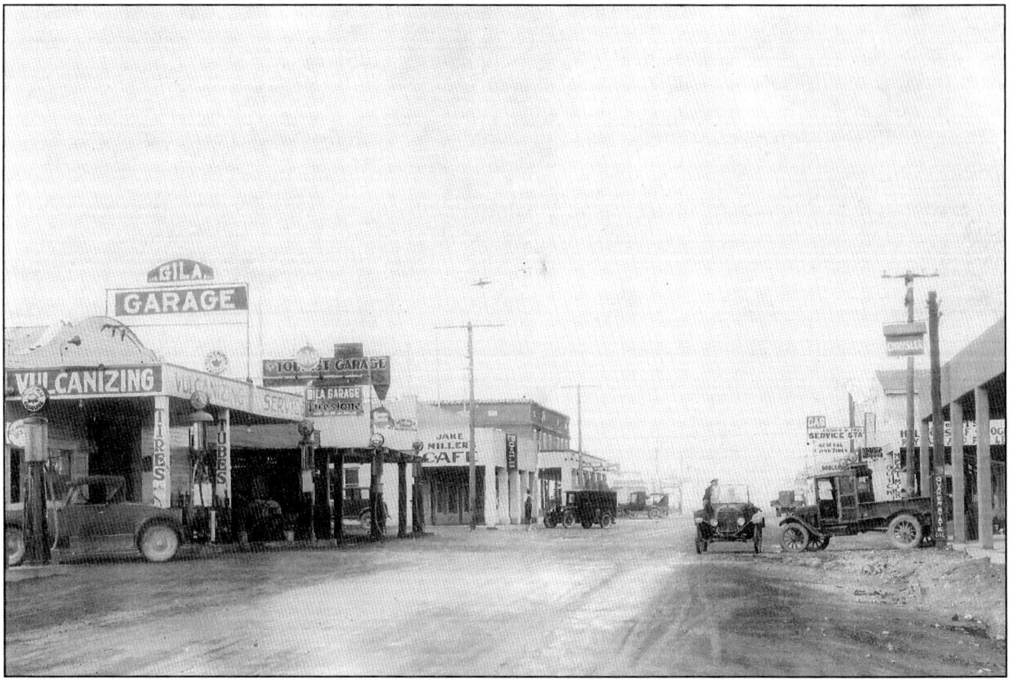

Competition developed quickly. Robert Singleton Gills opened his Gila Garage. Adjacent to Gills's establishment, John W. Bean and his brother opened the Tourist Garage in space leased from Jake Miller. (Courtesy of Daisy Bean Policy.)

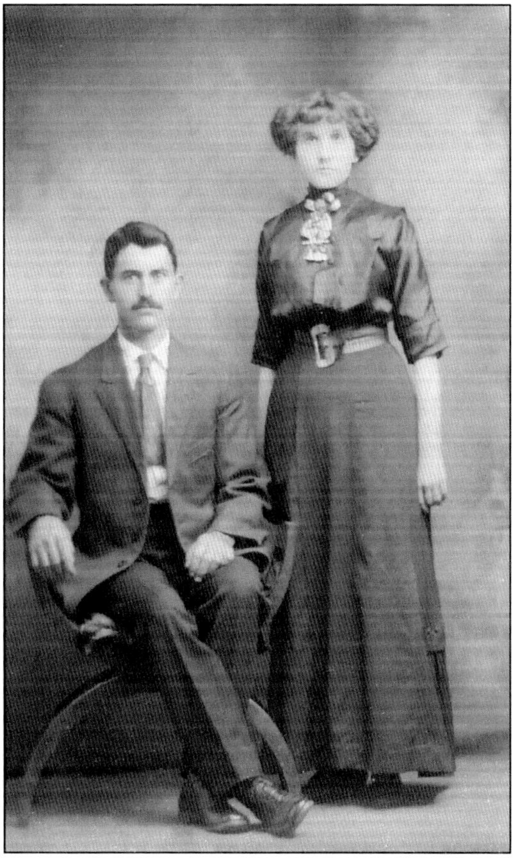

Robert Singleton Gills and wife, Martha "Virgie" Gills, came to Arizona from Arkansas around 1912 with Robert's parents. Gills's Gila Garage also employed his father, Robert Washington Gills, and his nephew Leonard Cole. Gills's son Silas also lived in Gila Bend and worked for the railroad. (Courtesy of Betty Gills.)

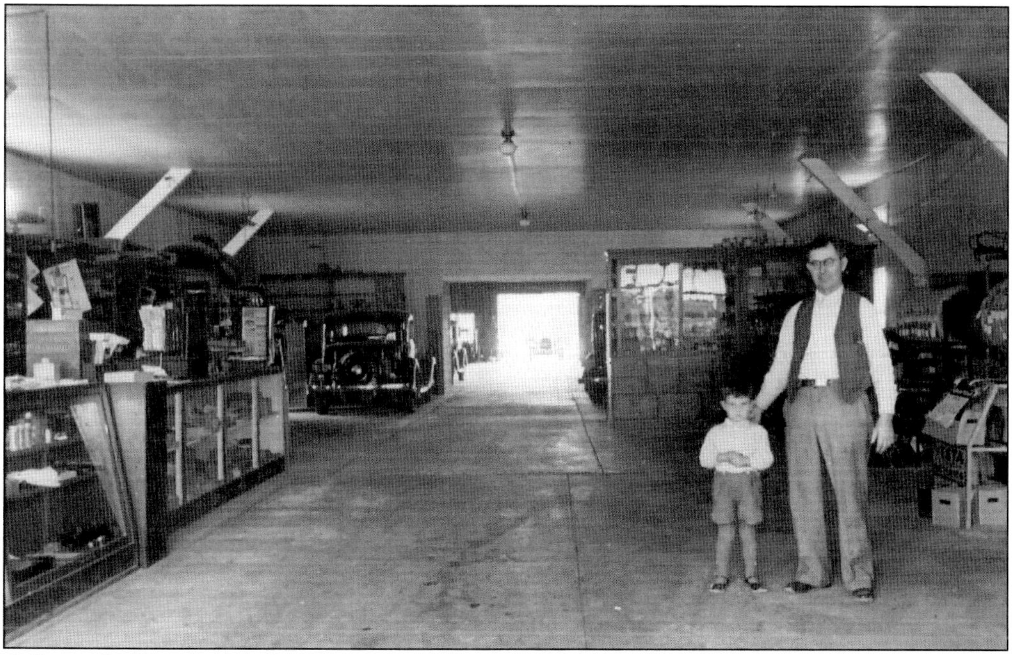

Gills's Gila Garage was the largest in Gila Bend, stretching from Pima Road on the north to Murphy Street on the south. Here, Robert shows the garage to grandson Doyle Gills. (Courtesy of Betty Gills.)

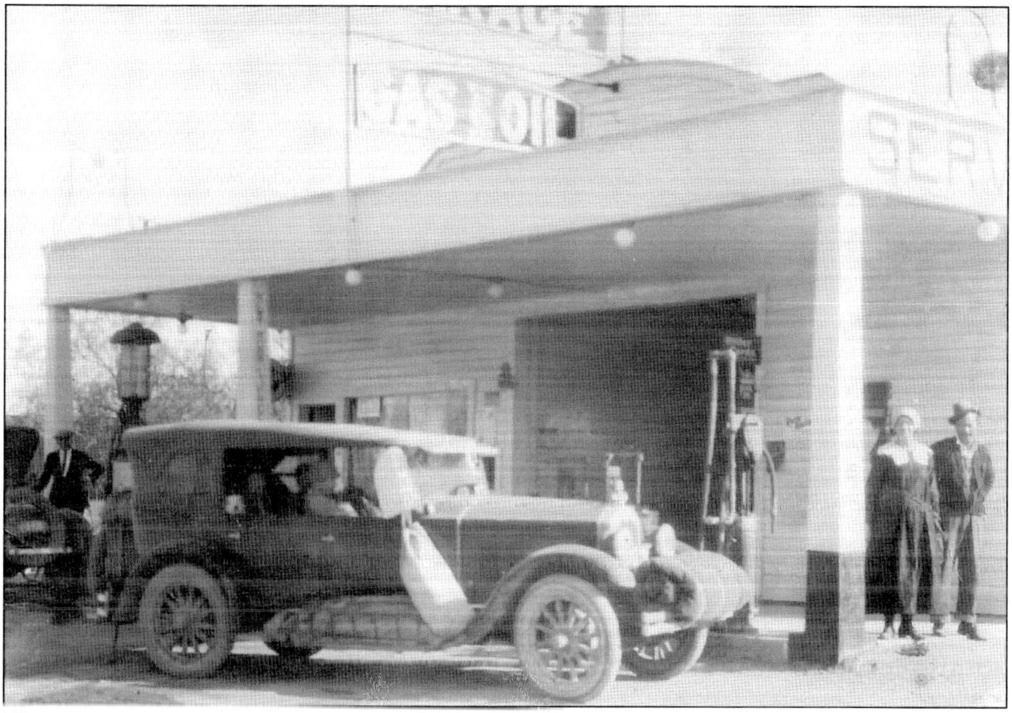

There were a number of families from Arkansas living in Gila Bend during the 1920s and 1930s, including the Gills, Coles, and Echolos. Virgie Gills and Steve Cole are in the far right of this photograph. (Courtesy of Betty Gills.)

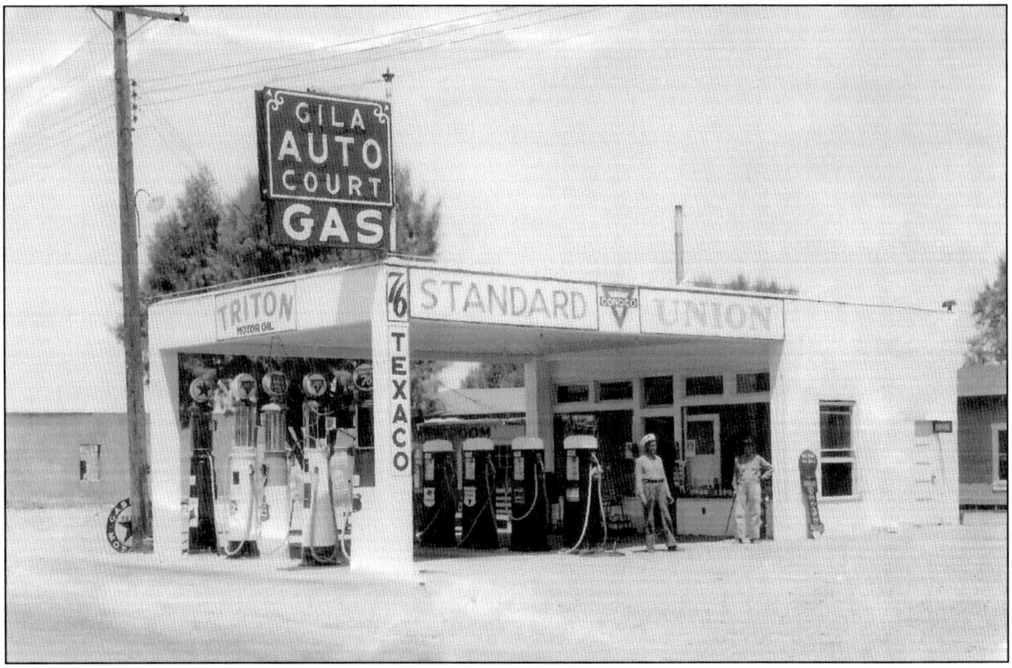

Gills eventually moved his garage across Pima Road to expand into the auto court business. Before the advent of auto courts, travelers' choices were limited. They could stay with family or friends, rent a room at a hotel or rooming house, or sleep under the stars at a tourist camp. The auto court eventually replaced the tourist camp as the favorite, affordable overnight accommodation. (Courtesy of Betty Gills.)

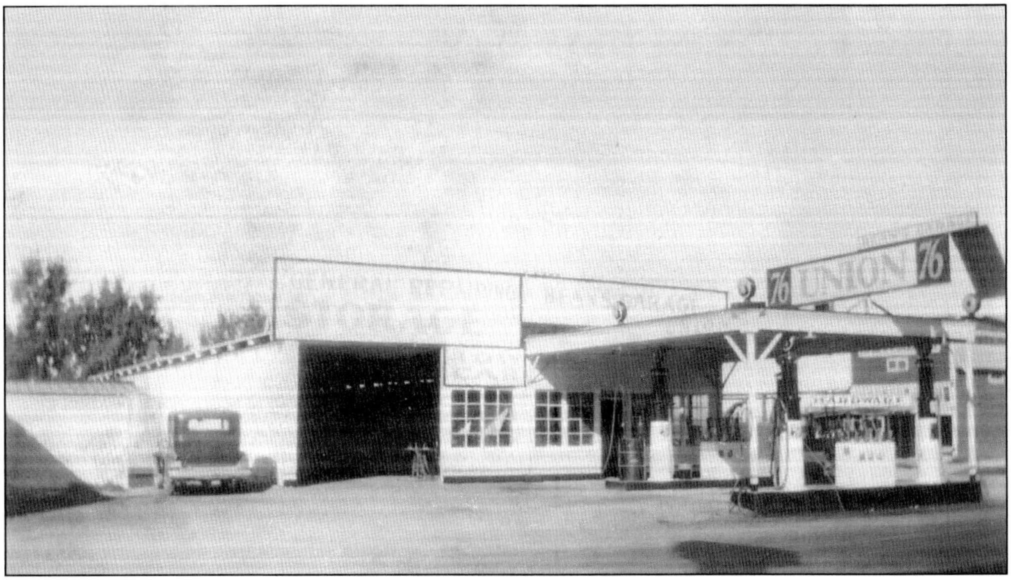

The Bean brothers eventually made enough money to also move to a new place across the street from their original location. (Courtesy of the Gila Bend Museum.)

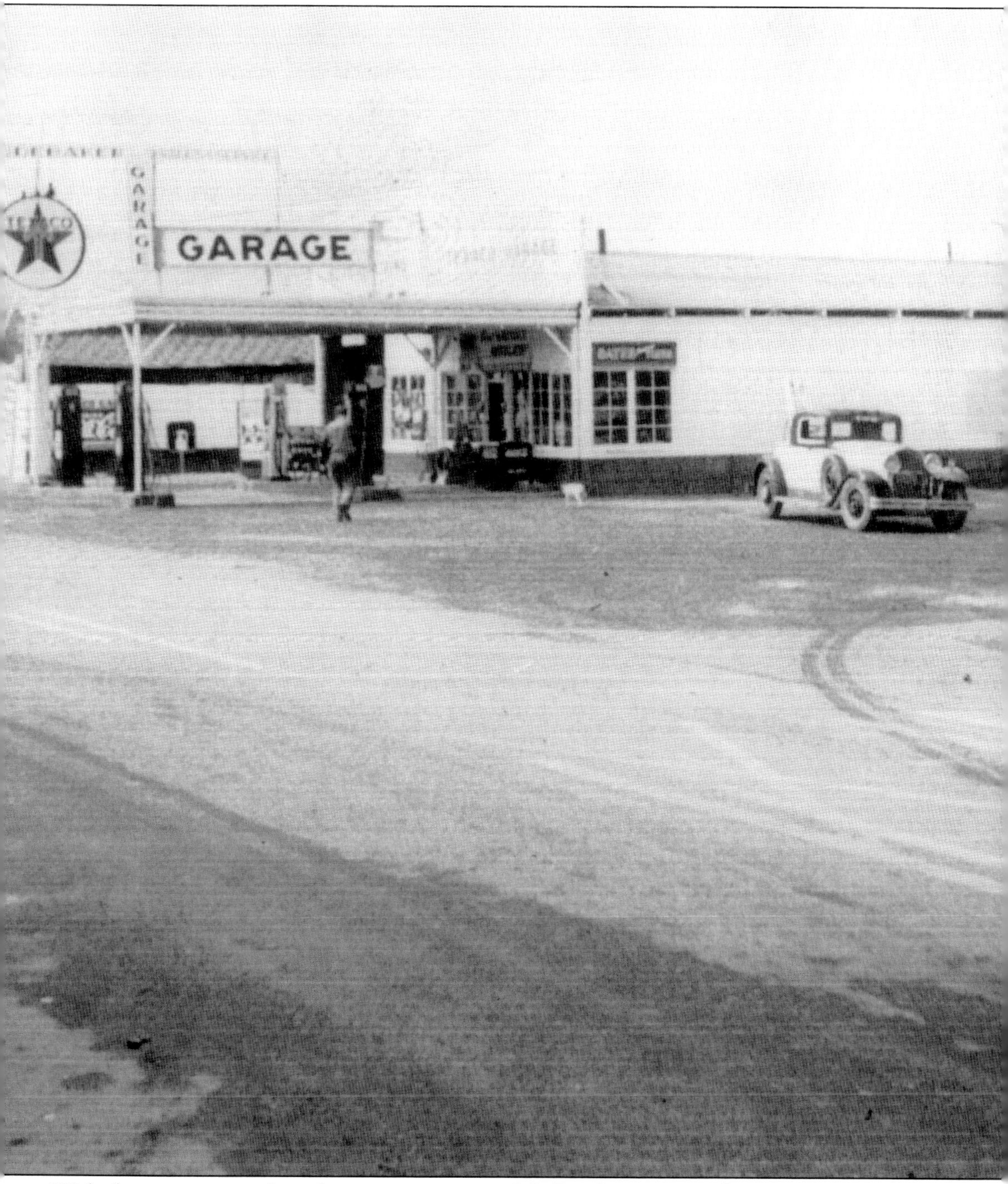

With the growing number of service stations in Gila Bend, companies began to specialize in the vehicles that they serviced and the fuel and petroleum products they offered—in this case, Studebakers and Texaco. (Courtesy of Betty Gills.)

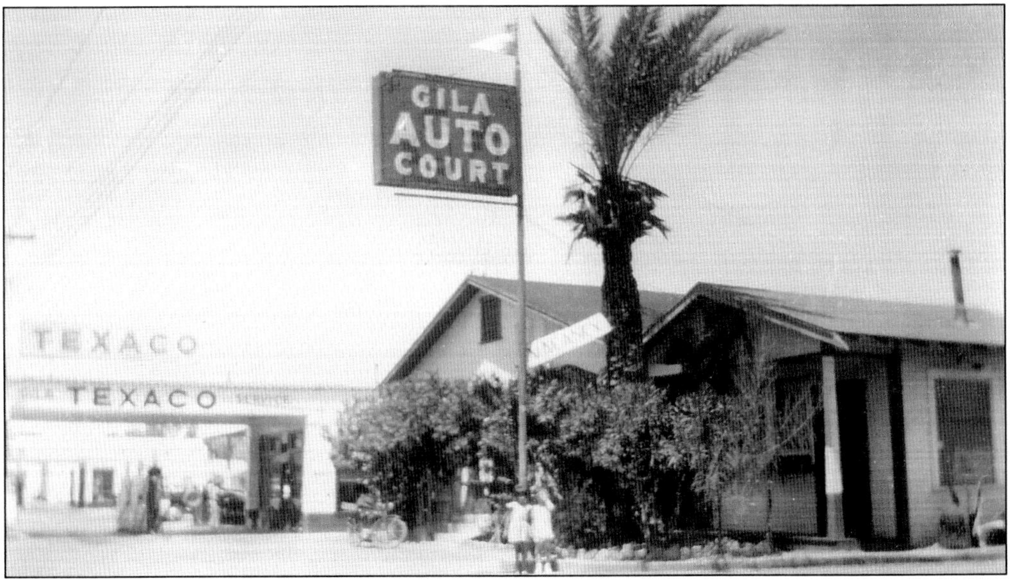

The Gila Auto Court included a main house for the owner-proprietors, a hotel, and auto court of over two dozen cabins. (Courtesy of Betty Gills.)

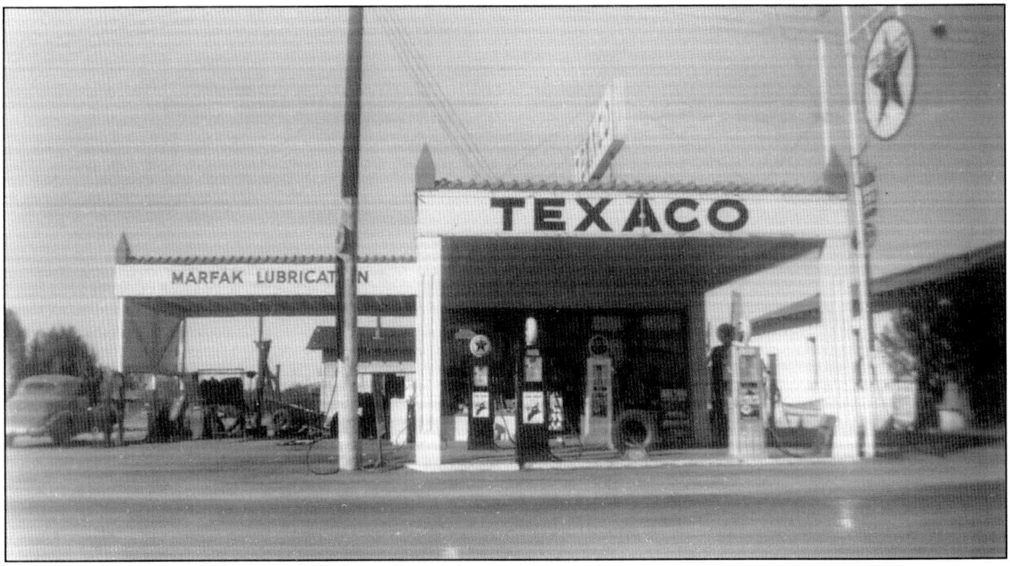

The Laird family came to Gila Bend to work on the railroad. Like many, they followed the trend and moved into the automobile service industry. (Courtesy of Johnny Laird.)

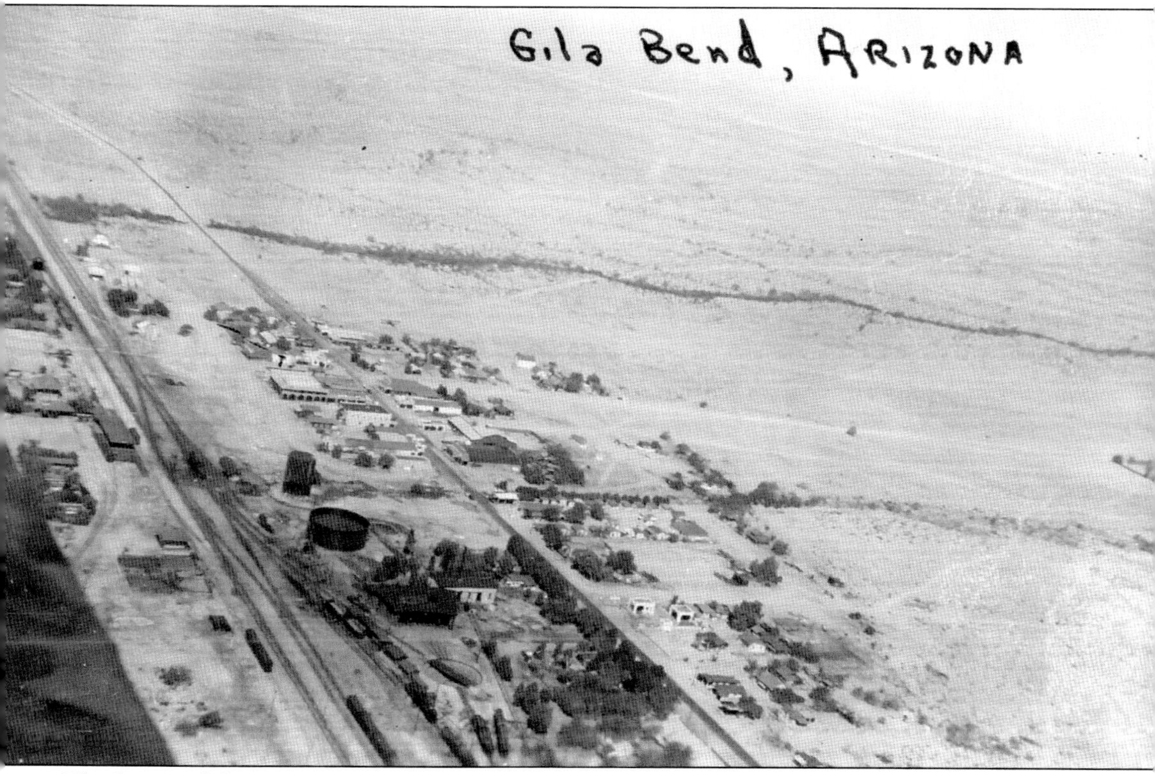

The layout of the town in 1930 is evident in this aerial photograph. Though the economy was very much automobile-related, the railroad remained the largest employer, with 200 employees out of a population of about 300. (Courtesy of the Gary Miller.)

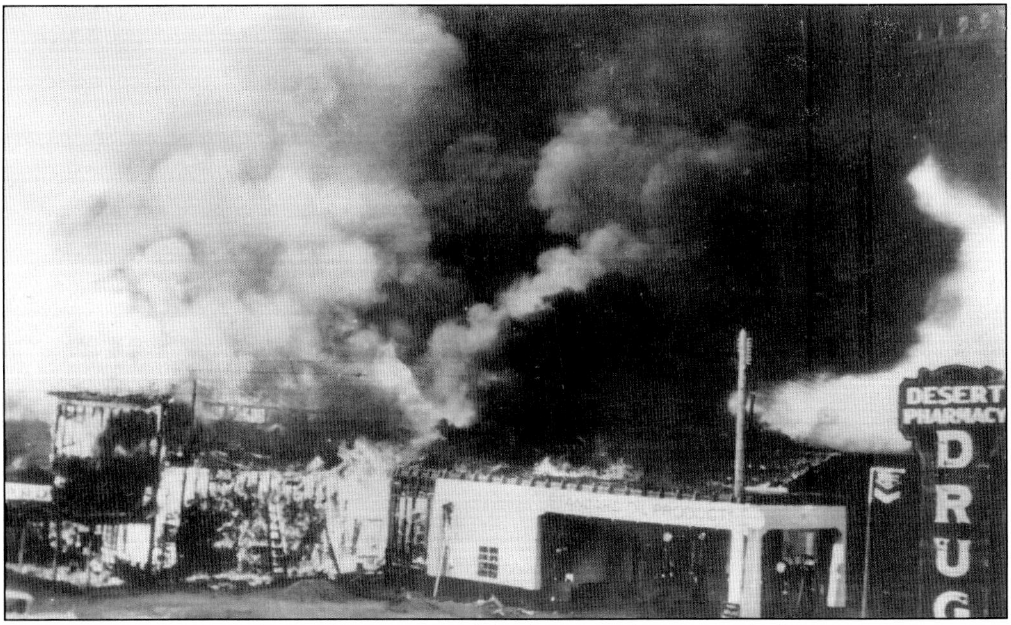

In 1936, a fire destroyed a sizable portion of the business district, including a service station, lumber company, mercantile, restaurant, and a house. The damages came to $80,000, which was considered quite a large sum at the time. (Courtesy of the Gila Bend Museum.)

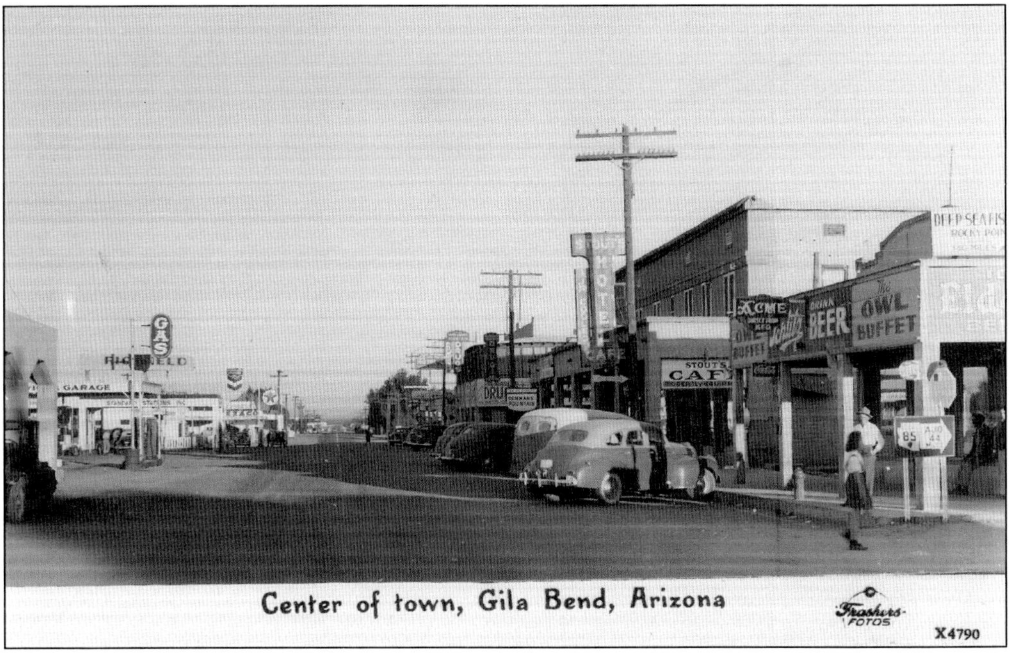

This photograph from the late 1940s shows the competition in downtown. Within just two blocks are three service stations, two hotels, two drugstores with soda fountains, and two cafés. (Courtesy of Ron Henry.)

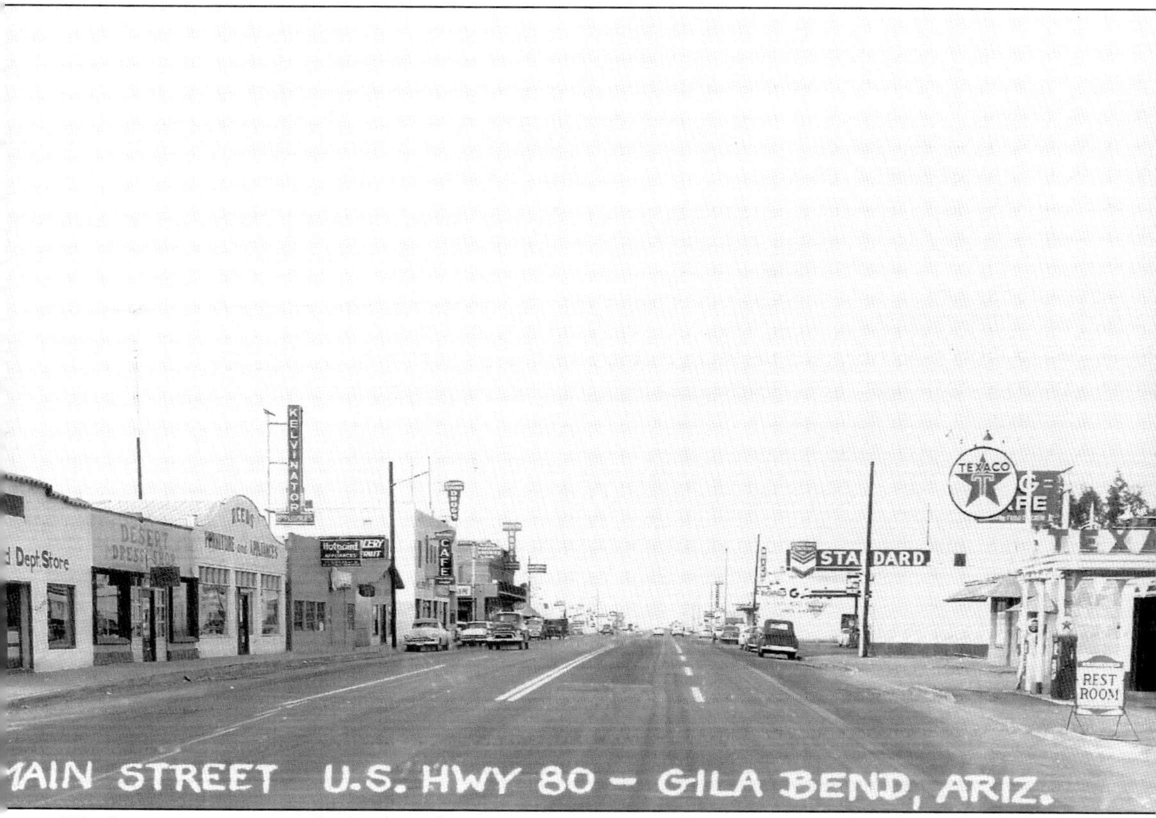

The booming economy also lead to a huge increase in population. Gila Bend grew from a population of 580 in 1950 to 1,844 in 1960. While the majority of the male populace worked in some facet of automobile service, some were employed in agriculture and the defense industry. Because of its location where US highways 80, 85, and 84 came together in the middle of the Sonoran Desert, more than 30 miles from any substantial cities, Gila Bend became known as the "Fan Belt Capital of the World," a moniker some lauded and others detested. With a widened road, the Gila Garage no longer had pumps and became an appliance store. Next door, occupying the former Tourist Garage, was Harold's. Miller's building also lost its large porch. (Courtesy of Betty Gills.)

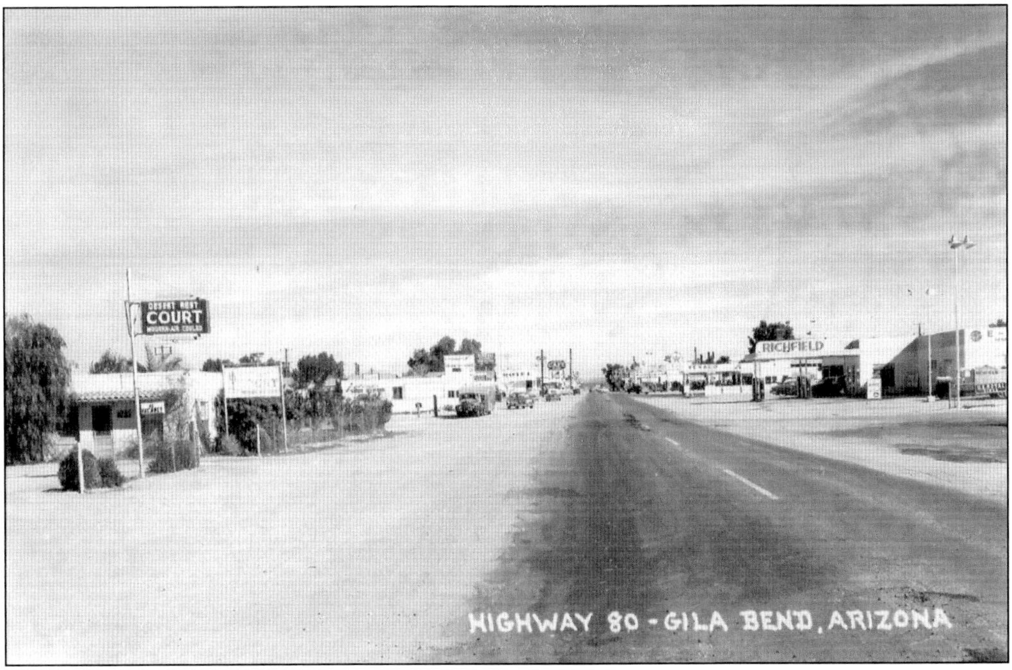

Gila Bend was growing, with plats for east and west Gila Bend being registered with the county recorder's office in 1931 and 1939 respectively. This photograph is of west Gila Bend, which was still considered outside of town in the early 1950s. (Courtesy of Betty Gills.)

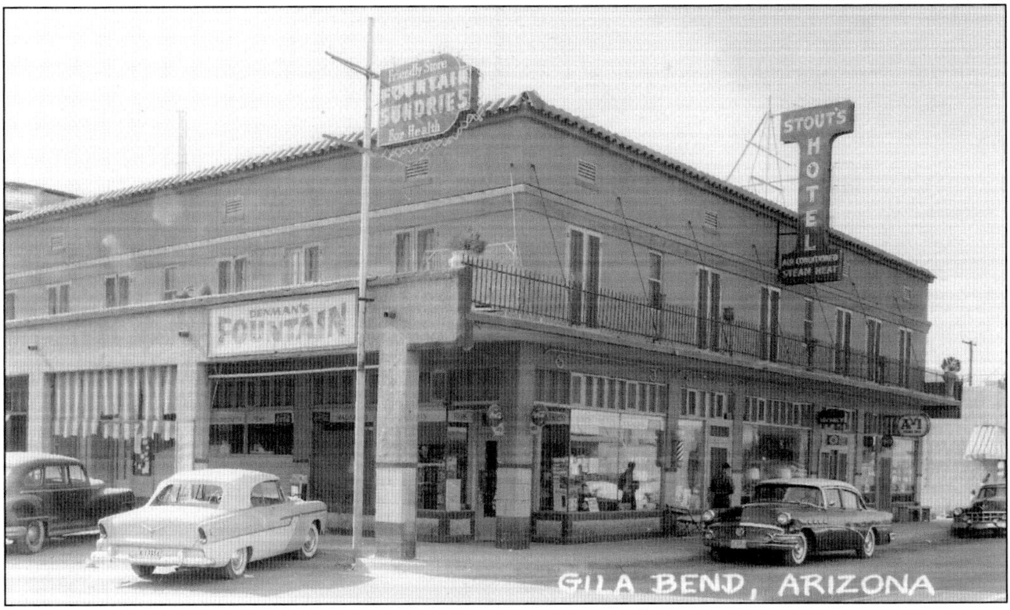

The growing number of accommodations for travelers and improvements in transportation continued to encourage more tourism. As additional people traveled through town, the number of service business increased until the end of the 1950s, when the town could boast three trailer parks, five grocery stores, 10 motels, 14 cafés, and 20 service stations. The widening of the highway also led to the removal of the facades from iconic buildings such as the Stout Hotel and Owl Buffet. (Courtesy of the Gila Bend Museum.)

By the 1950s, the Rio Drive-in Theater had opened in Gila Bend, providing a new and appropriate entertainment option for a town with an evolving automobile travel–based economy. (Courtesy of the Gila Bend Museum.)

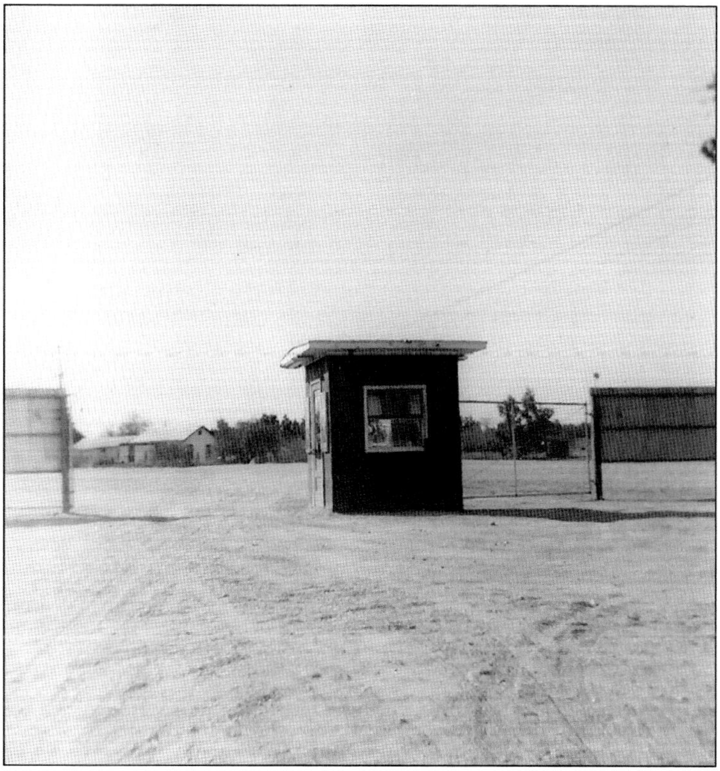

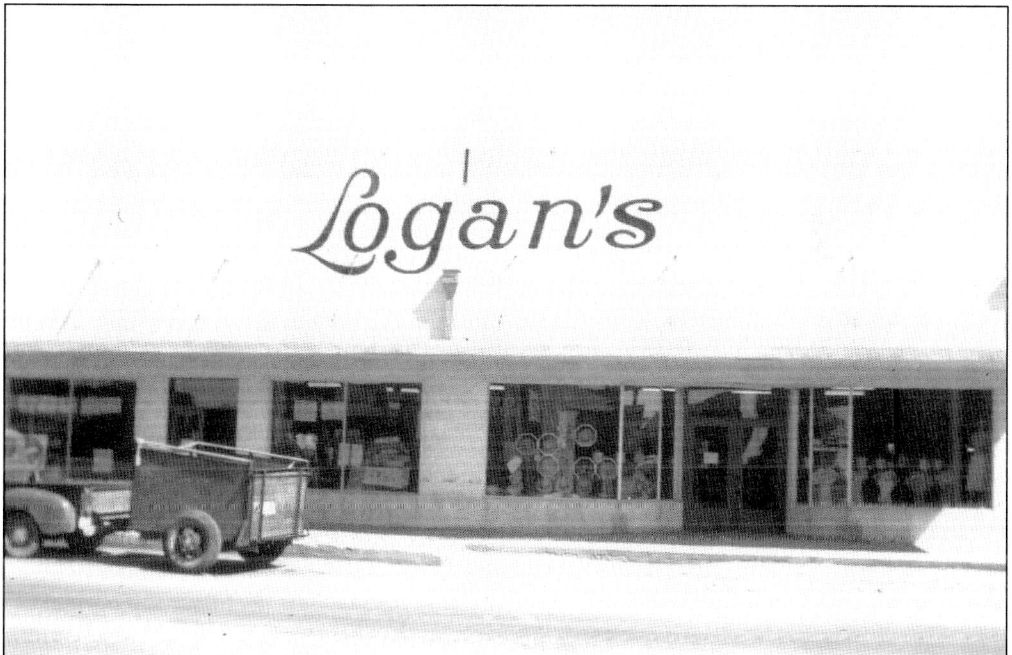

Logan's also made changes to its facade to adapt to the loss of its covered sidewalk. It was an ironic change, since the arcade was built with the designation of US 80. (Courtesy of the Gila Bend Museum.)

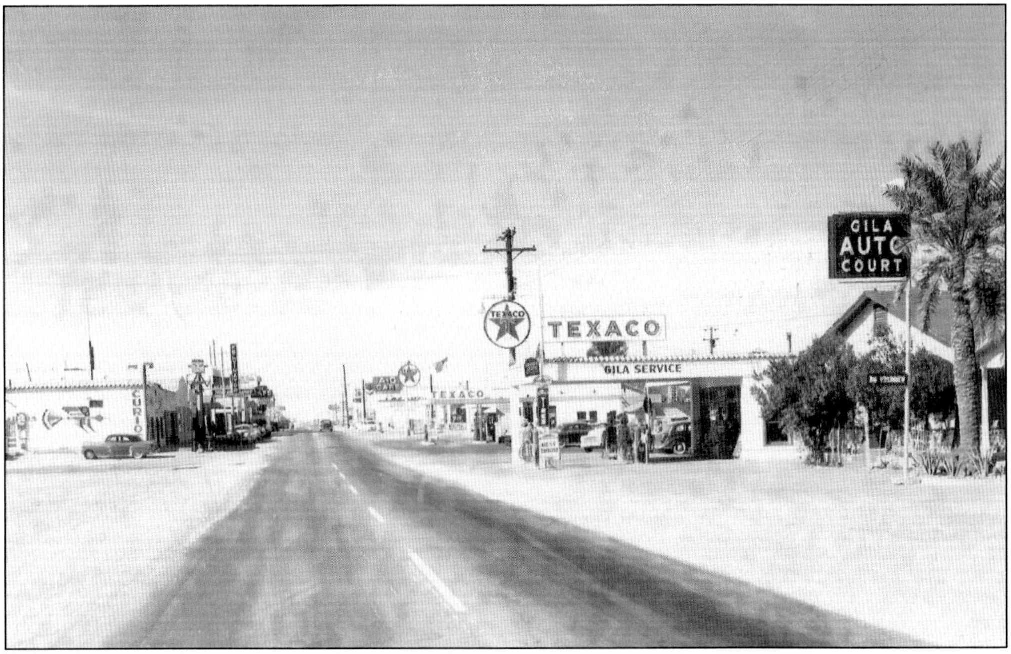

This photograph shows the highway through town in the early 1950s before the widening. Note the two Texaco stations. The au naturel shoulders are the substitutes for sidewalks. (Courtesy of Betty Gills.)

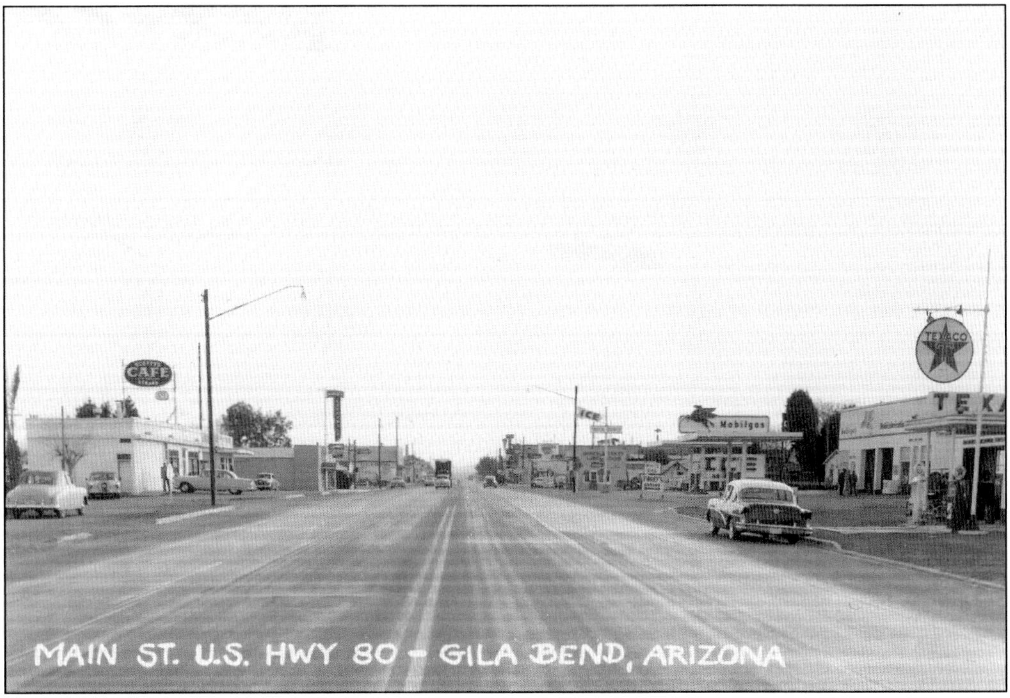

This view looks east down Gila Bend's "Main Street" (actually Pima Road) in the mid- to late 1950s. (Courtesy of Ron Henry.)

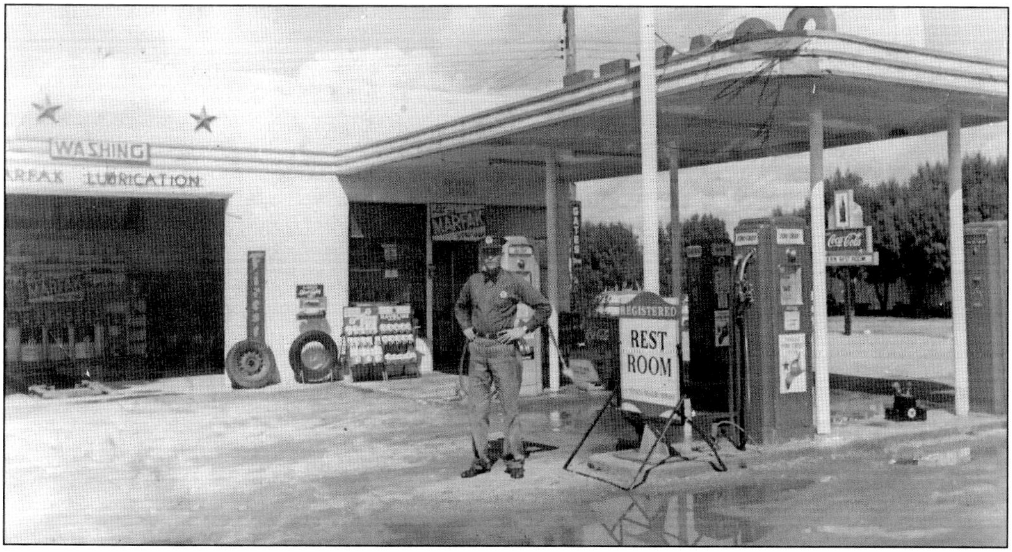

Here is an image of Charlie Bell's Texaco on the east end of town in the 1940s. As with most Texaco stations of the time, Marfak lubrication was a specialty. (Courtesy of Elva Mae McMahon.)

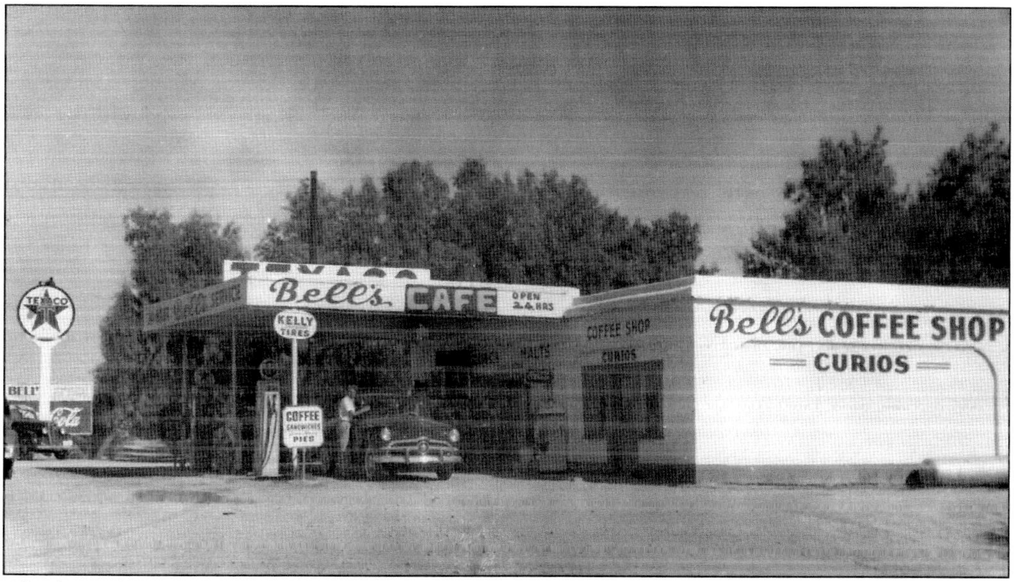

Charlie Bell's station was updated in the 1950s to include a snack bar and curio shop. It is not clear if Marfak lubrication is still available. (Courtesy of Elva Mae McMahon.)

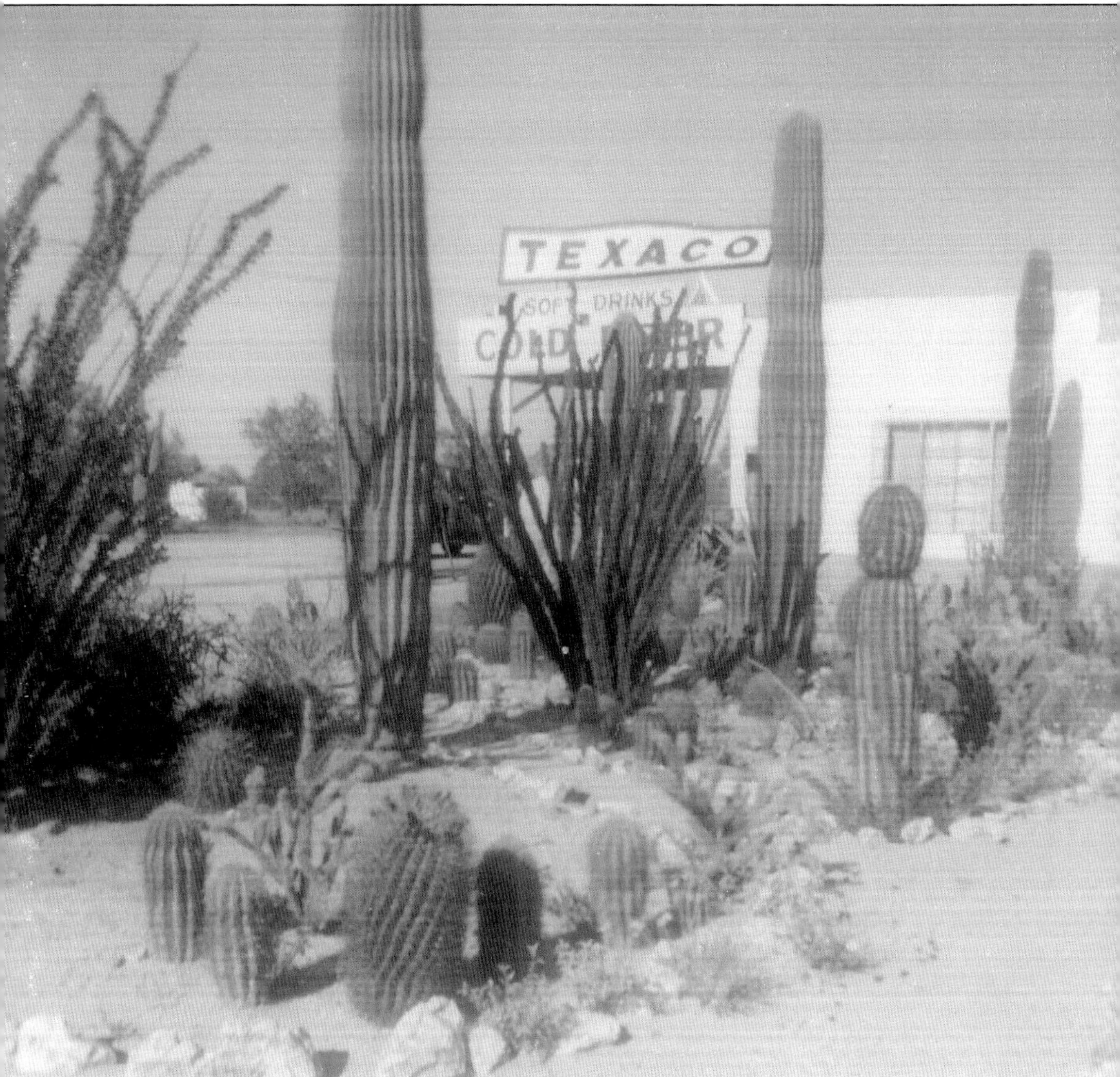

Curtis and Harold Hacker operated another Texaco station called Curtis' Place. It featured a cactus garden, as seen in this photograph. (Courtesy of Barbara Tillman.)

In this photograph, Barbara Tillman (the sister of Harold Hacker) is happily at work behind the counter at Curtis' Place. The station also offered a snack bar and served alcohol. (Courtesy of Barbara Tillman.)

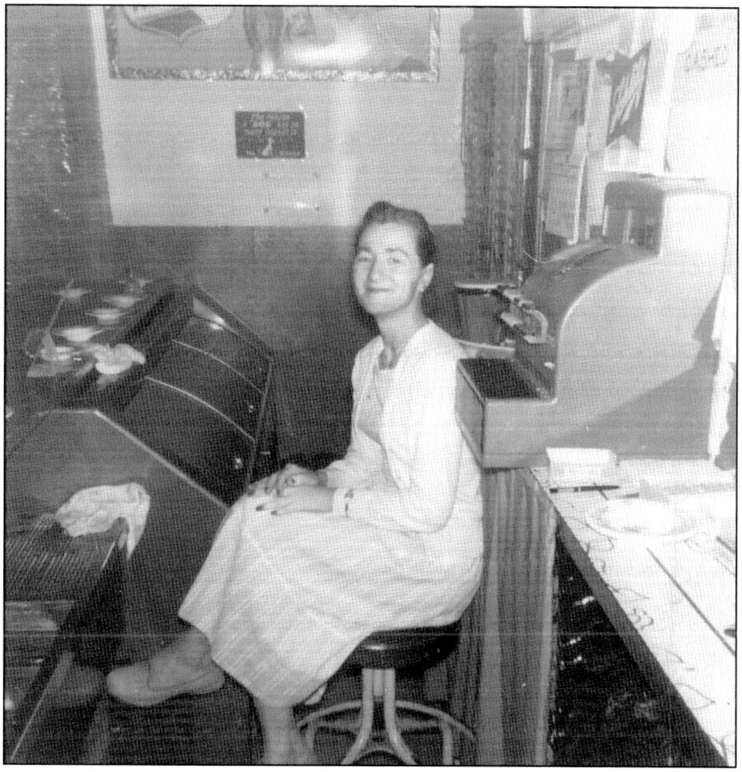

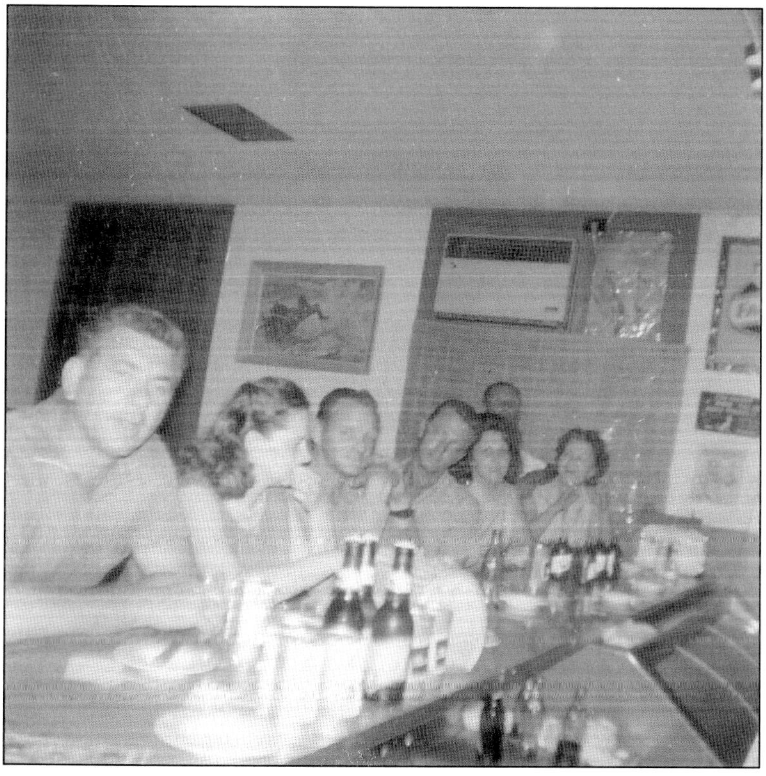

Curtis' Place was a small spot that could quickly fill with locals, as pictured here. (Courtesy of Barbara Tillman.)

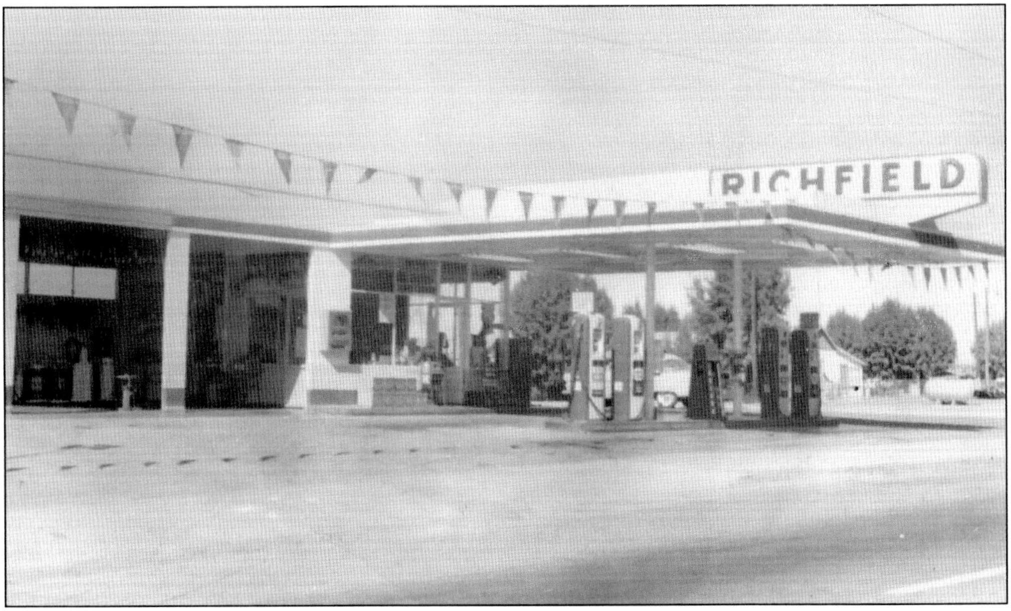

Thomas J. Harrison operated this Richfield station during the 1950s. (Courtesy of Bonnie Sandoval.)

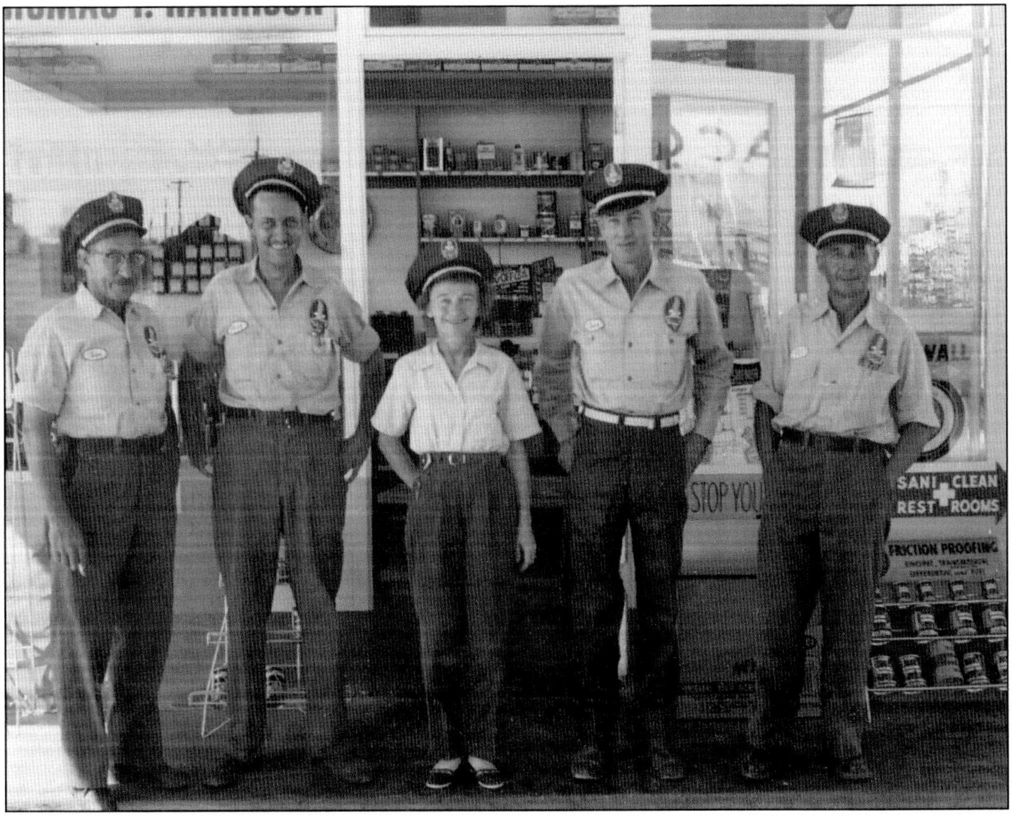

Harrison's operation was a family affair. This photograph includes, from left to right, Thomas, son Mick; Thomas's wife, Diane; and two unidentified employees. (Courtesy of Bonnie Sandoval.)

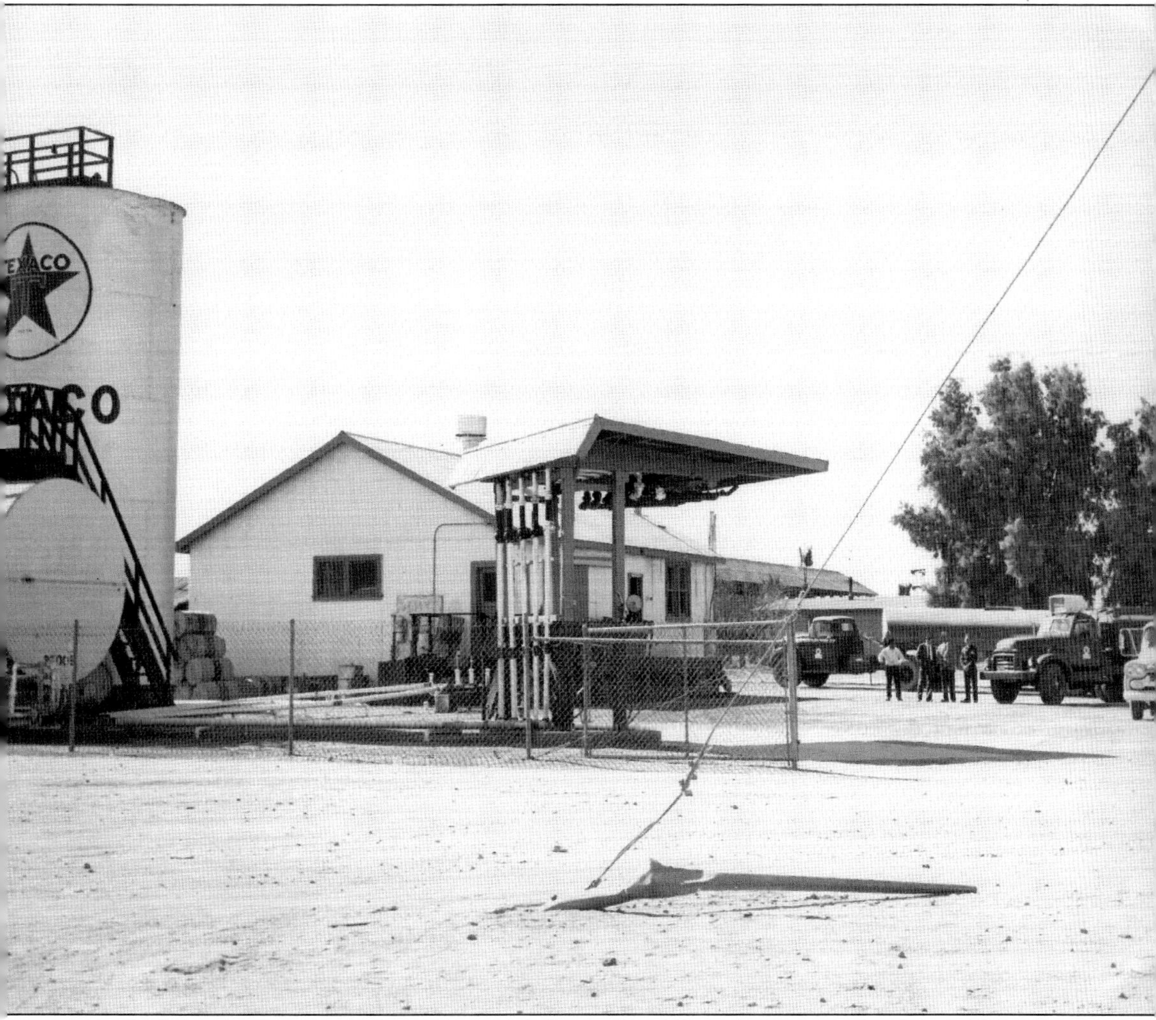

Texaco was obviously a popular business in town; the company also had a plant near the tracks. (Courtesy of Steven Holt.)

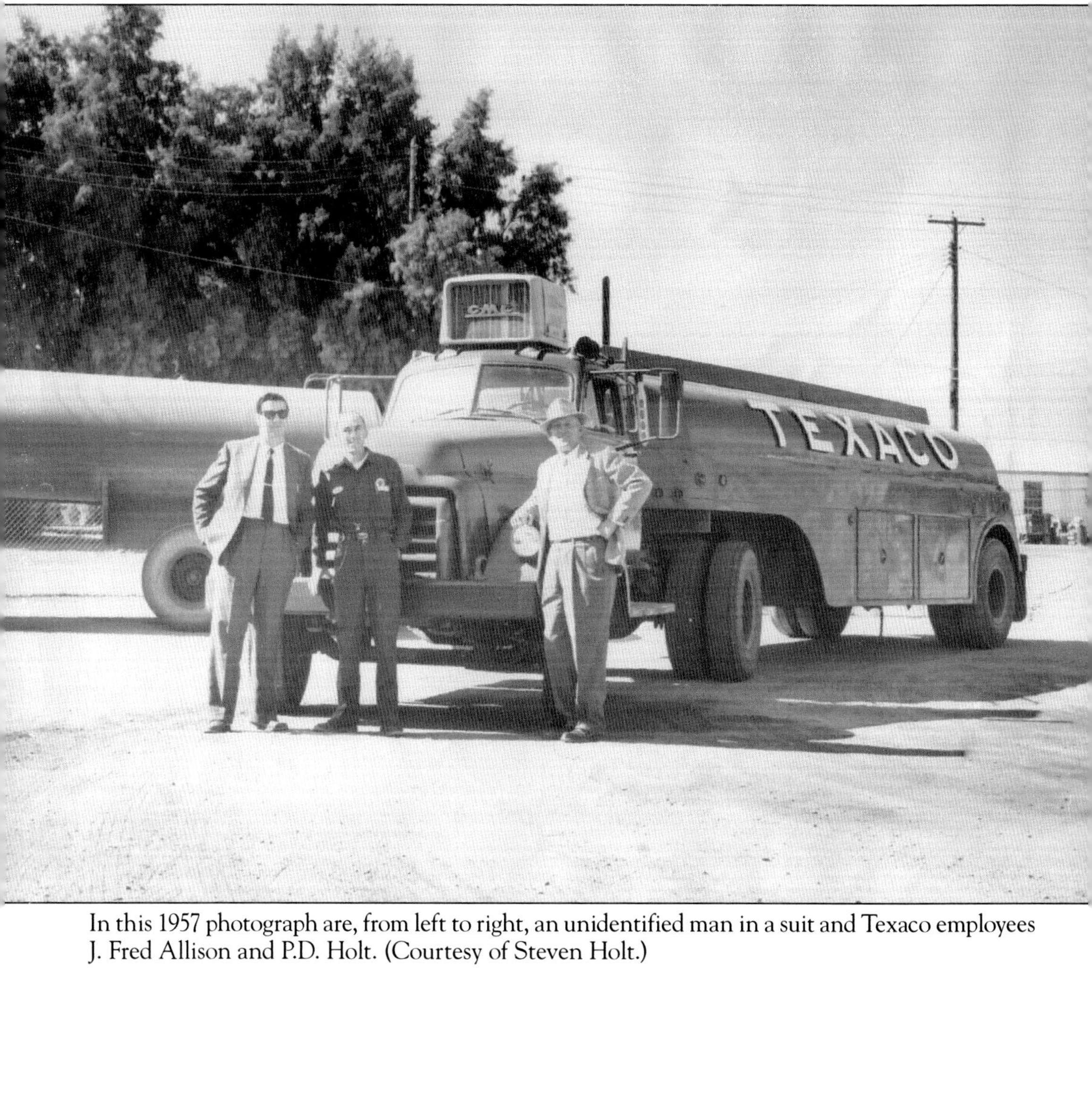

In this 1957 photograph are, from left to right, an unidentified man in a suit and Texaco employees J. Fred Allison and P.D. Holt. (Courtesy of Steven Holt.)

Five

Once a Gila Bender . . .

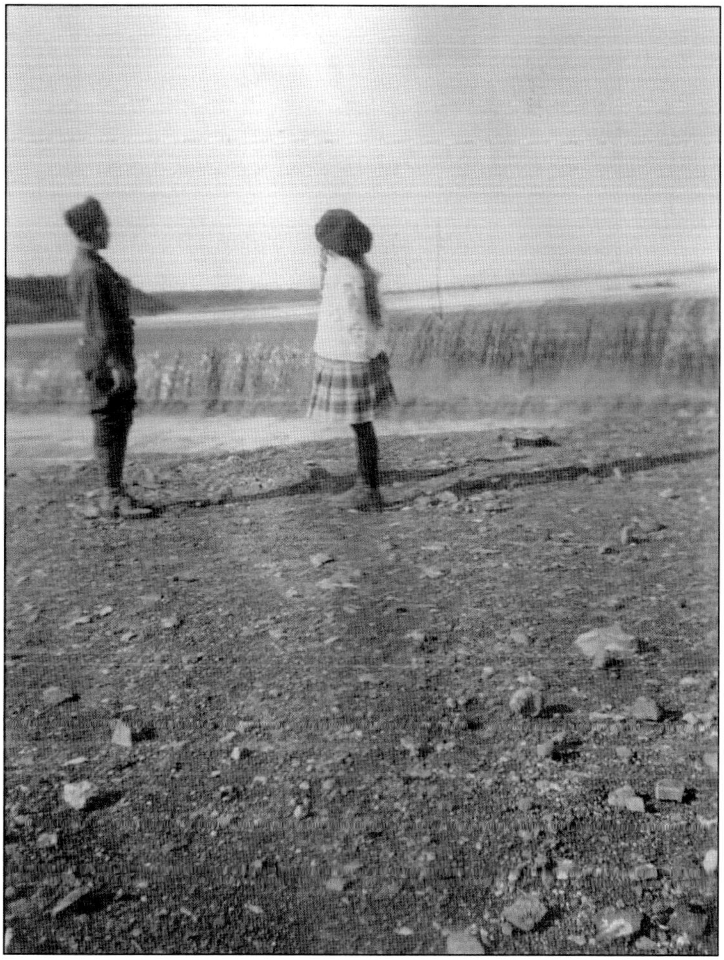

U. L. Logan Jr. and sister Louise visit the Gillespie Dam during high water. The flow of the Gila River was probably too deep to use the dam's apron for crossing. (Courtesy of the Gila Bend Museum.)

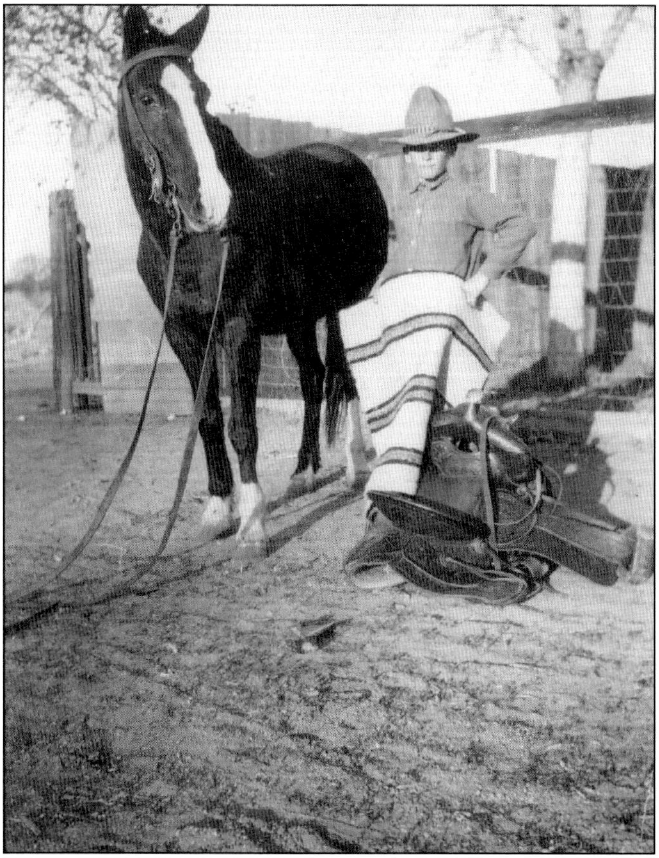

U.L. Logan Jr. is pictured in 1925 with a horse at the family ranch. (Courtesy of the Gila Bend Museum.)

Members of the extended Gills family include, from left to right, Kathy Gills, Silvester Chess Gills, Ruby Gills Neal, John Neal, Jack Neal, and Doyle Neal. (Courtesy of Betty Gills.)

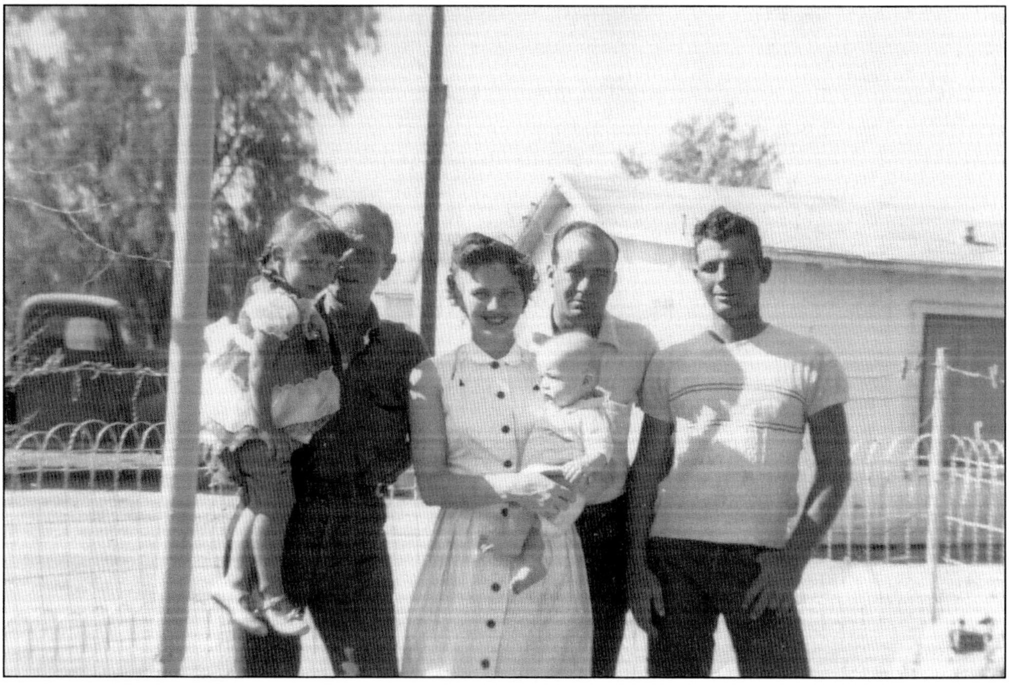

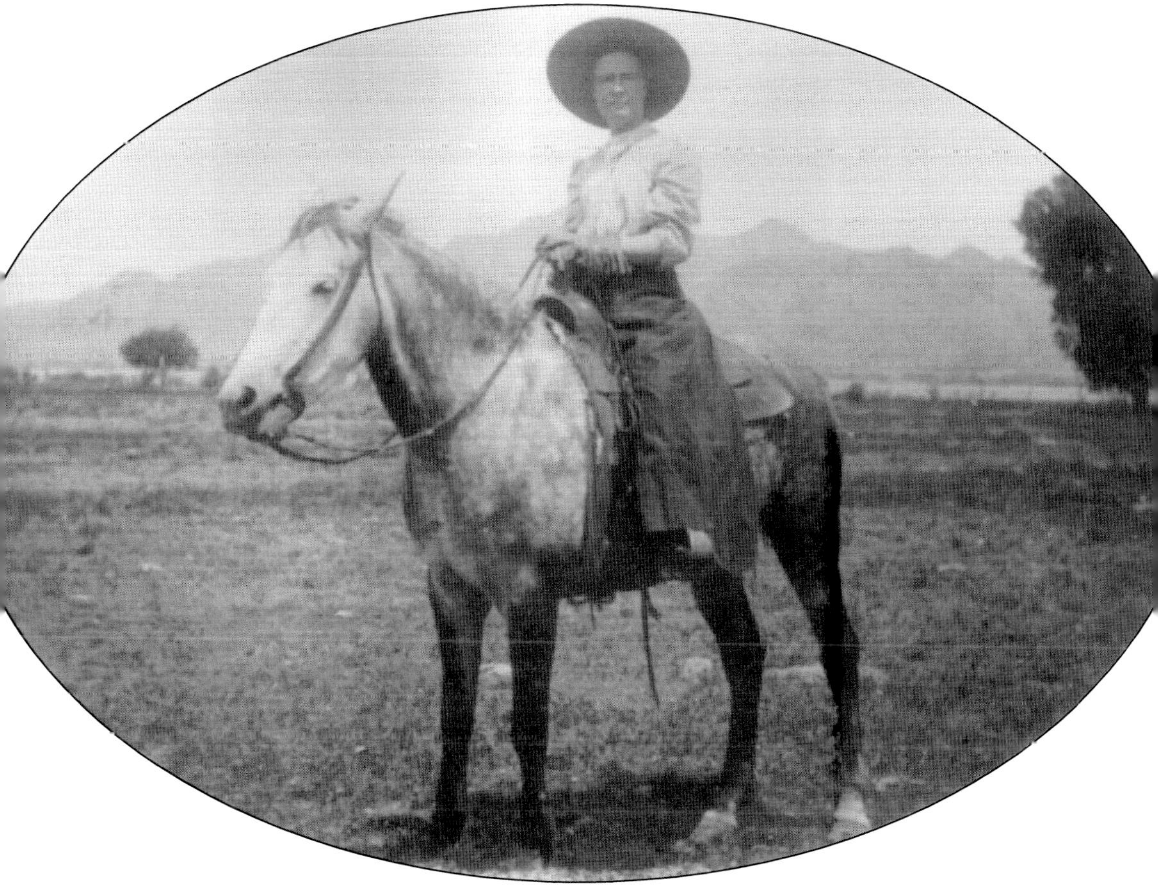

Pictured here in 1910 is Oklahoma "Okla" Anderson Noonan. Okla's parents were Irish immigrants much like those of her husband, Daniel Noonan Jr. In 1914, Okla was a livestock inspector and perhaps the only woman holding that position in the United States at the time. (Courtesy of the Gila Bend Museum.)

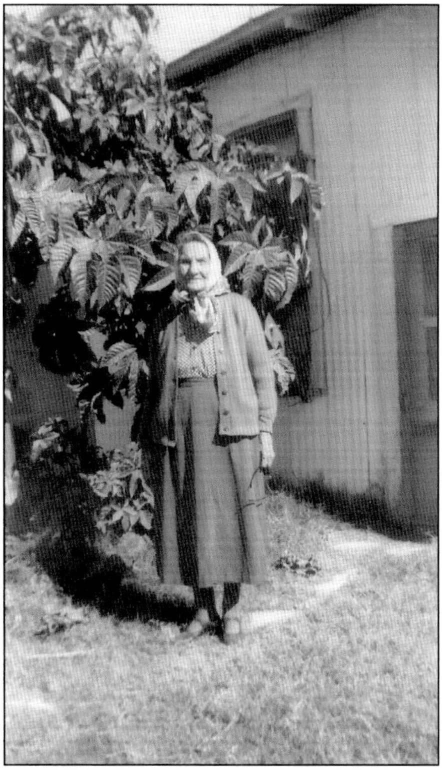

Marta "Virgie" Gills was one of the original Arkansas clan to immigrate to Gila Bend, where she lived out the rest of her life. She died in 1958 at the age of 80. (Courtesy of Betty Gills.)

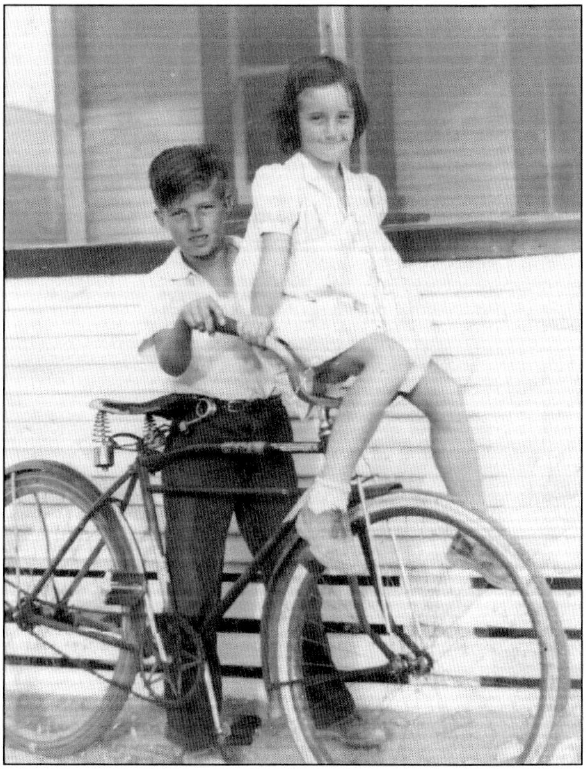

LaVerne and Daisy Bean were the children of service station owner John Bean and his wife, Lillie. In the early 20th century, paved streets in Gila Bend were far from the norm. However, Gila Bend was relatively flat and small, which made the bicycle a perfect means of transportation around town. This photograph was taken around 1931. (Courtesy of Daisy Bean Policy.)

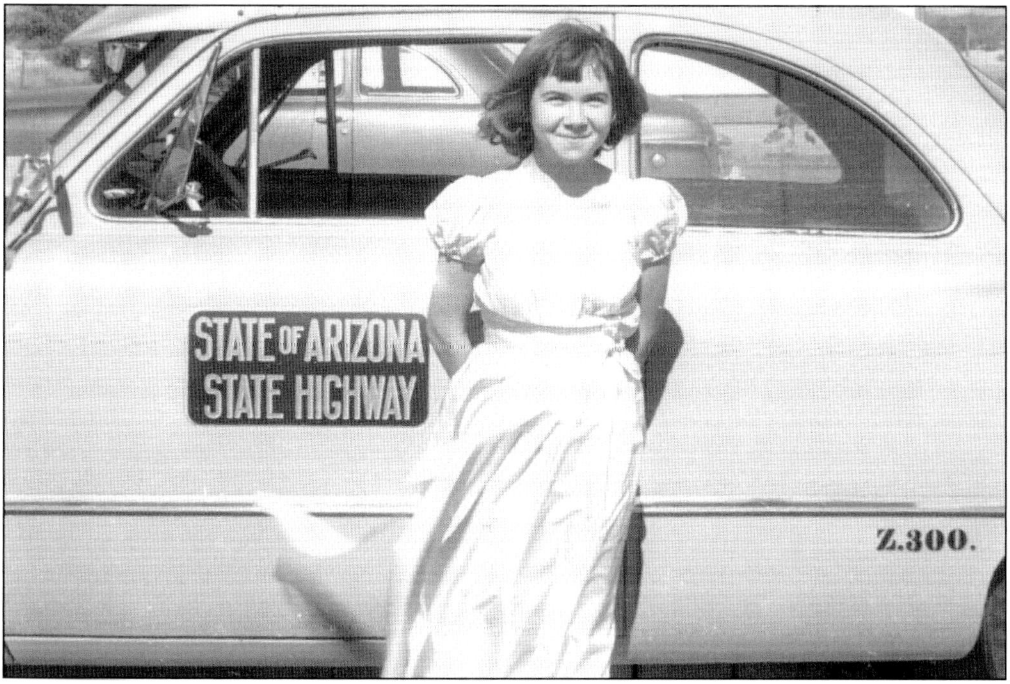

Elva Mae Palmer, daughter of Gene Palmer, stands in front of her father's squad car in 1950. (Courtesy of Elva Mae McMahon.)

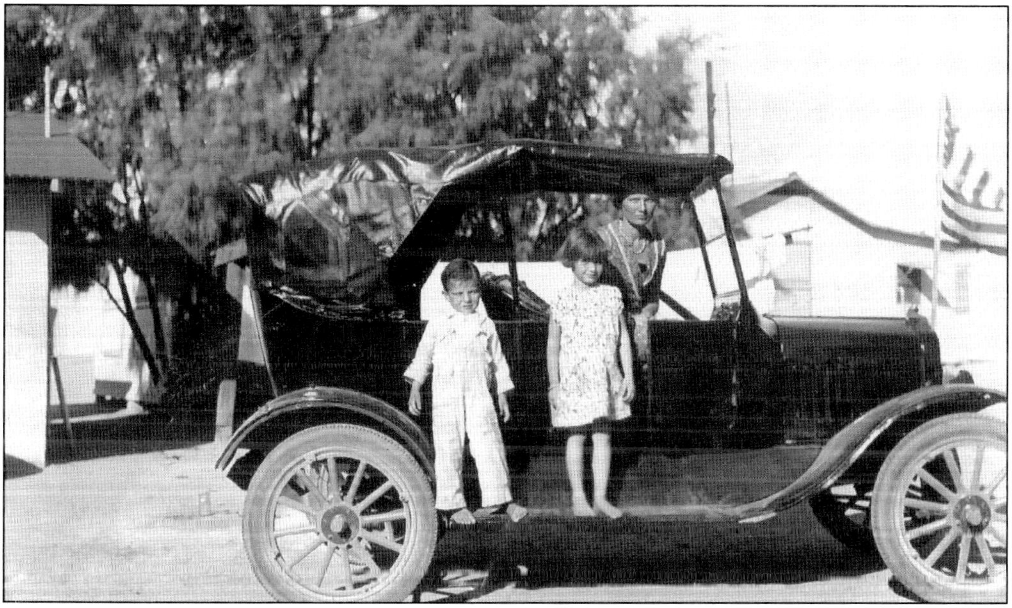
Thelma Gills, wife of Chess Gills, pauses for a photograph with their children, Ruby and Doyle. (Courtesy of Betty Gills.)

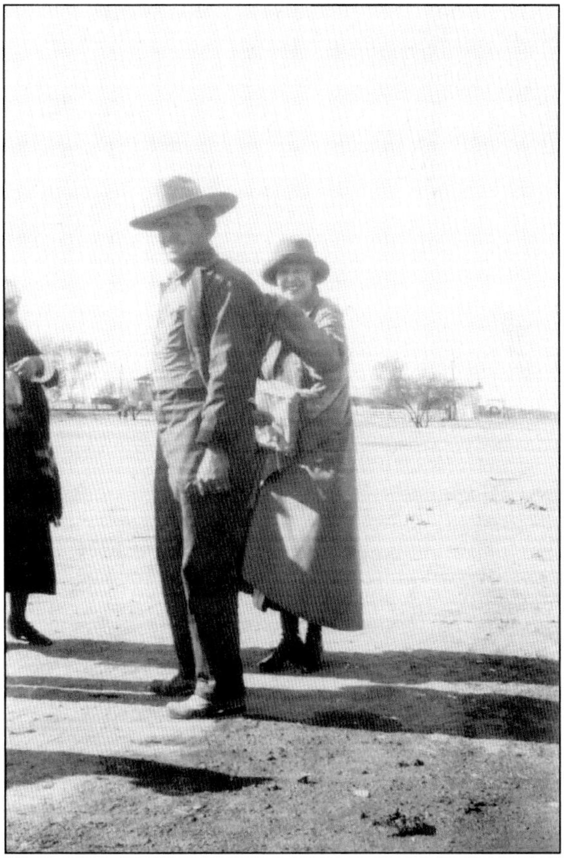

Positioned on the main highway to San Diego from points east, Gila Bend has had more than its share of celebrities pass through town. In this photograph, Clarke Gable poses with Gila Bend local Maudie Stout. (Courtesy of Edward Stout.)

The main highway was often blocked due to heavy traffic and plenty of accidents. Here, an overturned egg truck creates a picture-perfect moment east of town. (Courtesy of Elva Mae McMahon.)

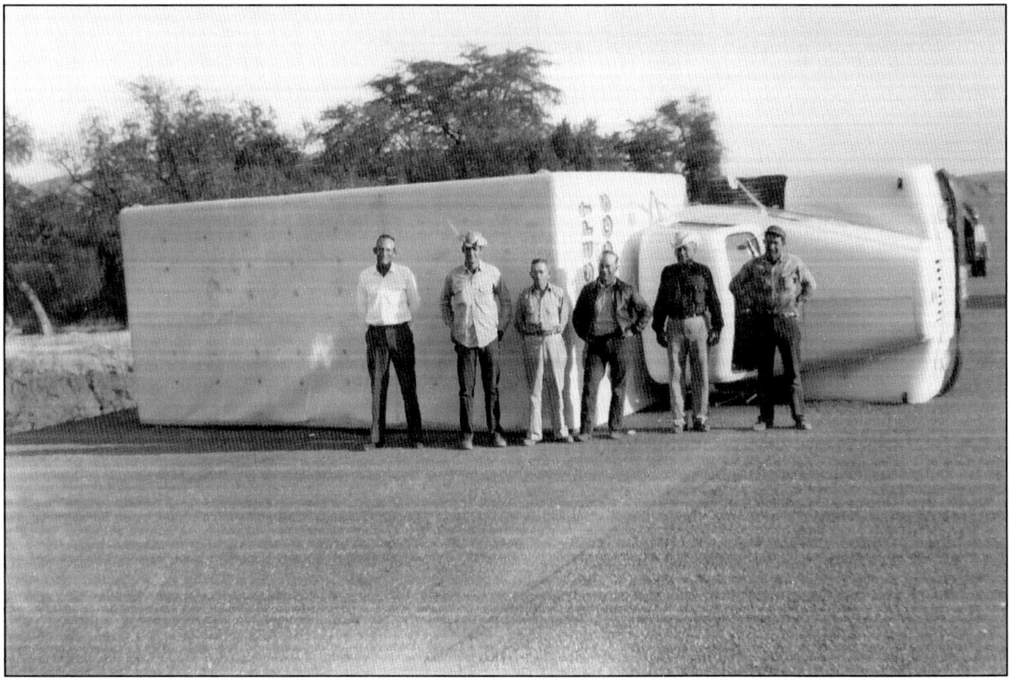

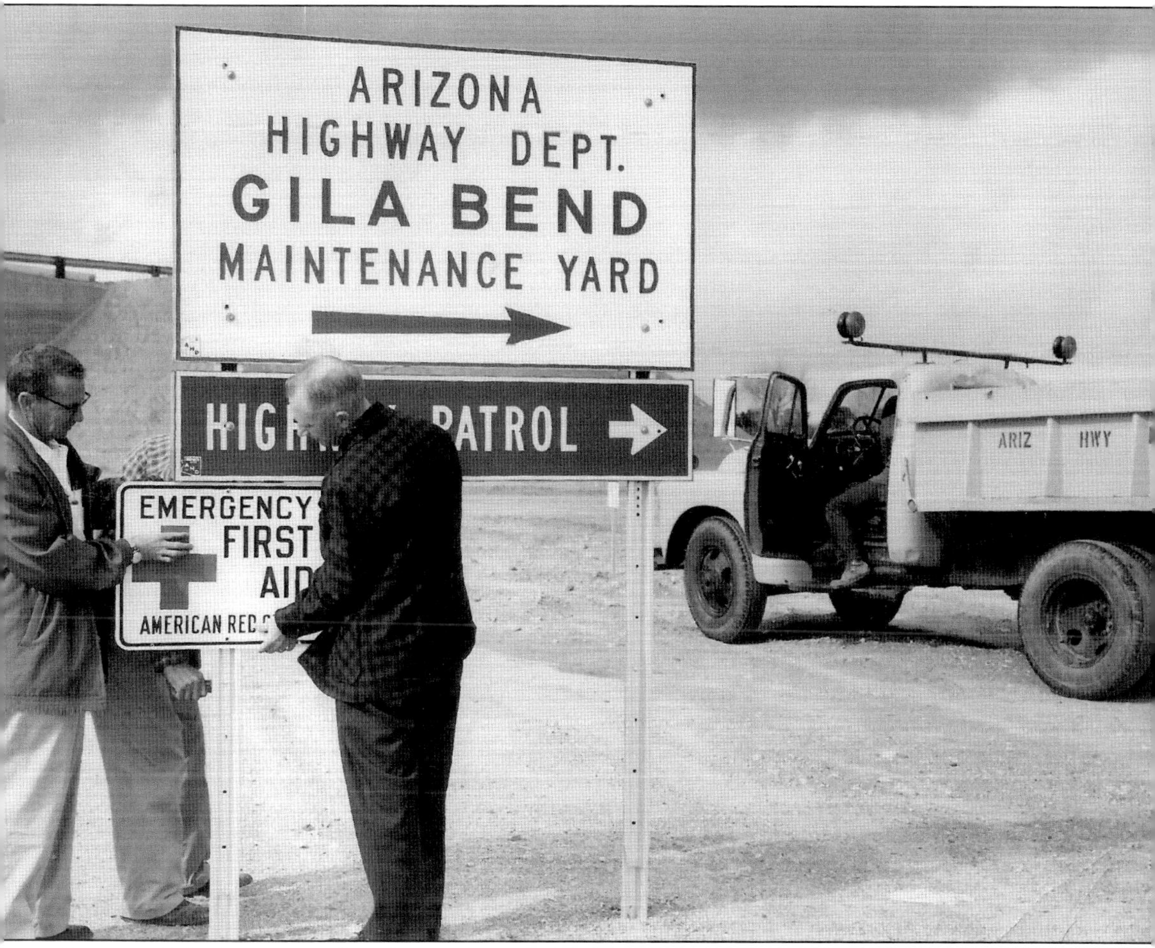

Because of the frequency of traffic accidents and the town's location in the middle of the Sonoran Desert, the Arizona Department of Transportation (ADOT) put up a sign directing travelers to the Red Cross–sponsored emergency first-aid station located east of town during the 1960s. (Courtesy of Elva Mae McMahon.)

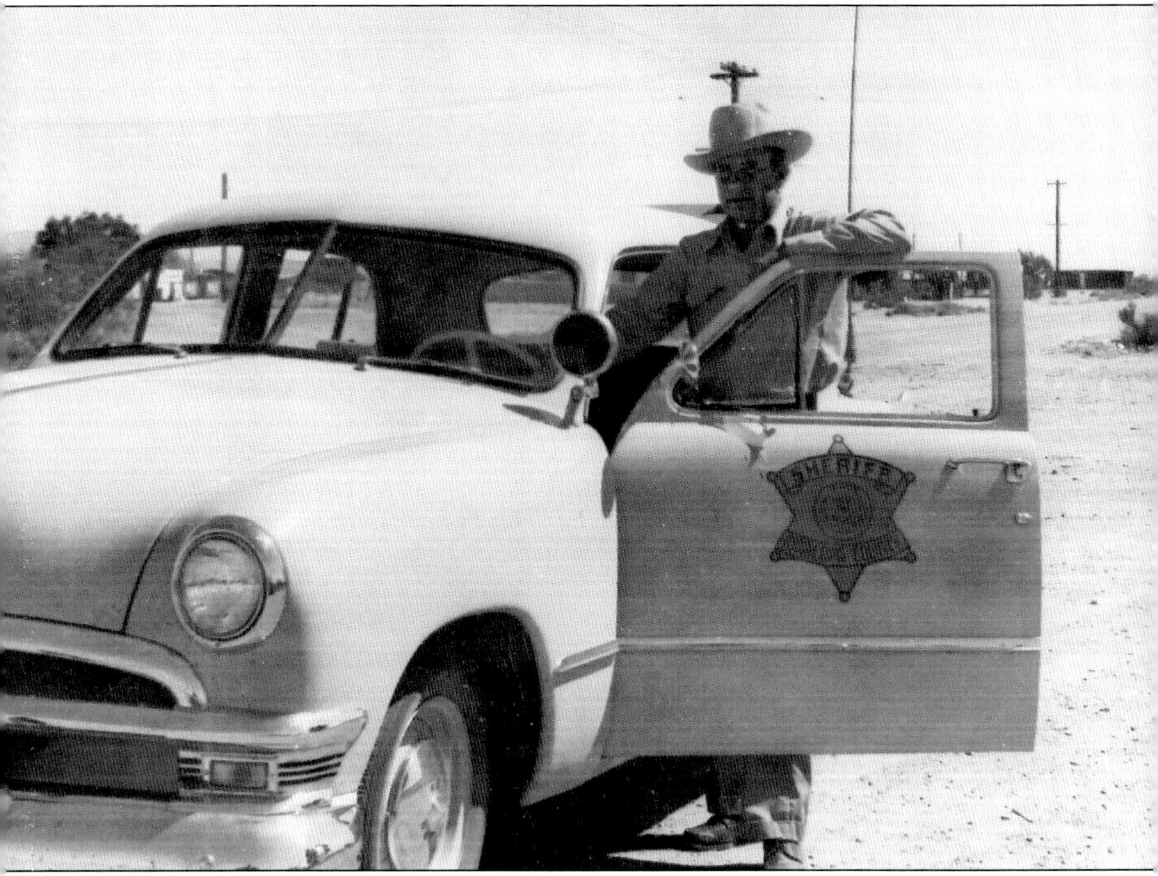

Deputy Thearl Tibbets was born is Oklahoma and came to Gila Bend by way of the town of Safford in eastern Arizona. He proudly served his country in World War II and died on the July, 4, 1989. (Courtesy of Elva Mae McMahon.)

Pictured here in 1945 is LaVerne Bean after maturing from the bicycle to the horse. Though Gila Bend's economy relied on the automobile and the train, its placement in the Sonoran Desert made it suitable for equestrian pursuits. (Courtesy of Daisy Bean Policy.)

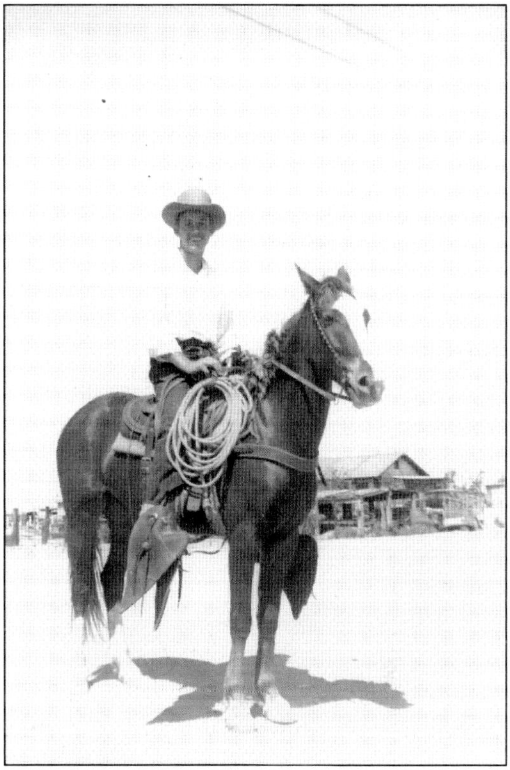

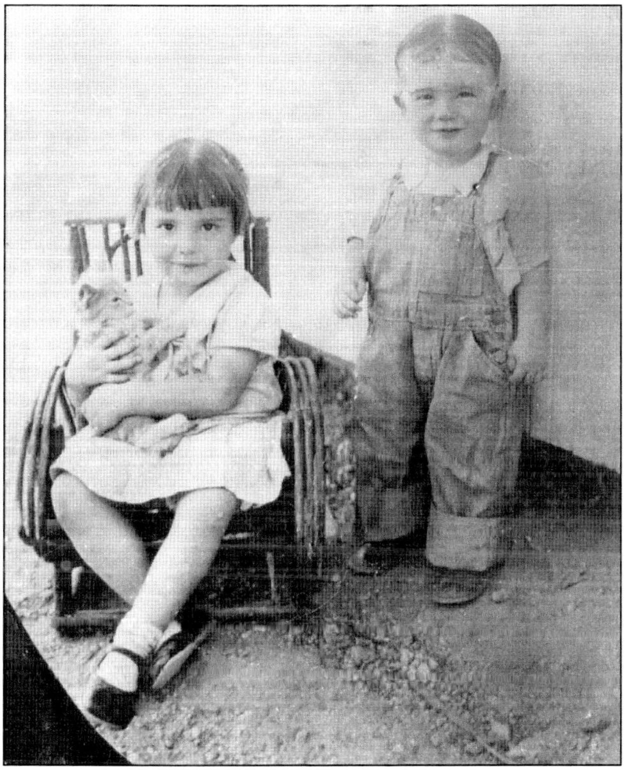

Young Ruby and Doyle Gills smile for the camera in 1931. Ruby was born in 1928, married local businessman Jack B. Neal, and worked for the Yuma School District No. 1 from 1969 to 2003. (Courtesy of Betty Gills.)

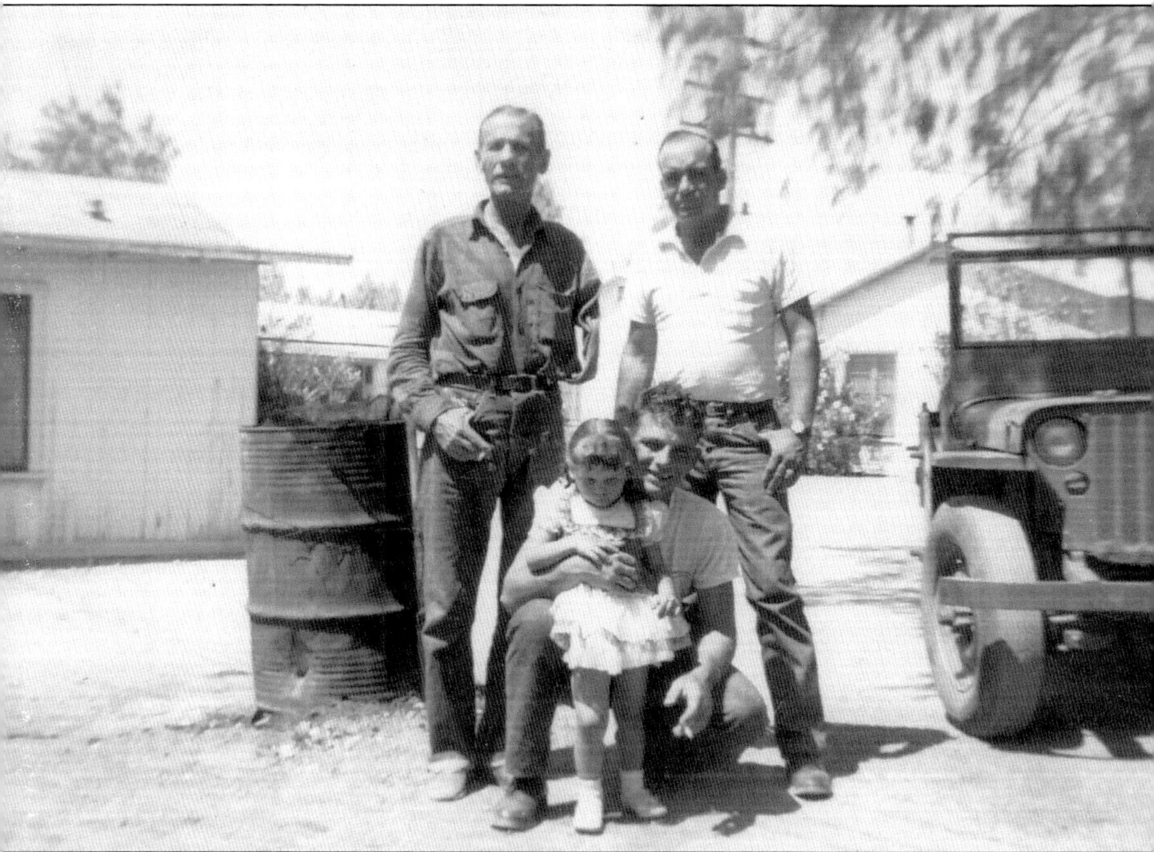

Generations of Benders in this photograph include, from left to right, (second row) Chess Gills, son-in-law Jack Neal, (first row) granddaughter Kathy Gills, and son Doyle Gills. (Courtesy of Betty Gills.)

Eight-year-old Doyle Gills poses with his Daisy Red Ryder. Hunting was considered a popular sport from a young age, and the BB gun was an ideal way for young shooters to hone their marksmanship. (Courtesy of Betty Gills.)

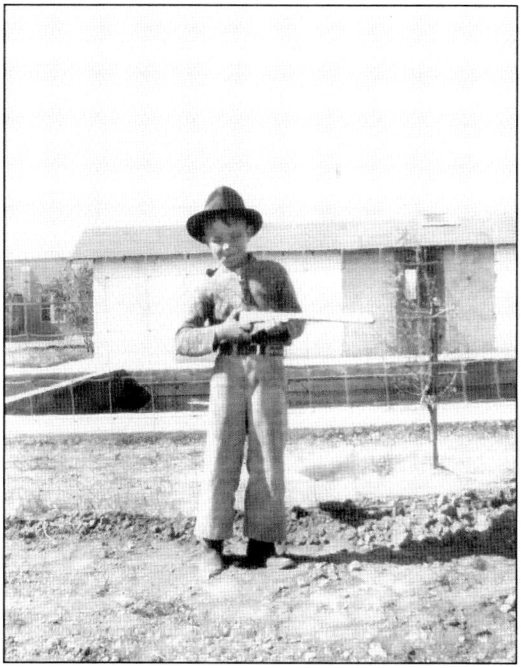

This image was captured during Sunday school studies with Virgie Gills (right). The girls on the couch are, from left to right, cousins Margie Brisby, Ruby Gills, and Helen Phillips. (Courtesy of Betty Gills.)

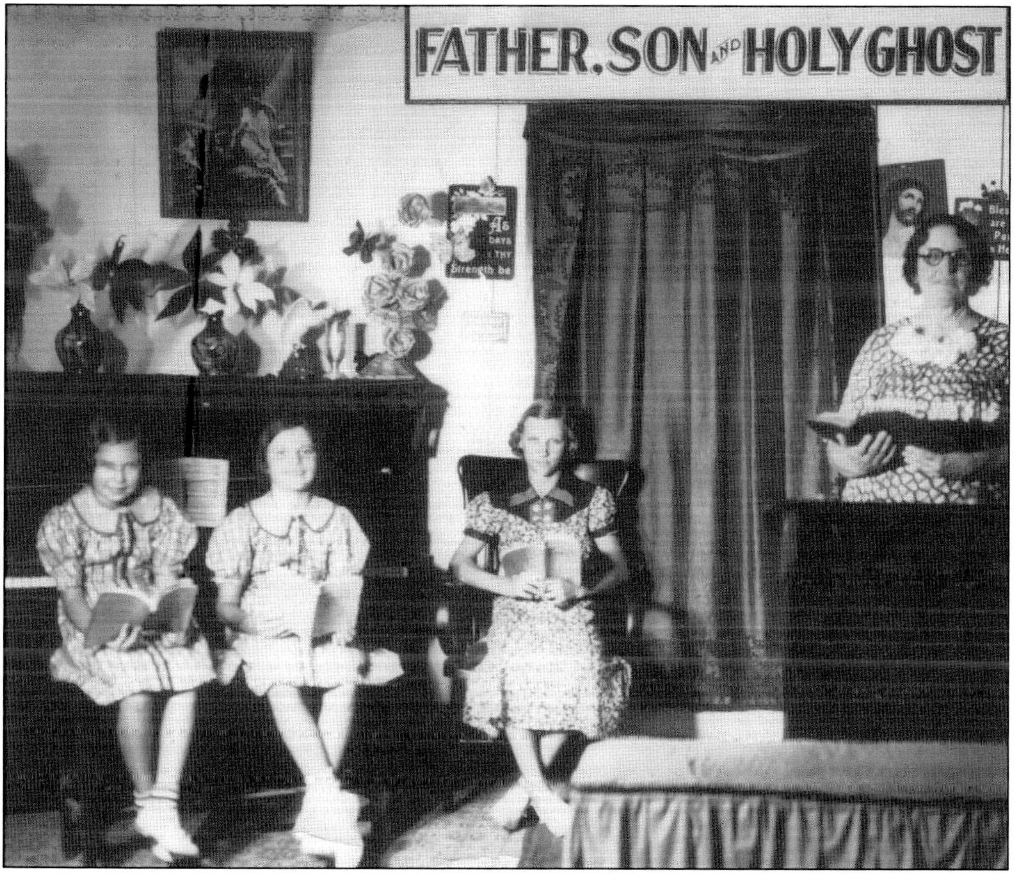

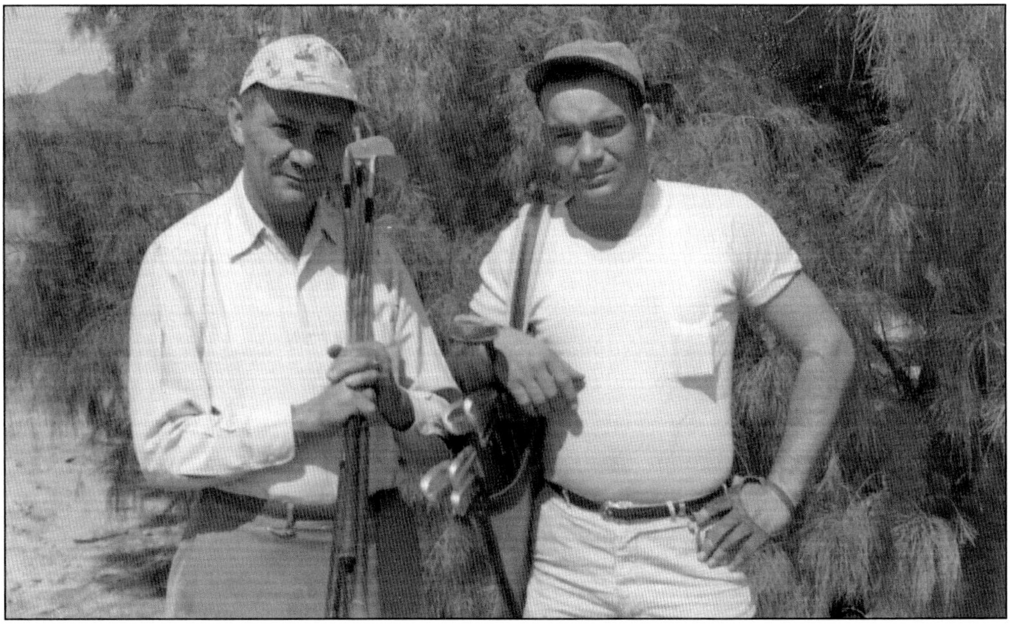

Golf buddies and fellow coworkers at the Owl, Bill Bentel (left) and Jack Neal pause for a photograph. (Courtesy of Betty Gills.)

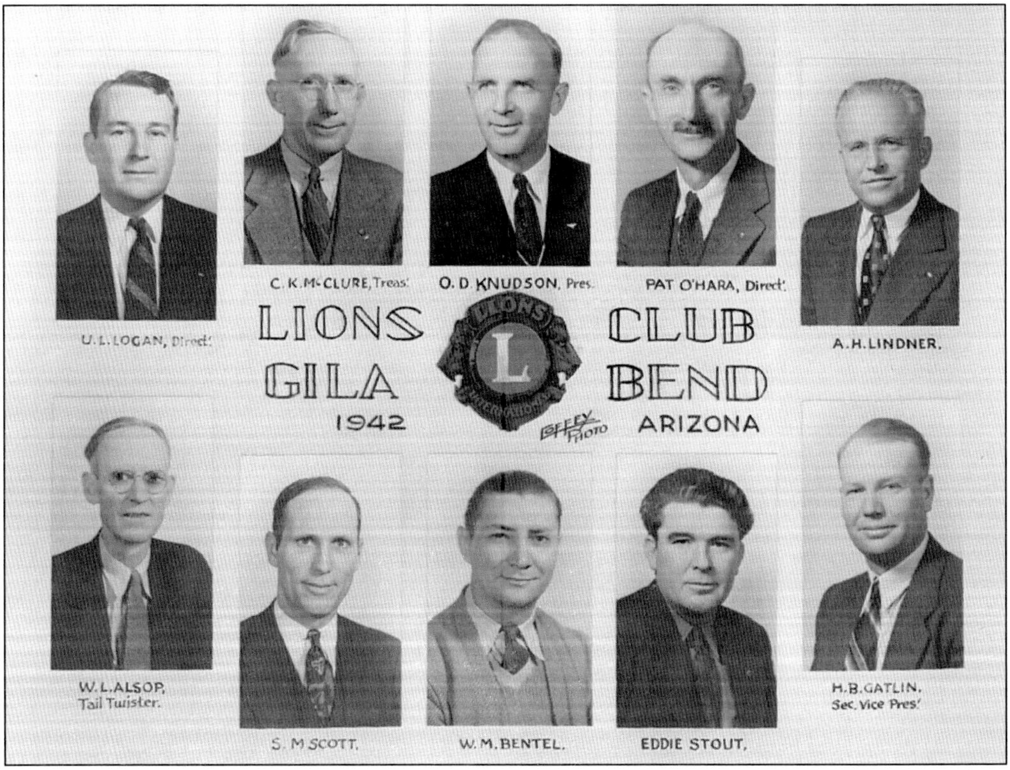

The Lions Club of 1942 include some of Gila Bend's most affluent and colorful men, including merchant U.L. Logan Jr., hotelier Eddie Stout, and Owl Cafe owner Bill Bentel. (Courtesy of the Gila Bend Museum.)

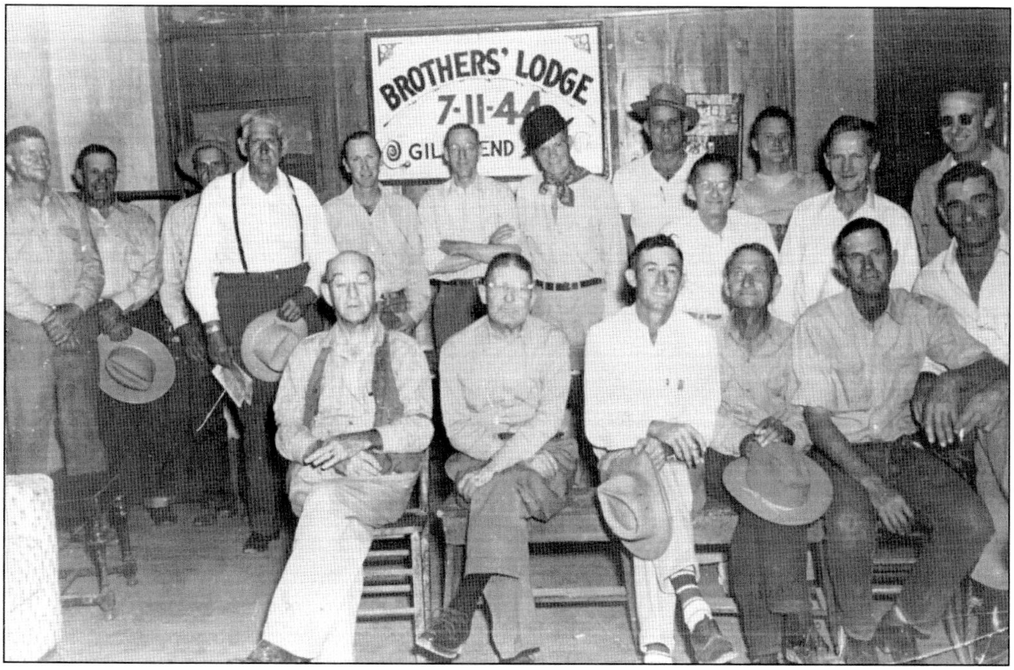

The Brother's Lodge was formed on July 11, 1944. This was probably the Brotherhood of Locomotive Firemen and Enginemen. Initially a mutual support society for railroad firemen and engineers, the brotherhood became involved in labor relations at the fin de siècle. (Courtesy of Johnny Laird.)

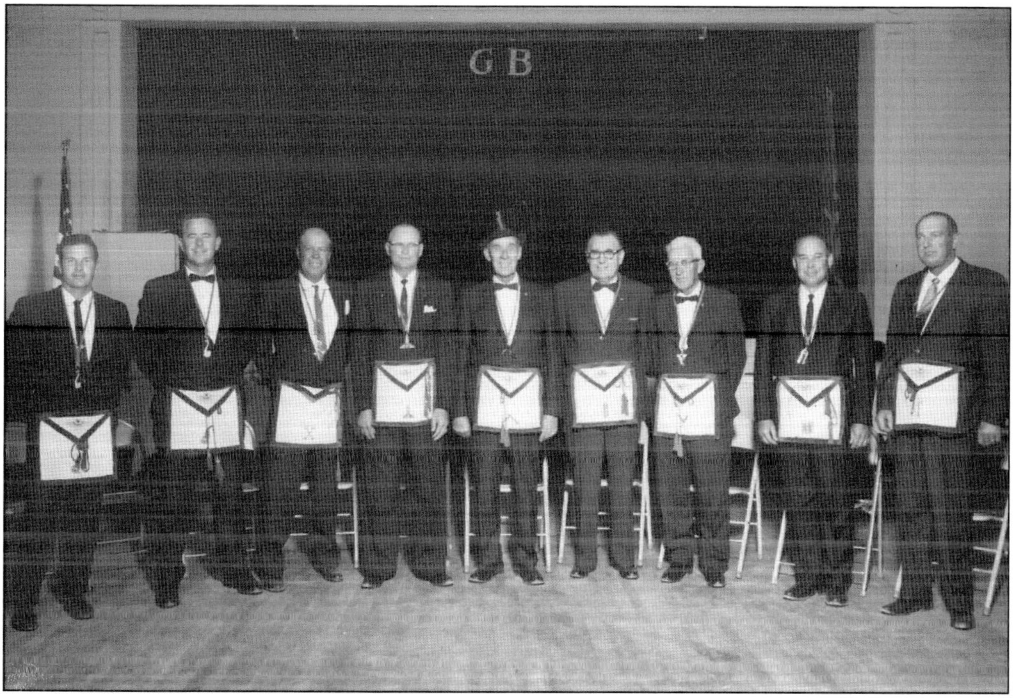

The Masons established the Mac McClure Lodge, No. 65 on May 11, 1968. (Courtesy of Johnny Laird.)

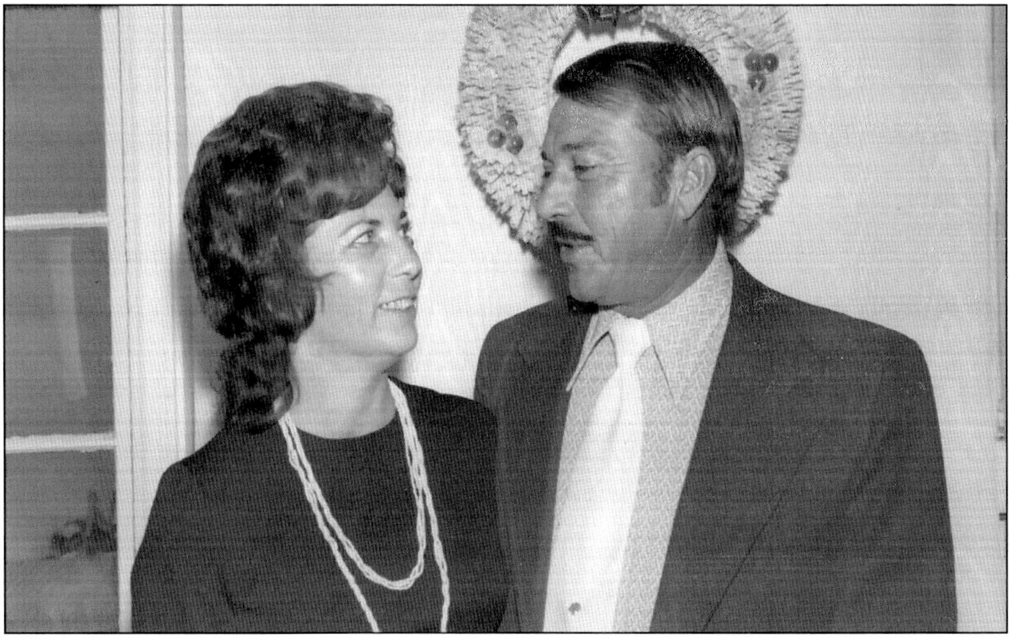

Pictured are Gila Bend resident Mulford "Sonny" Winsor with his wife, Virginia. Sonny was the Gila Bend Mason Lodge's first exalted ruler and the lodge's first repeat ruler 25 years later. He was also Gila Bend's justice of the peace for over two decades. (Courtesy of Cyndi Eisenberger.)

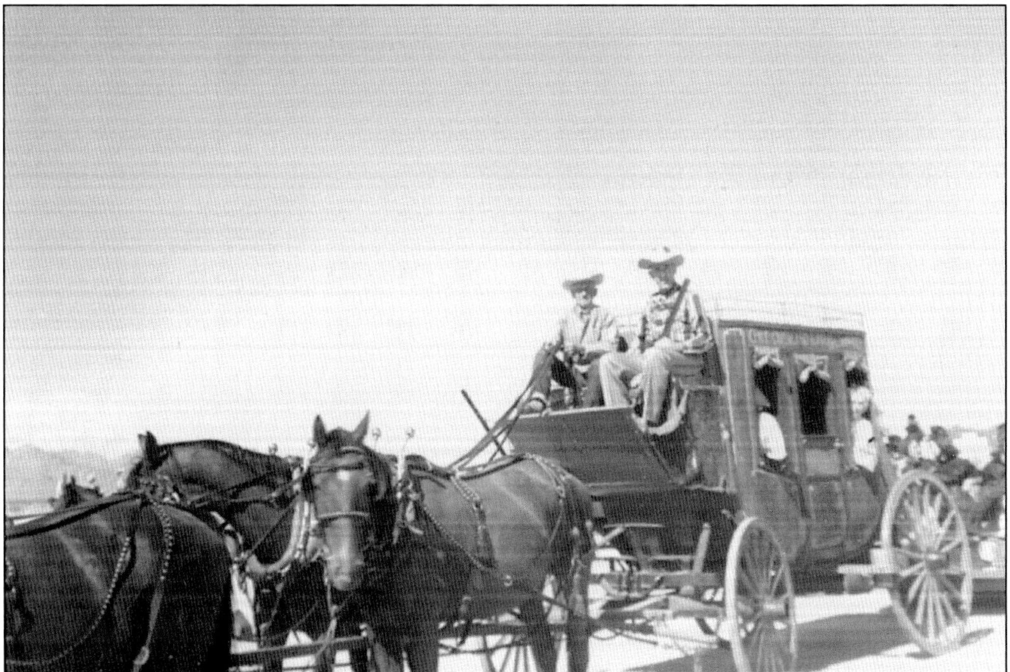

To add authenticity to the Butterfield Stage Days Parade, Louise Logan (seated in the rear) often rented a stagecoach, as in this 1960s photograph. (Courtesy of the Gila Bend Museum.)

Betty Gills, left, is dressed for Butterfield Stage Days during 1964. Butterfield Stage Days began with the centennial celebration of the short-lived mail and stage line in 1957. It has been an annual event ever since. (Courtesy of Betty Gills.)

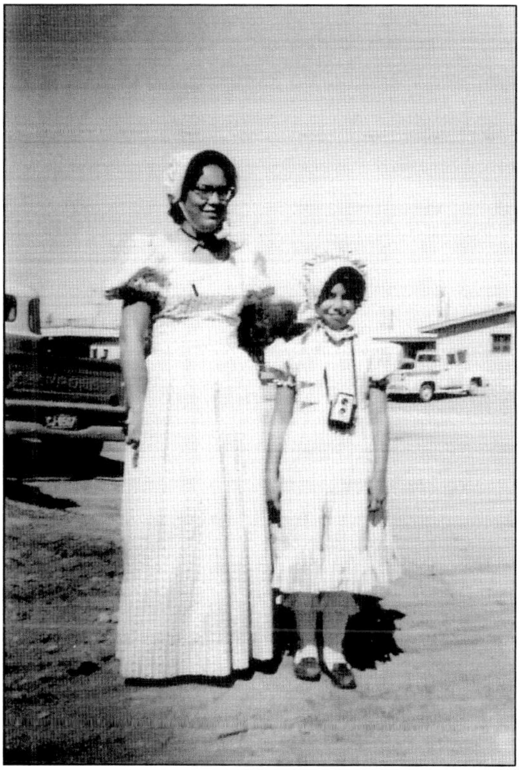

The photograph was taken during the Butterfield Stagecoach Days parade in 1966. Riding the float is Steve Stewart. Other activities during this festival typically include a rodeo and a dance. (Courtesy of Cyndi Eisenberger.)

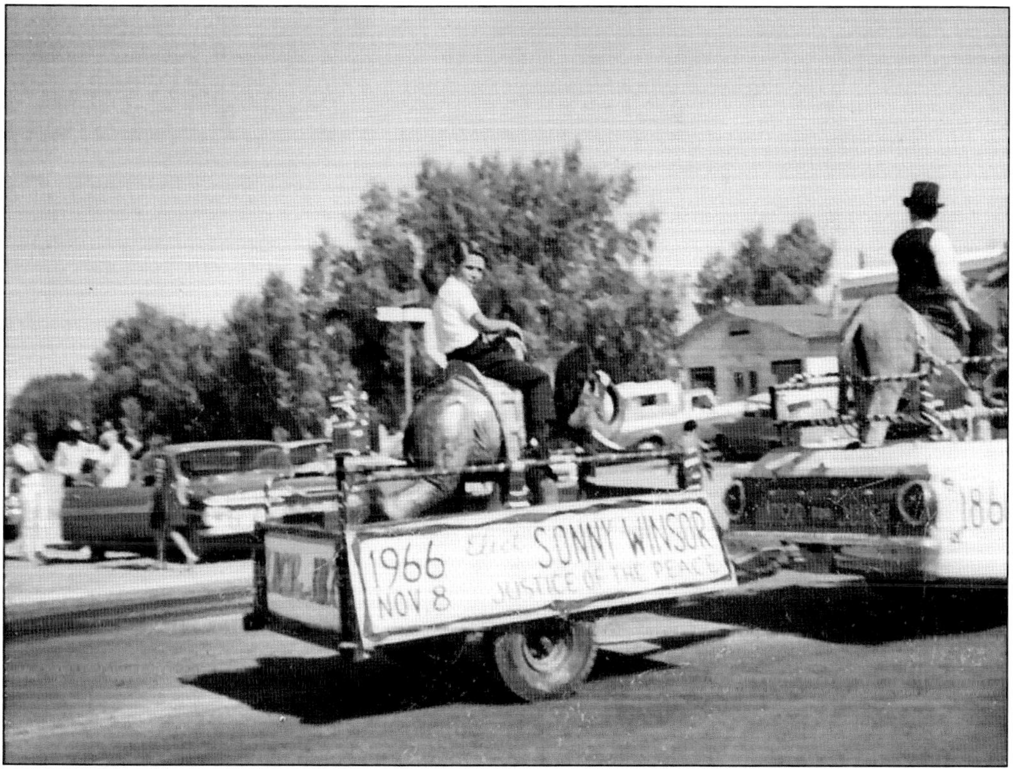

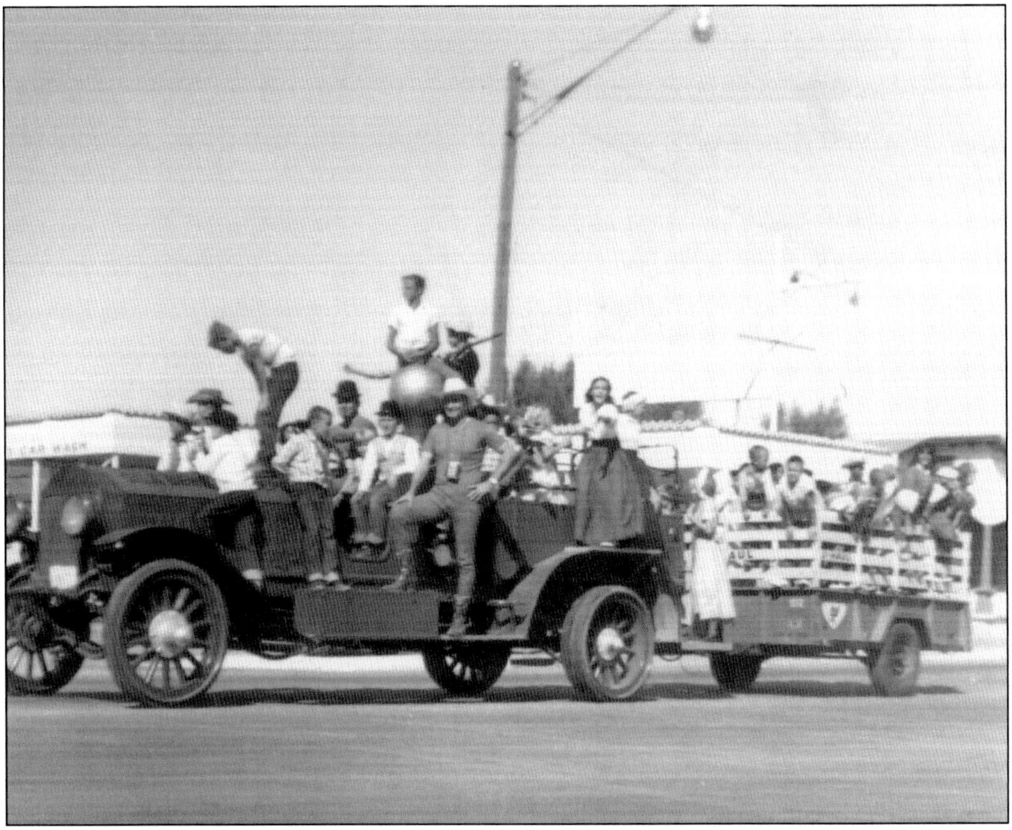

Enlisting the use of an antique fire engine and a U-Haul trailer, Benders proudly parade down Pima Street in this image of an early Butterfield Stage Days celebration. (Courtesy of Betty Gills.)

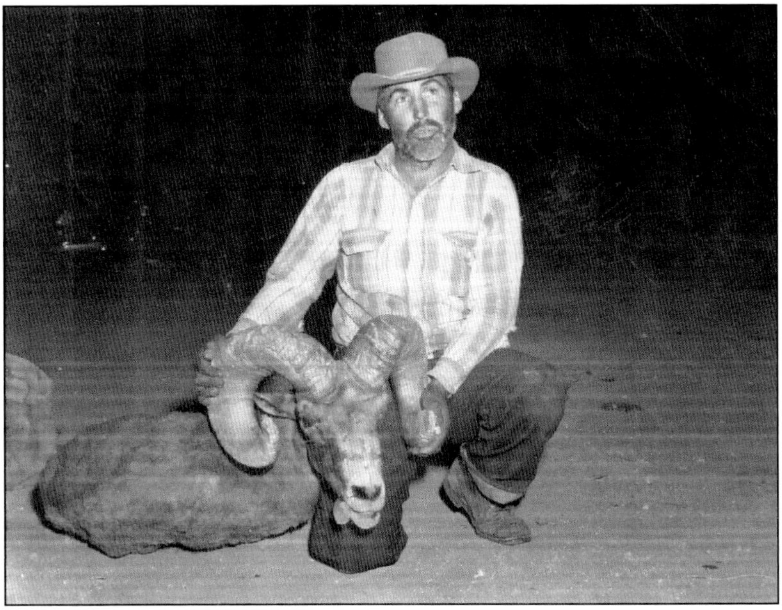

One of the more colorful people in the annuals of Gila Bend history is Lynn Cool. Cool was a hunter, trapper, and outfitter who was just as at home in the desert as he was in his unusual house. Here, Cool has taken down a big horn sheep in Arizona's first legal hunt of that species in 1952. (Courtesy of Gary Miller.)

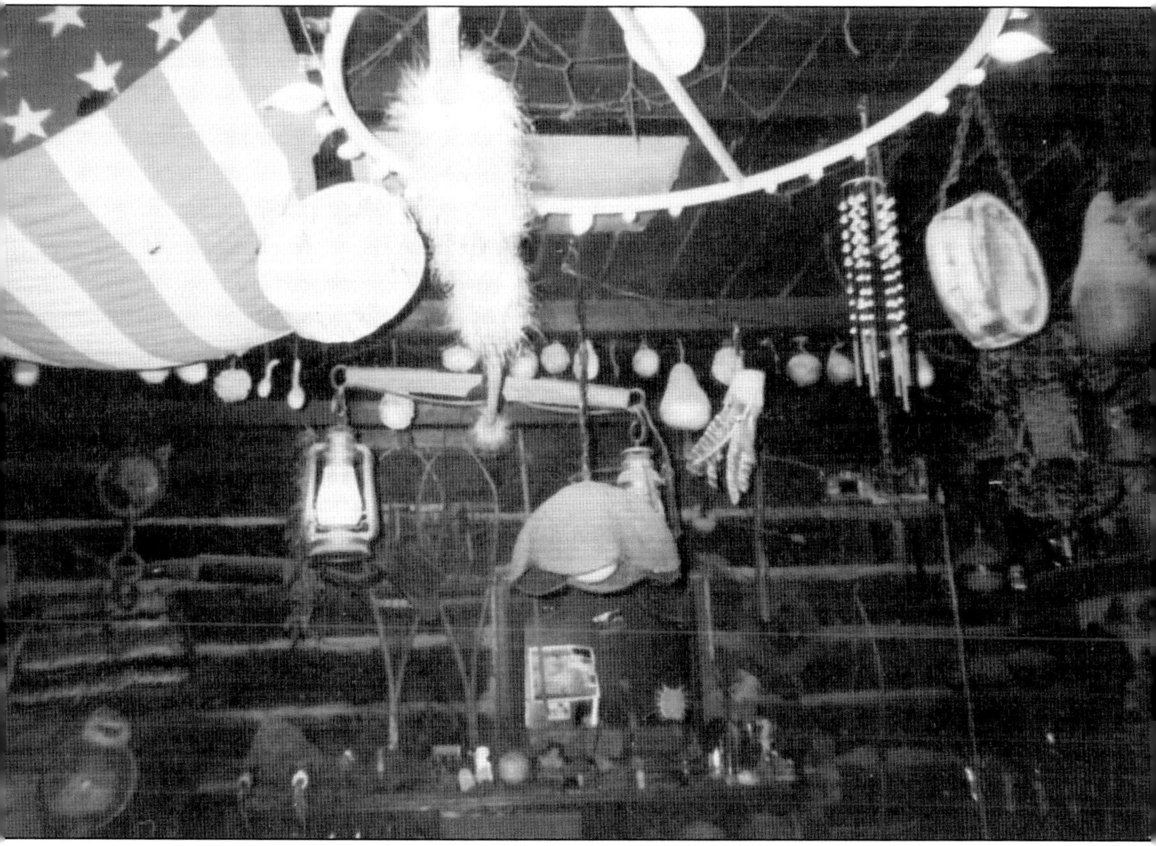

Cool built his home from railroad ties, a relatively peculiar, though locally ubiquitous, building material. The residence included a fireplace with a door to the outside for the gathering of firewood. It was also decorated in an eclectic fashion, as seen in this photograph. (Courtesy of Gary Miller.)

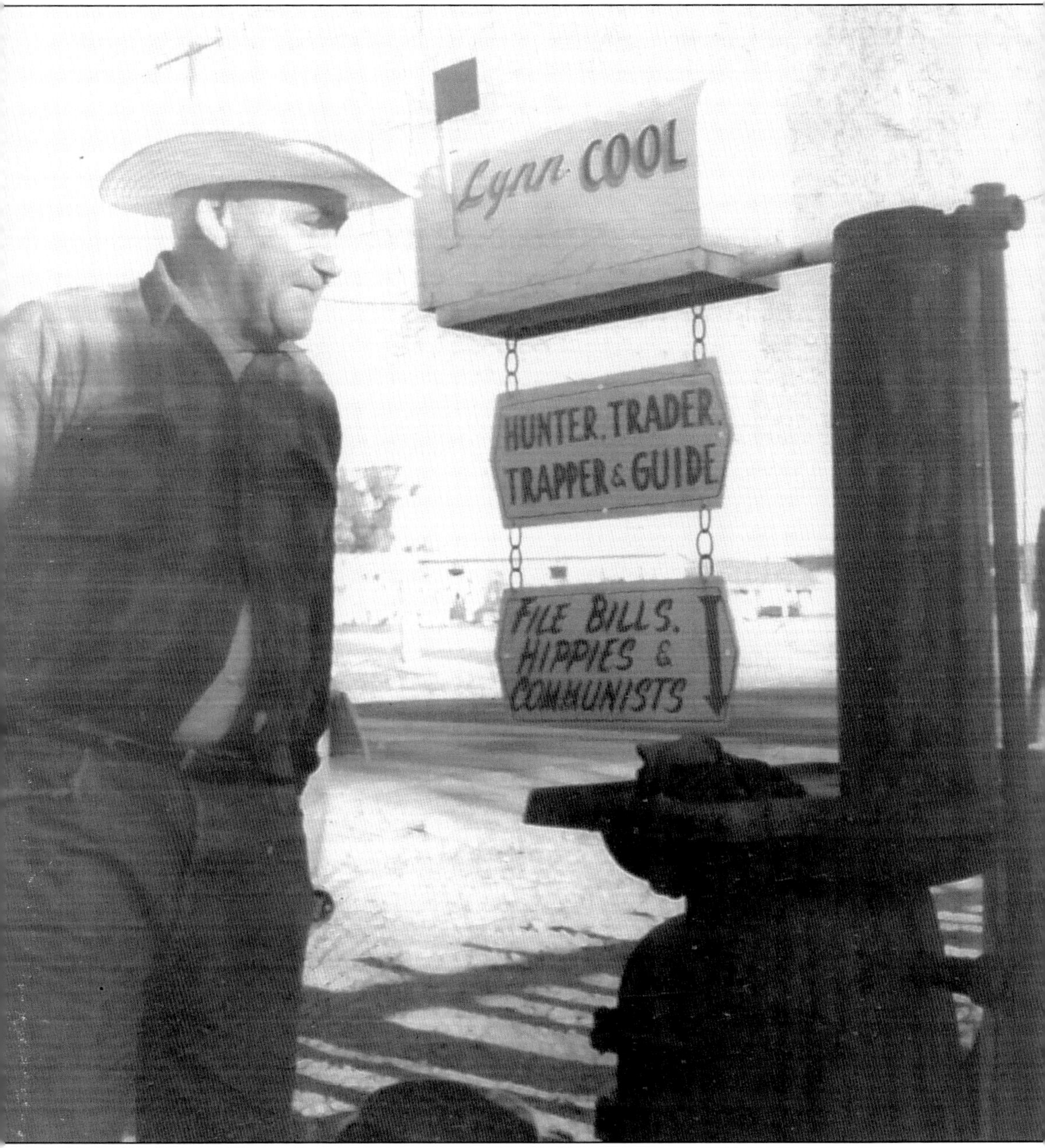

Lynn Cool checks his mailbox in this photograph from the 1960s. Mounted to the stovepipe of a potbellied range, Cool had a filing system for "bills, hippies, & communists," though it is not clear that he ever used it. (Courtesy of Elizabeth Cool.)

Six

GILA BUILDINGS

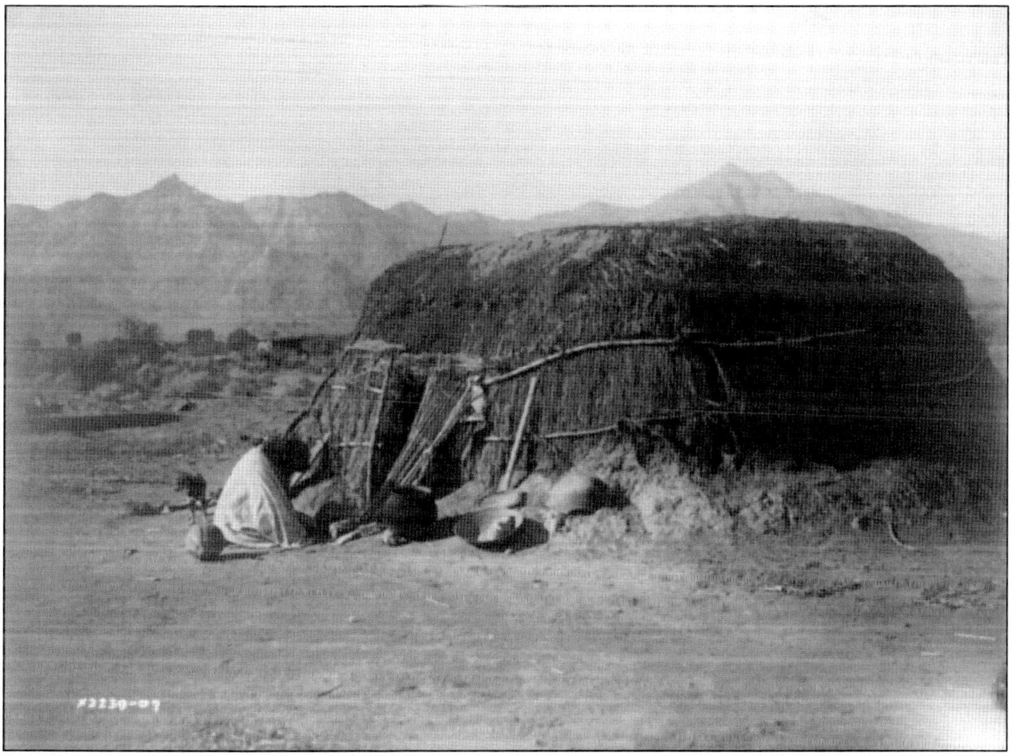

Earlier inhabitants created pit houses similar to this Akimel O'odham ki. They were relatively stable structures; the curvature deflects wind and supports the weight of the mud and daub. (Courtesy of the Library of Congress, Prints & Photographs Division, Edward S. Curtis Collection, LC-USZ62-83600.)

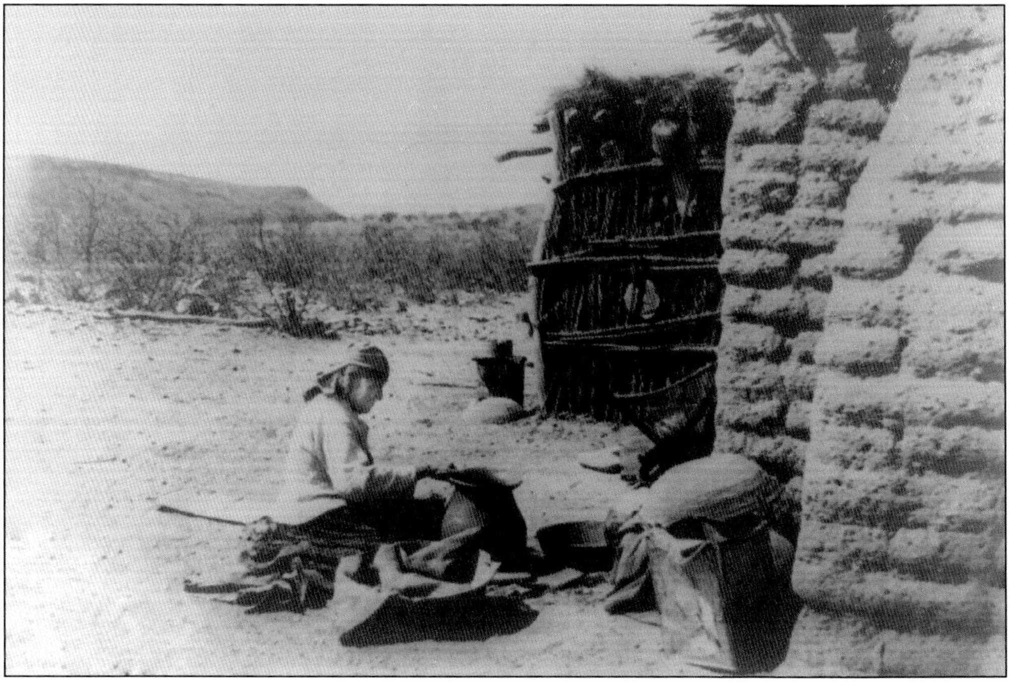

Adobe brick later became common in construction, as shown in this Tohono O'odham house. (Courtesy of the Library of Congress, Prints & Photographs Division, Reproduction LC-USZ62-94598.)

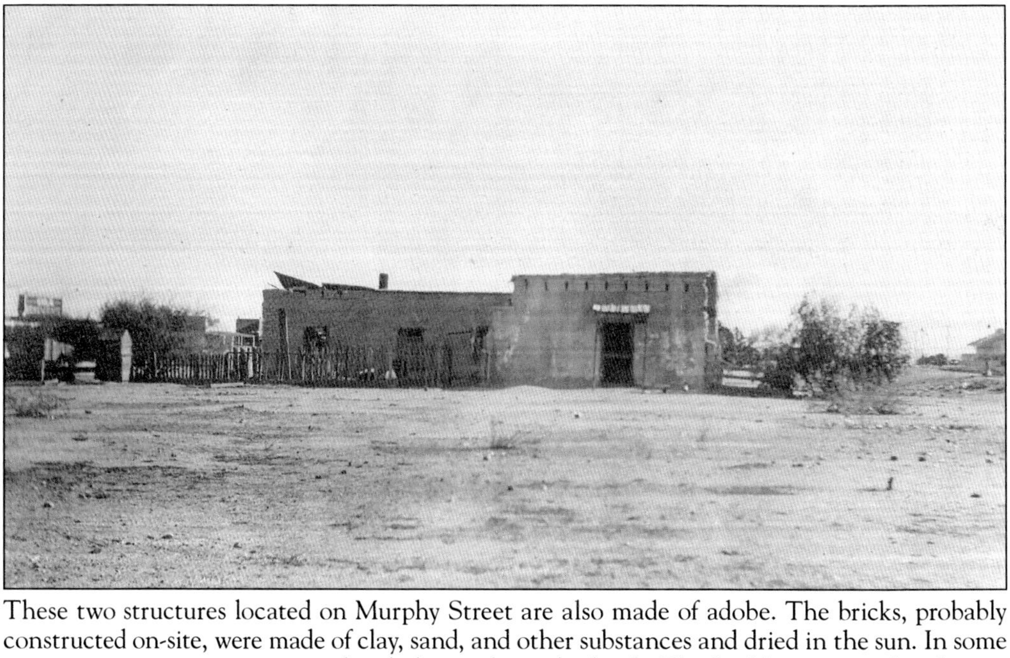

These two structures located on Murphy Street are also made of adobe. The bricks, probably constructed on-site, were made of clay, sand, and other substances and dried in the sun. In some cases, manure or straw was used to help reinforce the brick. The buildings were already in a dilapidated state when this photograph was taken in the 1890s. The structures were likely built shortly after the arrival of the railroad but before completion of the line, when other building materials such as wood and brick would be more readily available. (Courtesy of Johnny Laird.)

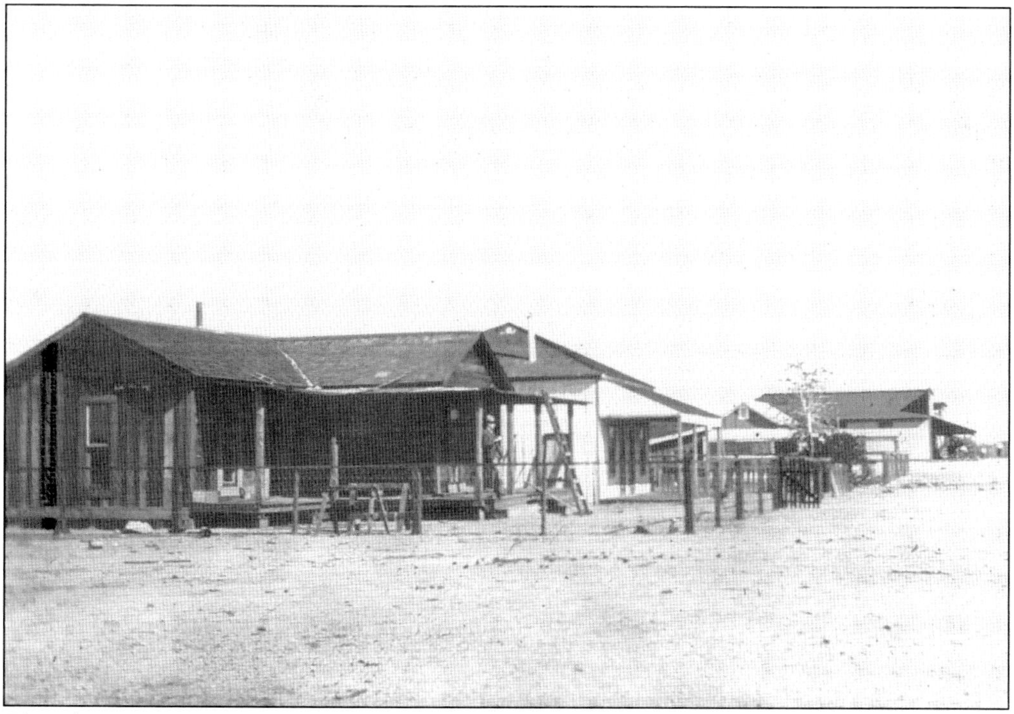

This photograph is of the north side of Pima Street facing east. The house on the left is possibly that of E.C. Caruthers. This turn-of-the-century house is vernacular in its design, though it is influenced by National Folk–style elements such as the lack of detailing and the full-facade porch. The house on the right is more in the National Folk style, which typically has a hipped roof. The Caruthers-Logan Store can be seen in the distance. (Courtesy of Johnny Laird.)

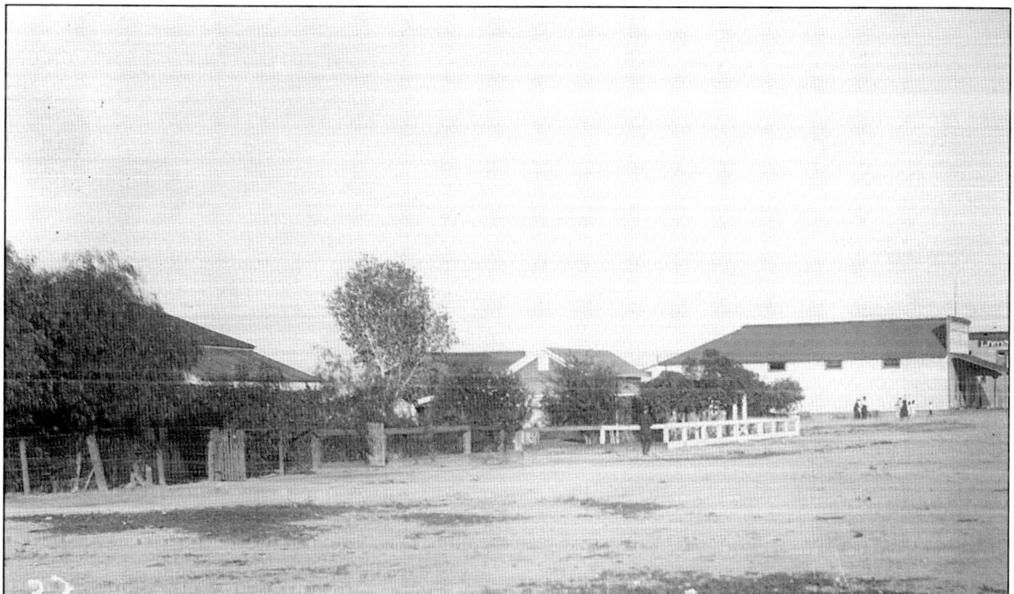

This is a similar photograph to the preceding one, though it was captured a little to the east on Pima Street. The landscape has matured significantly. (Courtesy of the Gila Bend Museum.)

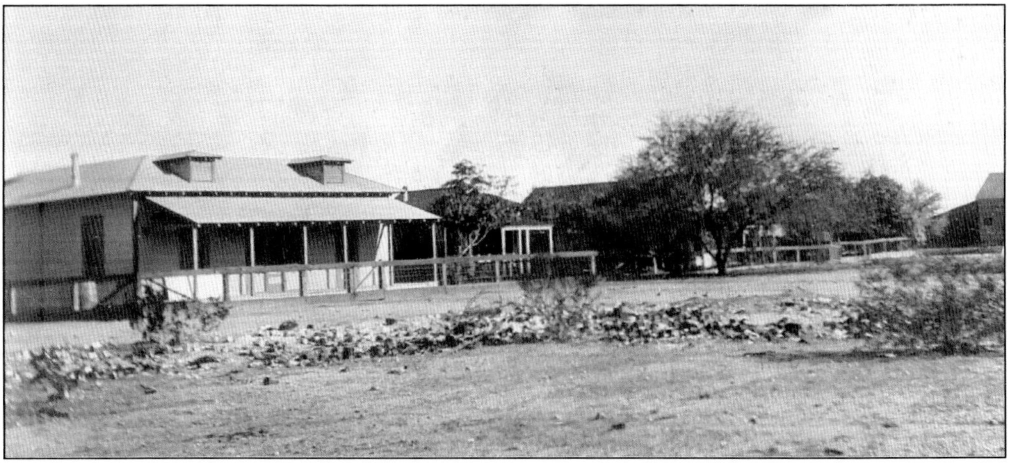

While the exact location of this photograph is unknown, it was more than likely taken of the north side of Pima Street. The design of the house, while unusual with a hipped-desk roof and twin dormer vents, is of National Folk–style influence. (Courtesy of Johnny Laird.)

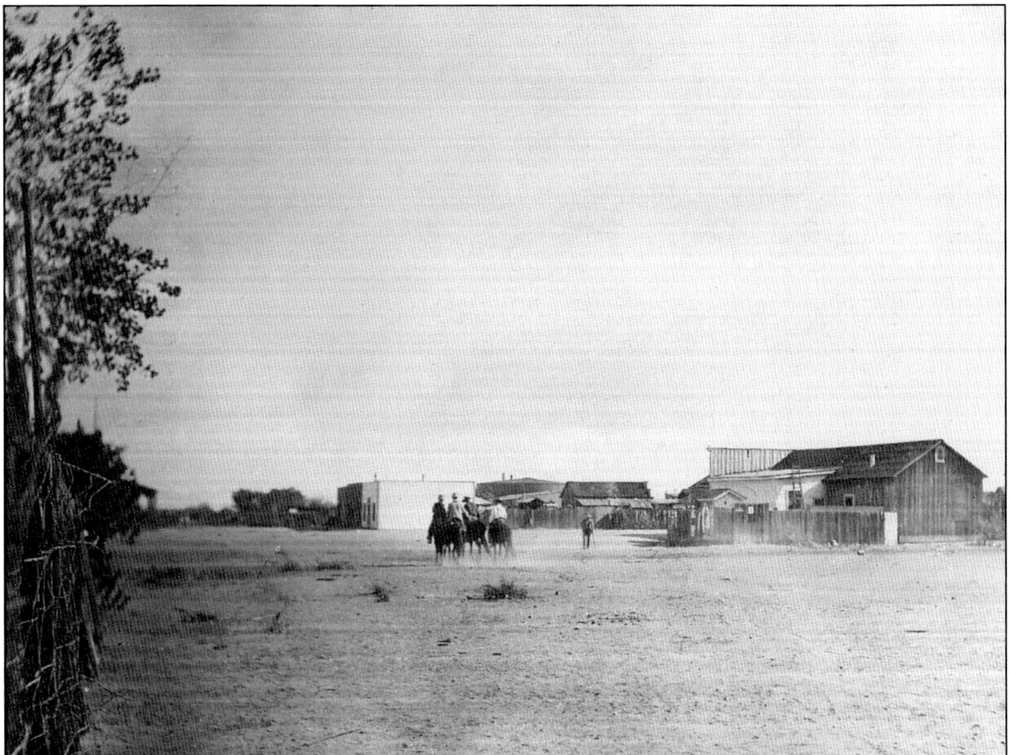

This is possibly the south side of Pima Road, looking east. The huge Southern and Pacific fuel tank is in the distance. The idea of zoning is decades away, and most are using horses as a regular mode of transportation. (Courtesy of Johnny Laird.)

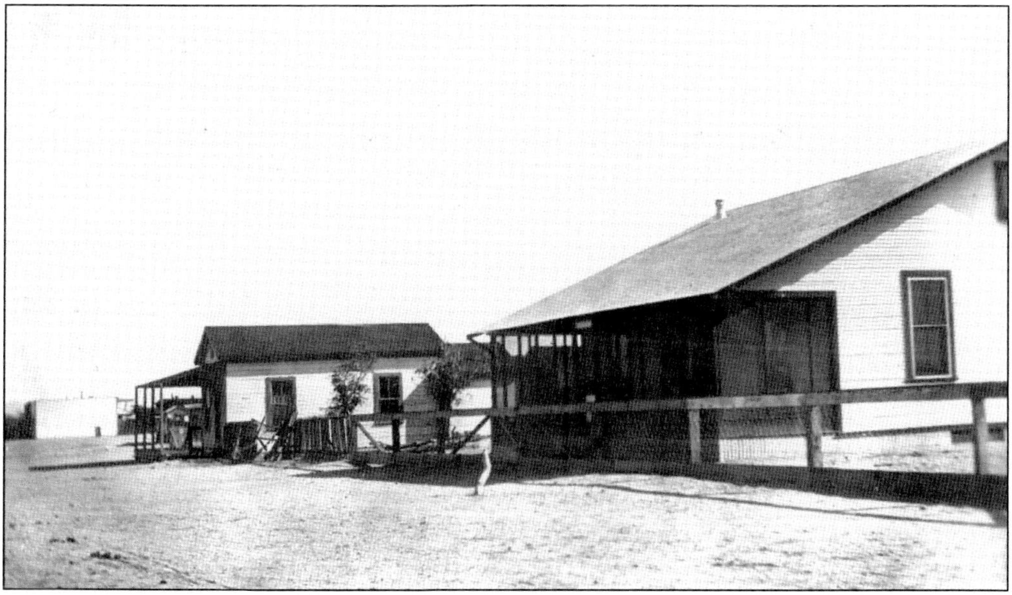

The house on the left is a modest structure known as a shotgun house, a popular style after the Civil War. These structures, often found in railroad towns such as Gila Bend, were small with three or four rooms. Supposedly, the name comes from the layout of a door on each end and the idea that one could fire a shotgun at the front door and the pellets would come out the back. The house on the right is a National Folk–influenced structure with an enclosed porch across the facade. The porch was probably used for sleeping during the hotter times of the year. (Courtesy of Johnny Laird.)

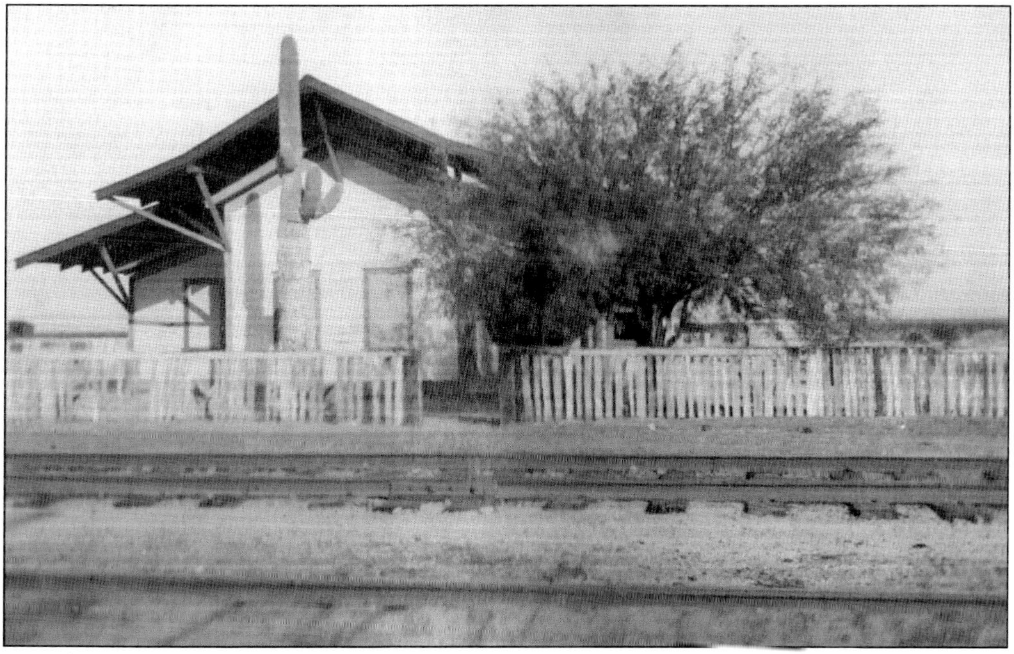

Some homes were once located along the tracks, providing a close and quite audible experience for their residents. This home, designed in the National Folk style, possesses a double roof designed to reduce the heat of the summer. (Courtesy of the Gila Bend Museum.)

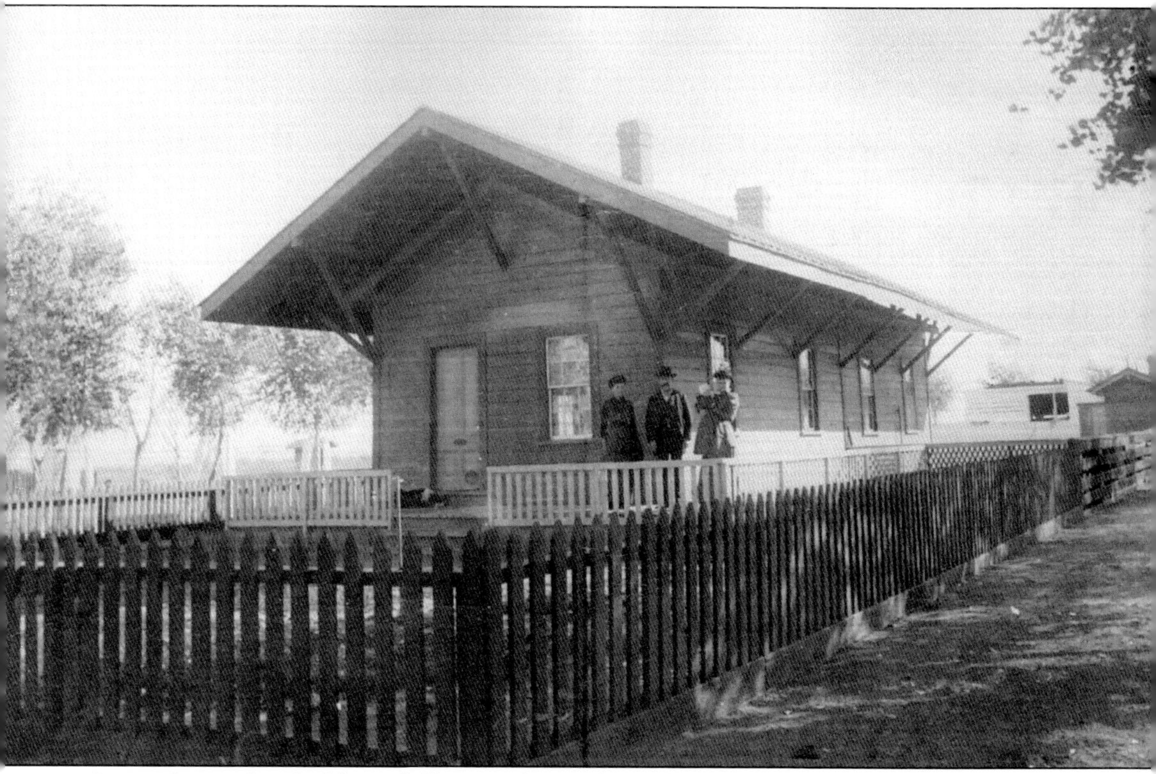

Pictured is another double-roofed house. The ample windows allowed for cross ventilation, another method for cooling the home. (Courtesy of the Gila Bend Museum.)

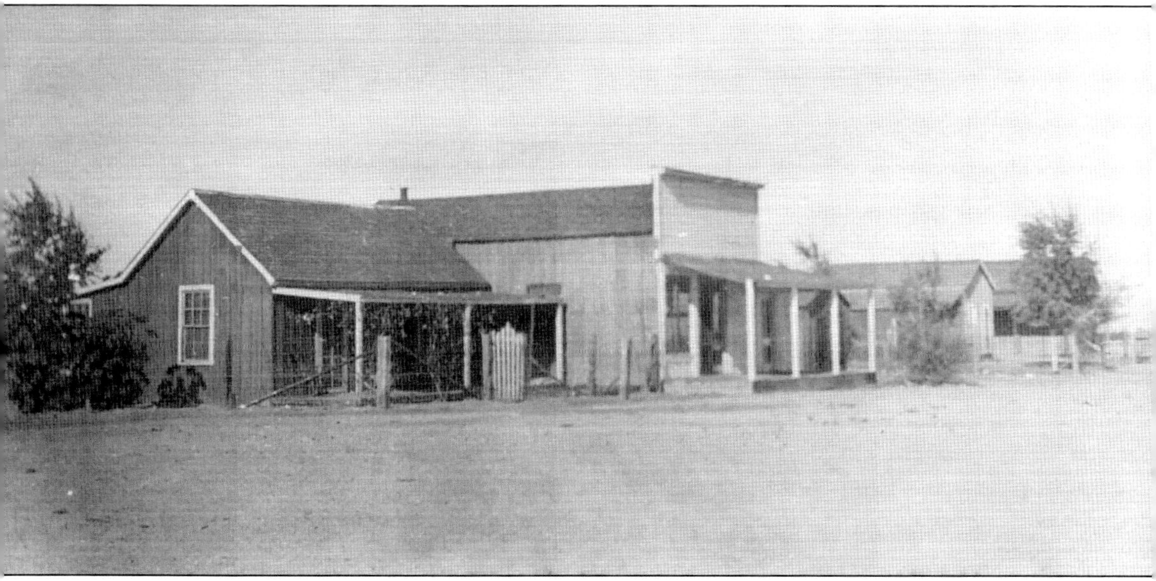

The house on the left resembles the popular saltbox style of New England. The commercial building to its right is of Boomtown style, accentuated by its false front. Boomtown storefronts were popular between 1870 and 1915. (Courtesy of Johnny Laird.)

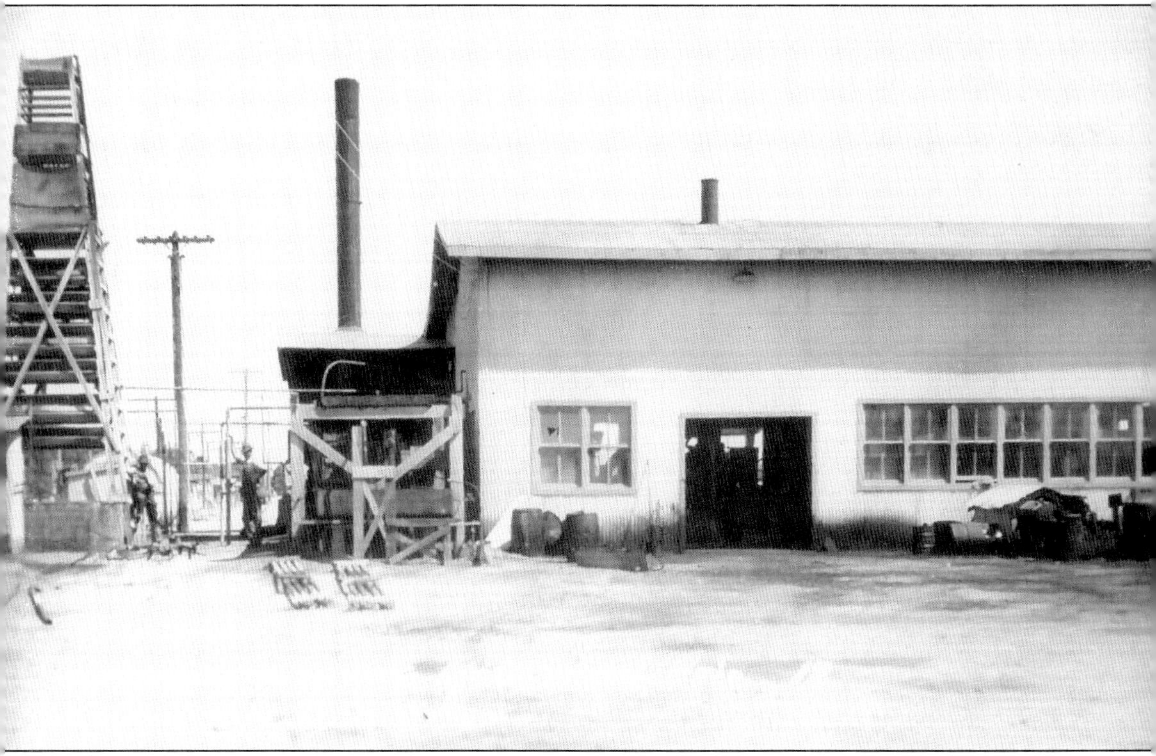

Electricity was important to the burgeoning community. This plant, pictured around 1930, was operated by the Arizona Edison Company, which had similar operations in small towns throughout Arizona. (Courtesy of Elva Mae McMahon.)

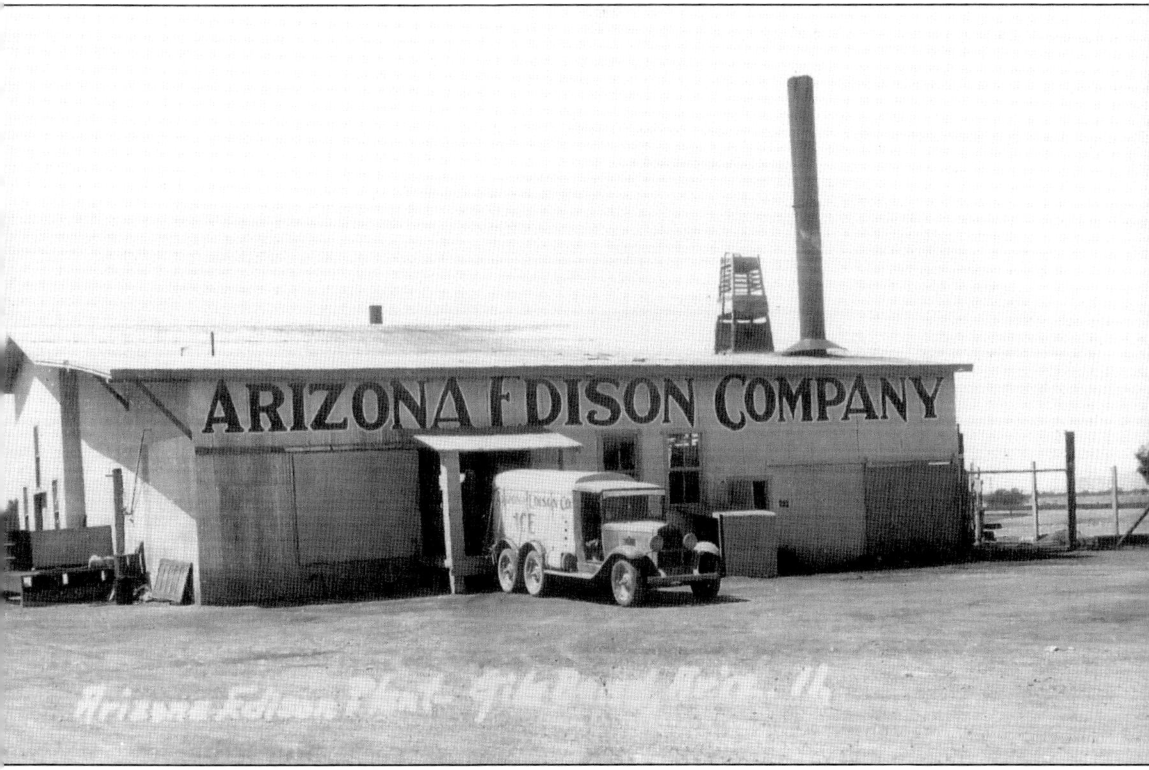

Ice was a welcome by-product of the electric company, especially in what was considered the hottest place in the United States. The ice was used for commercial and residential use. (Courtesy of Elva Mae McMahon.)

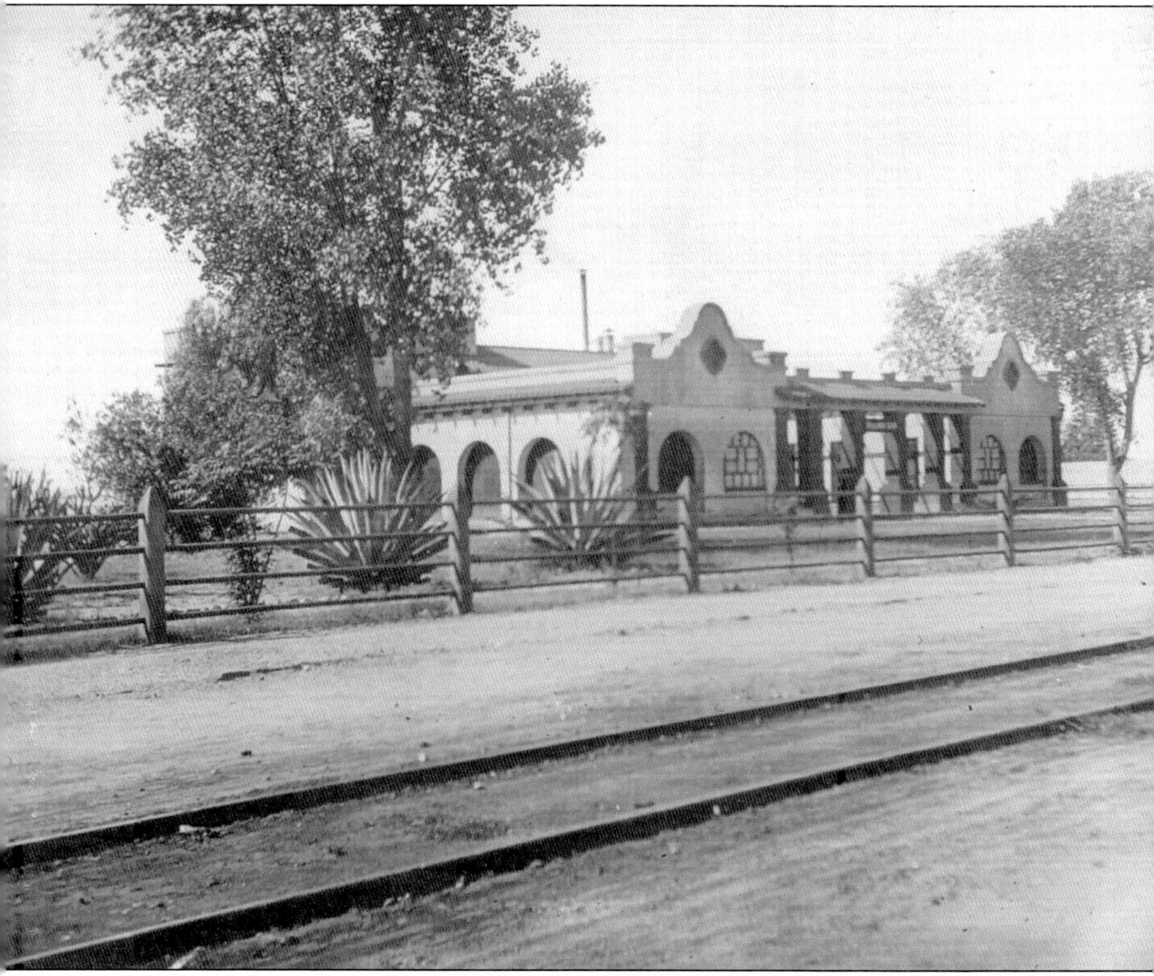

The Southern Pacific Club House was a unique example of Spanish Colonial Revival–influenced architecture. It is unfortunate that the building, like almost all of the railroad-related structures, no longer exists. (Courtesy of the Gila Bend Museum.)

Seven

Then and Now

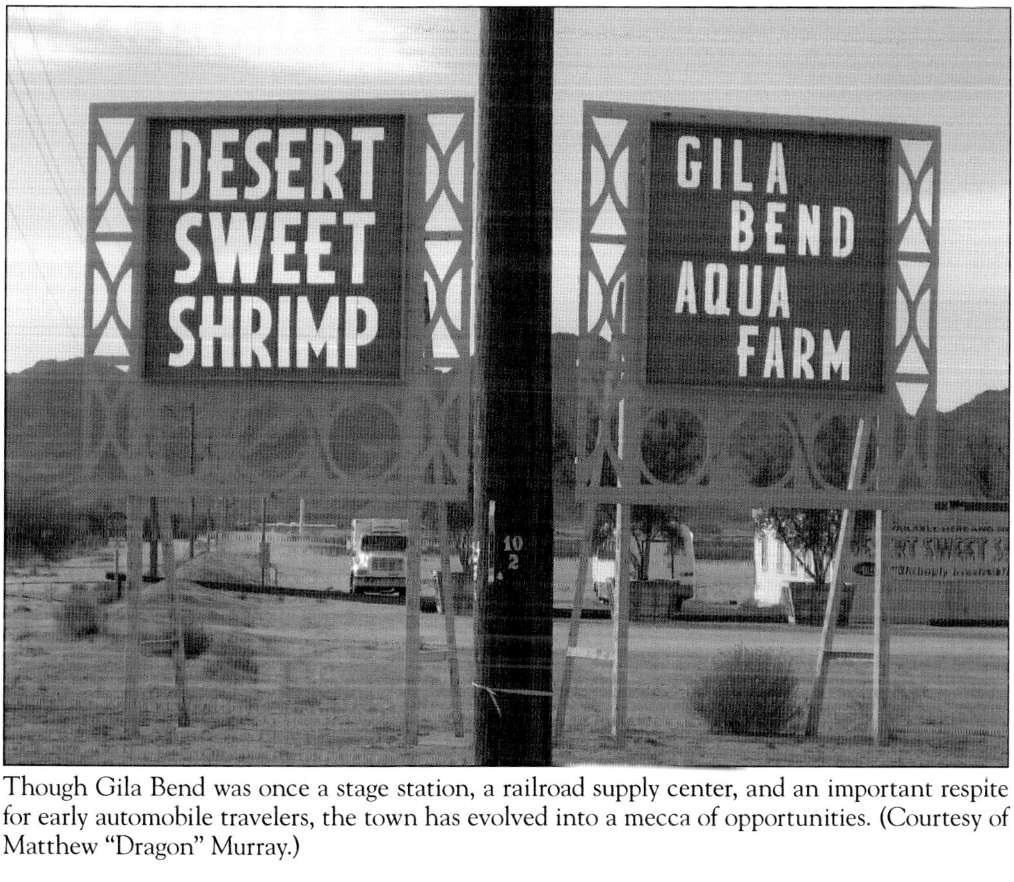

Though Gila Bend was once a stage station, a railroad supply center, and an important respite for early automobile travelers, the town has evolved into a mecca of opportunities. (Courtesy of Matthew "Dragon" Murray.)

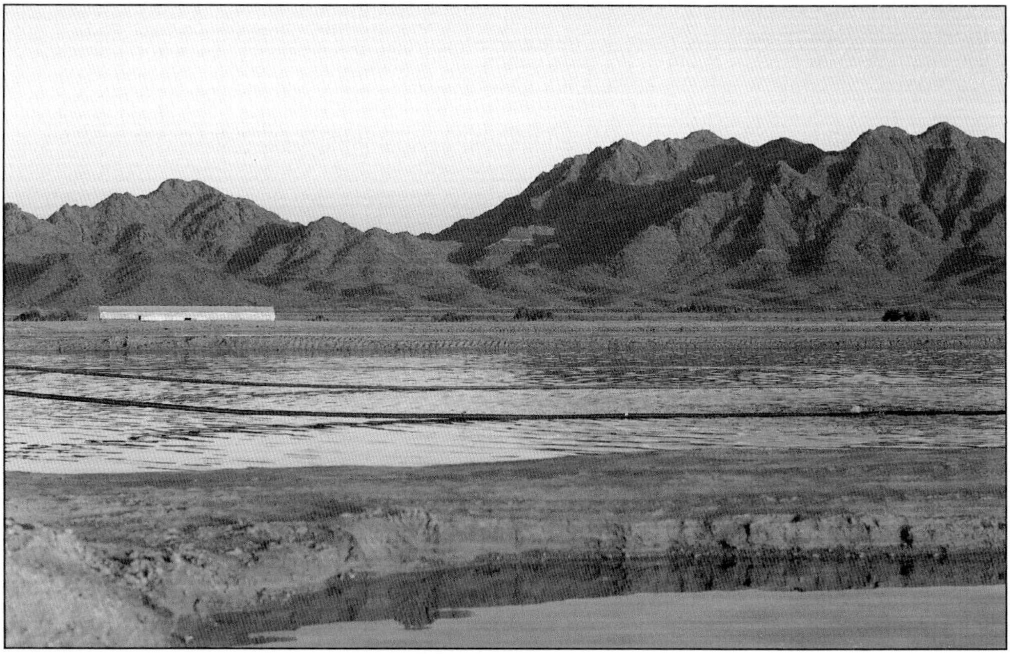

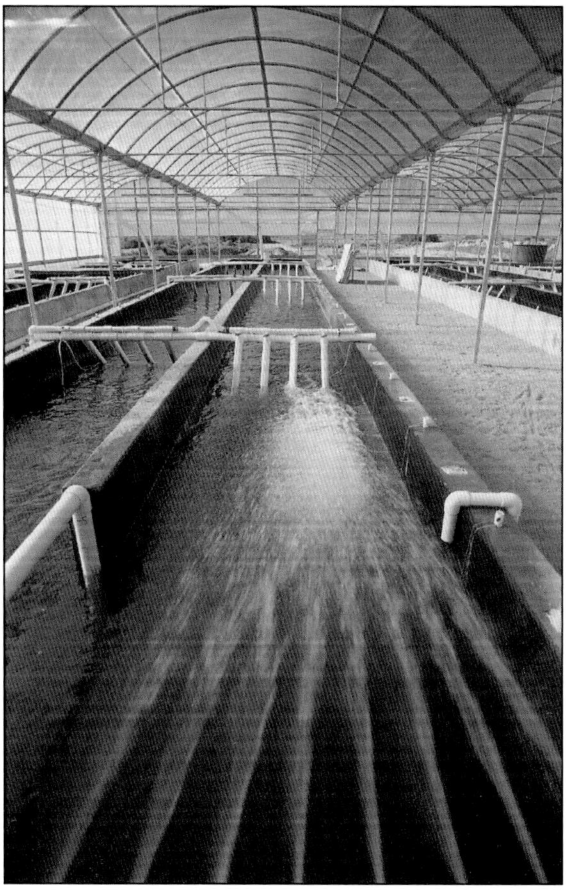

What began in the 1990s as an experiment became a culinary sensation that would have seafood aficionados scratching their heads: shrimp from the desert. These ponds are used for growing shrimp without the worries of oil spills and overfishing. (Courtesy of Desert Sweet Shrimp.)

Part of the hatchery process, these runs are similar to those used in fish farming. Developed by the New Alchemy Institute in the 1970s, this technique creates a by-product that is used for irrigating and fertilizing local crops. (Courtesy of Desert Sweet Shrimp.)

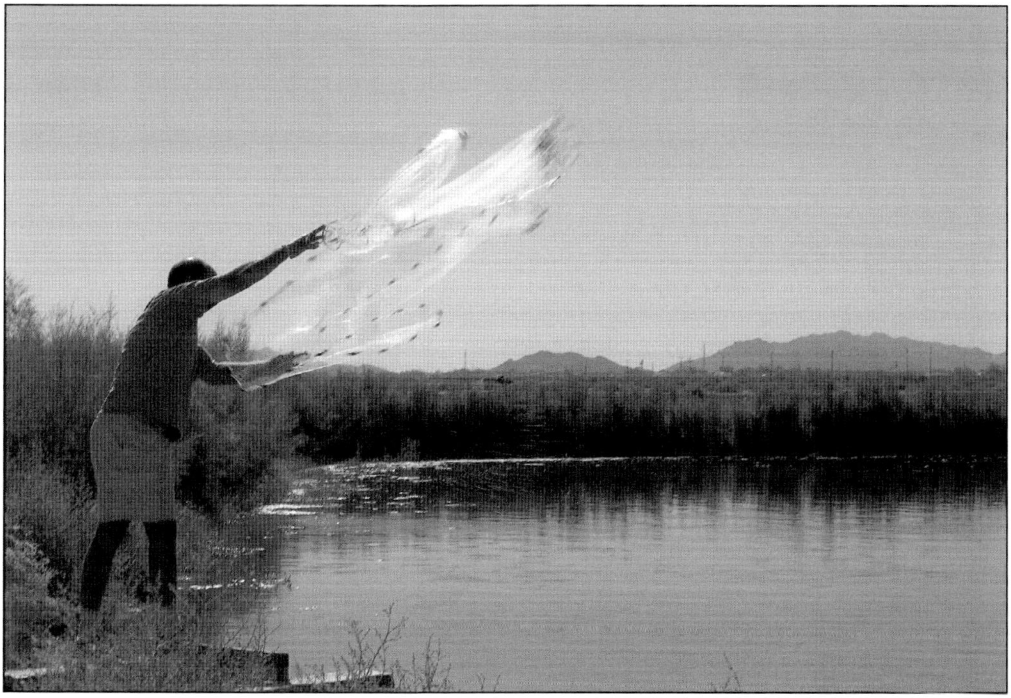

Harvesting the shrimp farm is easier than driving a tractor. The main labor involved is the casting of a net. (Courtesy of Desert Sweet Shrimp.)

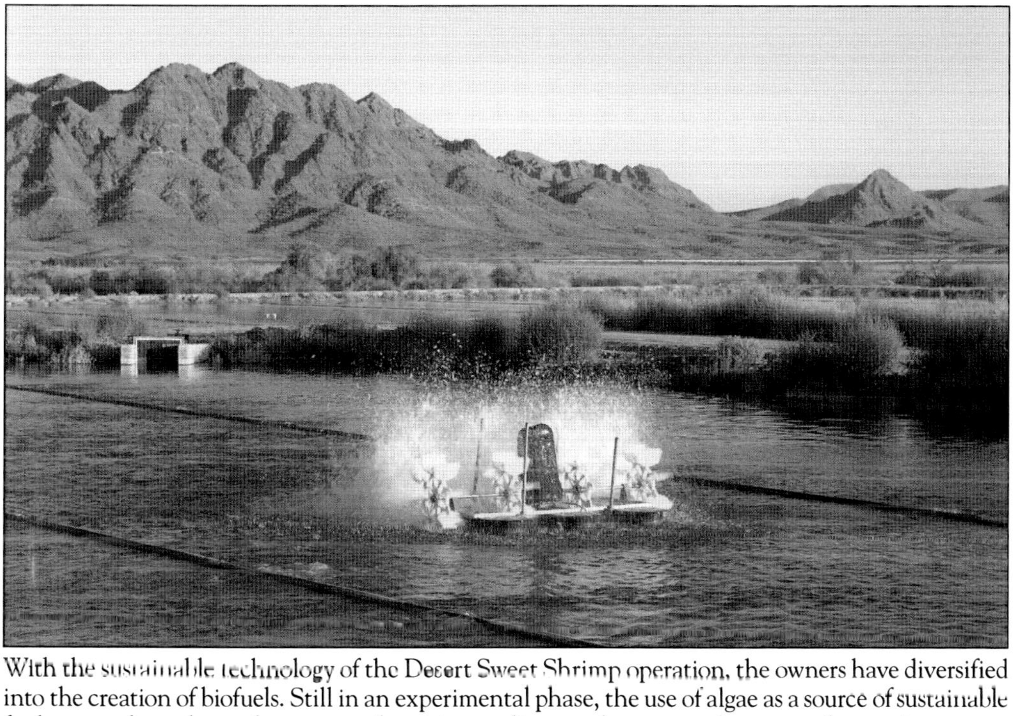

With the sustainable technology of the Desert Sweet Shrimp operation, the owners have diversified into the creation of biofuels. Still in an experimental phase, the use of algae as a source of sustainable fuel can reduce dependence on oil, mitigate climate change, and protect the environment. (Courtesy of Desert Sweet Biofuels.)

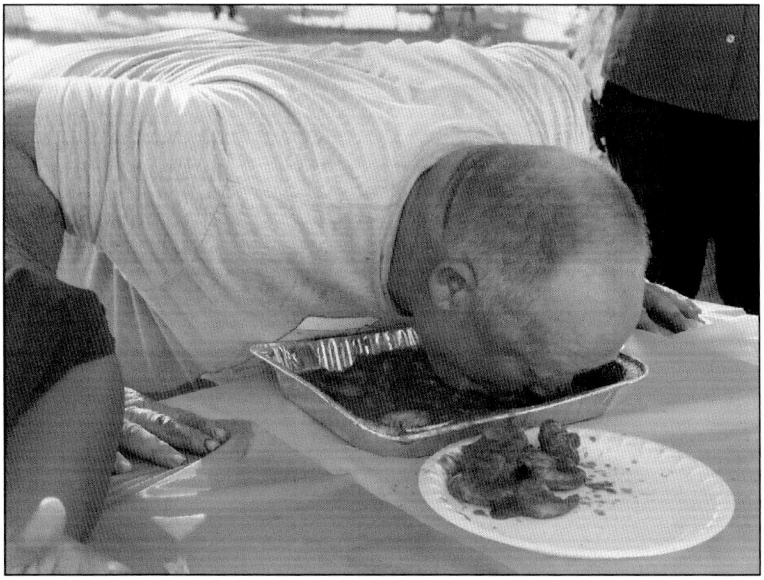

With Desert Sweet Shrimp as a growing industry, it seemed only natural to highlight this important segment of Gila Bend's economy with the Desert Shrimp Festival. In this 2010 photograph, a contestant bobs for shrimp. (Courtesy of Cyndi Eisenberger.)

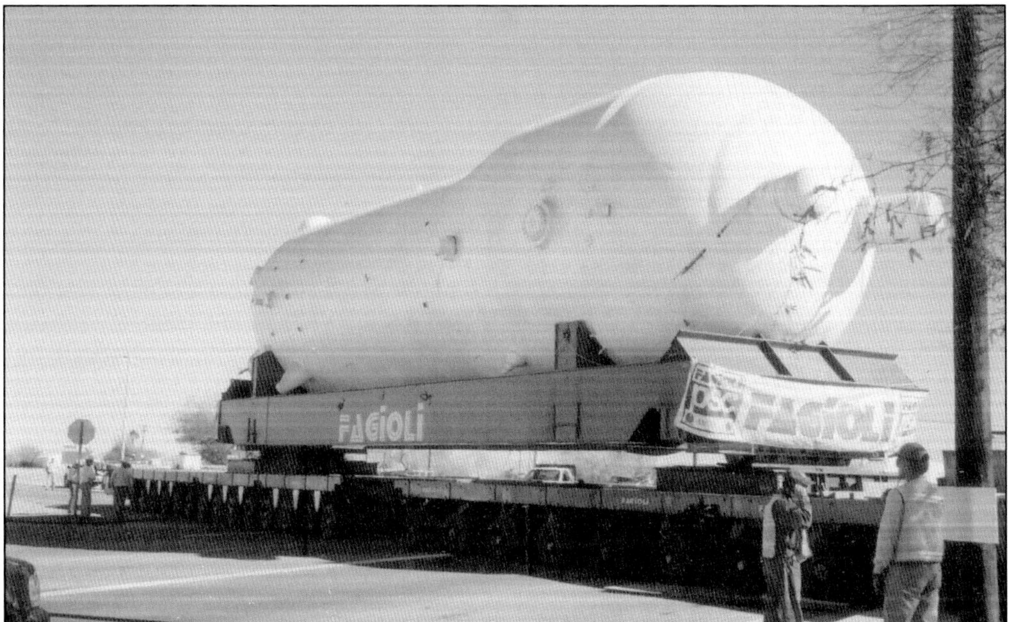

When the Palo Verde nuclear plant needs new parts, they usually come by way of the Gulf of California on ship and then through Mexico, following the route from Sonoita, Sonora, through Ajo and Gila Bend to the plant. This is an ideal route given the size of the components, as shown in this photograph. (Courtesy of Clyde Kreeger.)

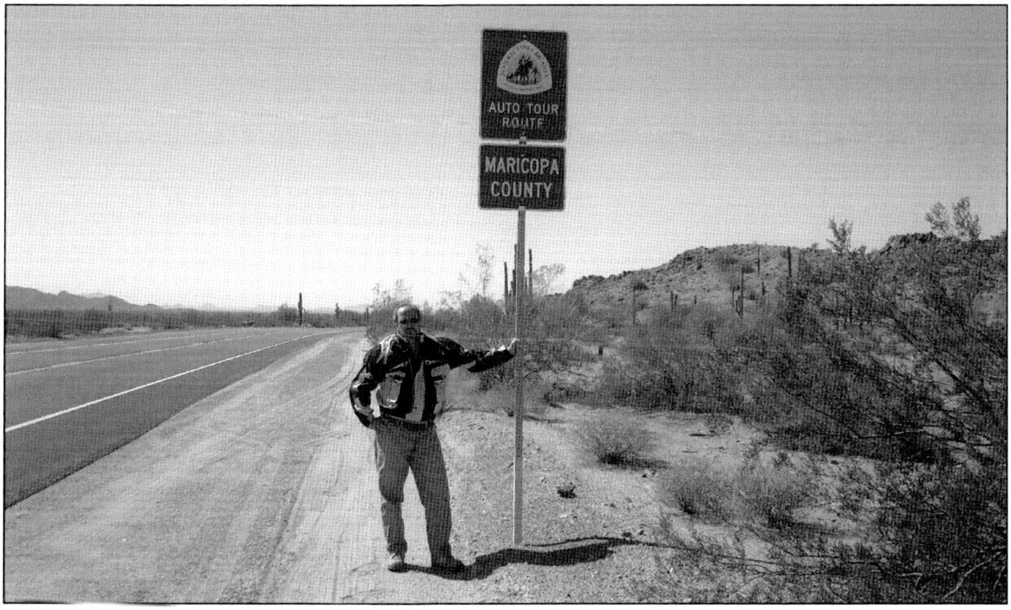

For those would like to follow the trail of the 1775–1776 expedition led by Juan Bautista de Anza without leaving the confines of their cars, an auto route has been developed with a portion running near Gila Bend. The author was instrumental in the selection of this portion of the road through Maricopa County, which closely parallels the actual route to the north. (Courtesy of Matthew "Dragon" Murray.)

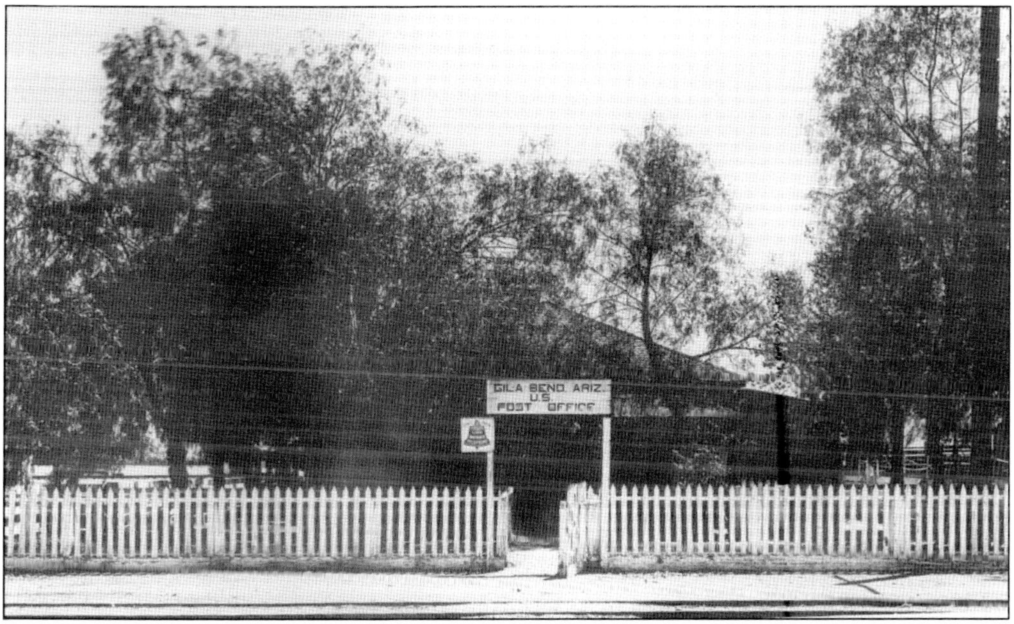

One of Gila Bend's early post offices also provided access to a public phone. Located on the tracks, its address was probably on Main Street. (Courtesy of the Gila Bend Museum.)

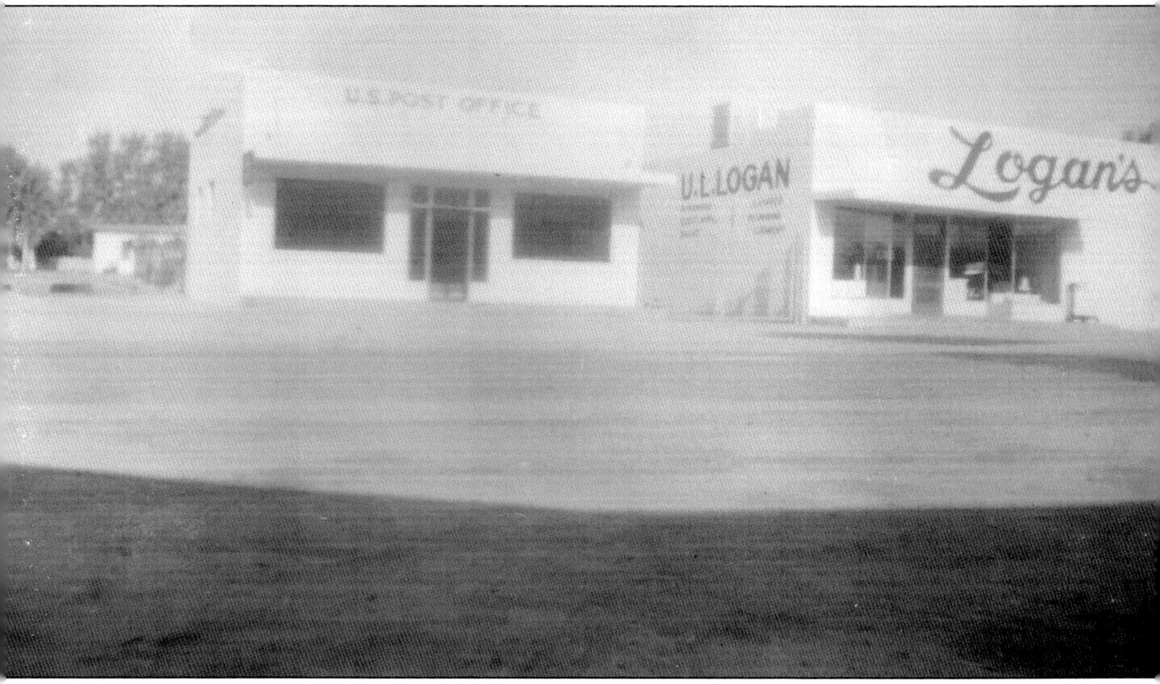

In this c. 1940s photograph, the post office is located on Pima Street next to Logan's General Store. The two buildings shared architectural similarities, but neither structure currently exists. (Courtesy of Gila Bend Museum.)

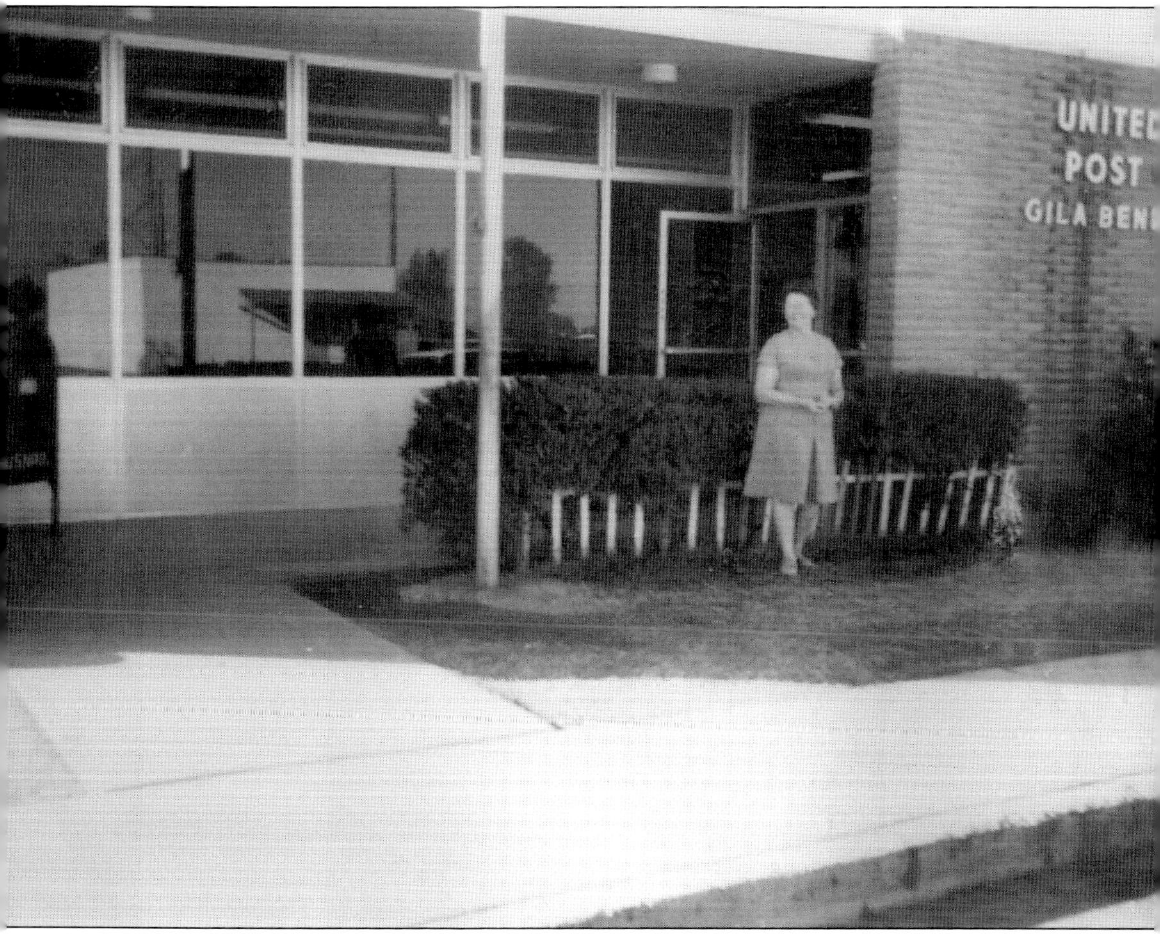

In the late 1960s, the post office moved to its current location on Papago Street. (Courtesy of Gila Bend Museum.)

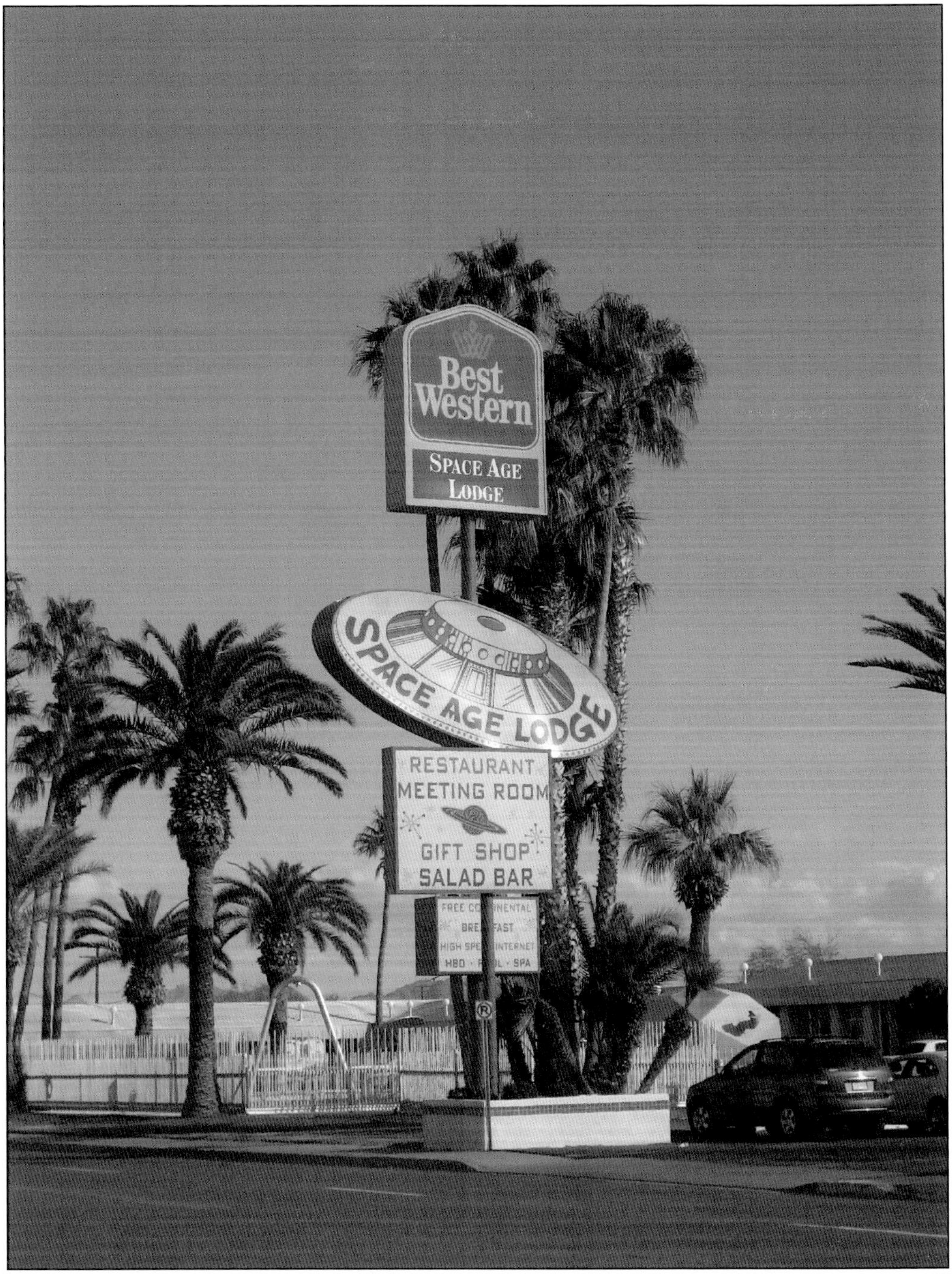

One of the most iconic places in Gila Bend is the Space Age Lodge. Built in 1963, it was well known for its unique Sputnik-style "satellite" attached to the roof to add to the outer space theme. The satellite has been replaced with a spacecraft. (Courtesy of Matthew "Dragon" Murray.)

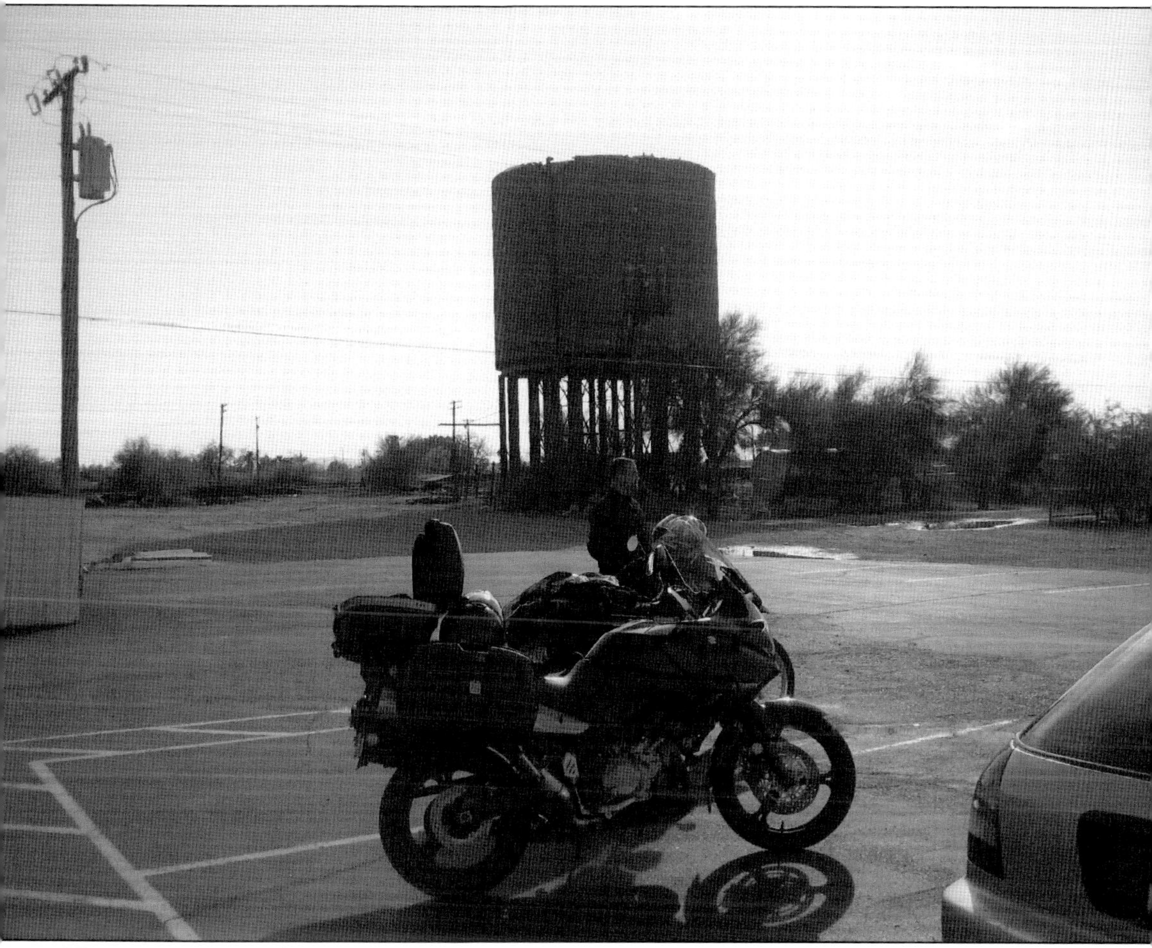

The water tower is the only Union Pacific structure remaining from Gila Bend's heyday as a railroad supply center. It was later used to supply water for the city. No longer in use, the water tower serves as a monument to an important facet of the town's past. (Courtesy of Matthew "Dragon" Murray.)

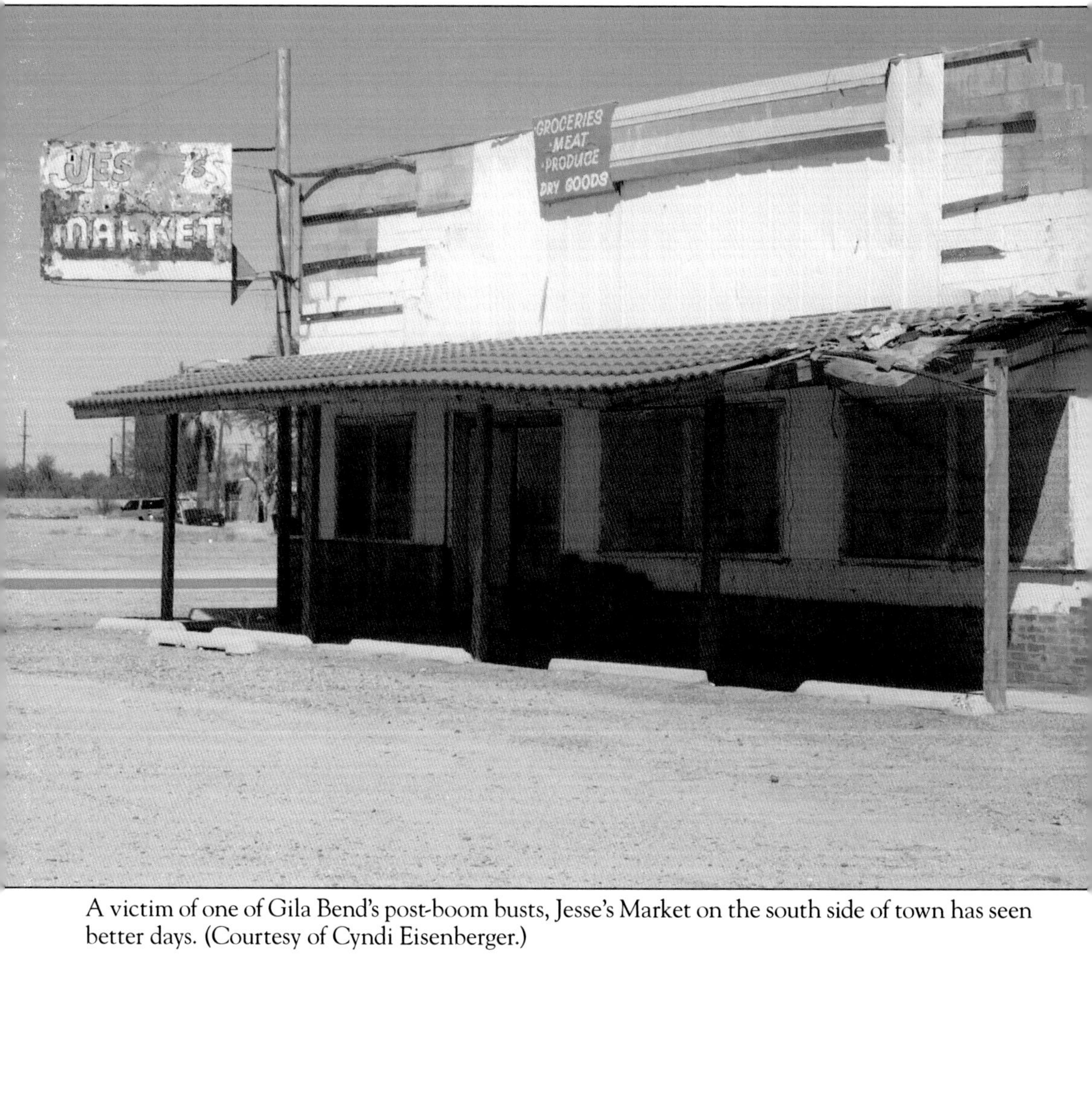

A victim of one of Gila Bend's post-boom busts, Jesse's Market on the south side of town has seen better days. (Courtesy of Cyndi Eisenberger.)

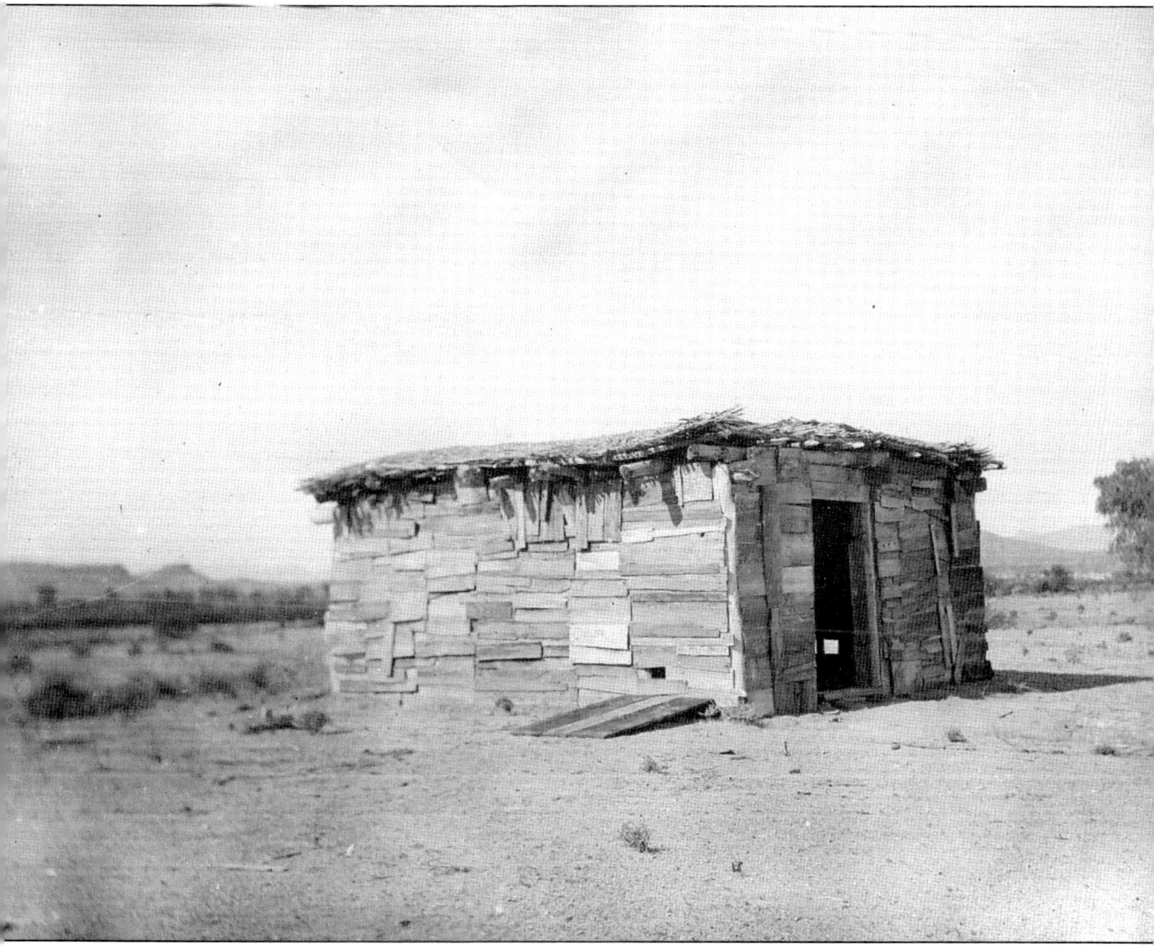

This photograph is from the Tohono O'odham village of Sil Murk. When the Painted Rock Dam was constructed in the early 1960s, the villagers found themselves living in the floodplain. The federal government provided a 40-acre tract next to Gila Bend, and some of the residents moved to what is now called the San Lucy Village. (Courtesy of Johnny Laird.)

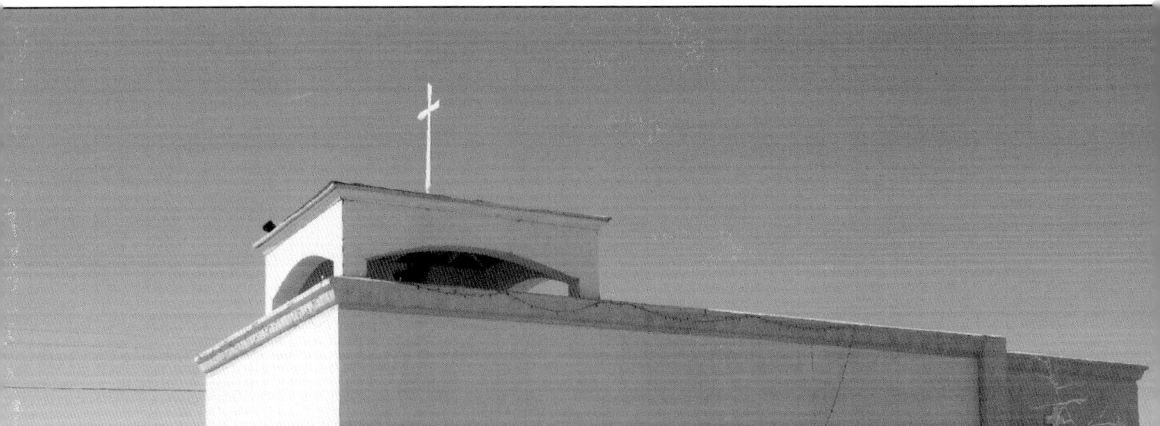

The San Lucy Village gets its name from the St. Lucy Parish, which has been a part of the culture of Gila Bend since 1885 when Diocesan priests from the Immaculate Conception Church established a mission to the Tohono O'odham. The village is adjacent to the town of Gila Bend, but it is a political subdivision, albeit a noncontiguous one, of the vast Tohono O'odham Nation. Created by Congress in 1882, the San Lucy District was originally over 22,000 acres. In 1960, the Painted Rock Dam rendered 9,880 acres unusable and forced the community from a 750-acre farm to a 40-acre parcel adjacent to the town. The current church was built as part of the relocation from what had been the Gila Bend Indian Reservation. The village has subsequently expanded its holdings, including the controversial purchase of a 135-acre parcel near Glendale. The Catholic church shown here continues to serve the community. (Courtesy of Cyndi Eisenberger.)

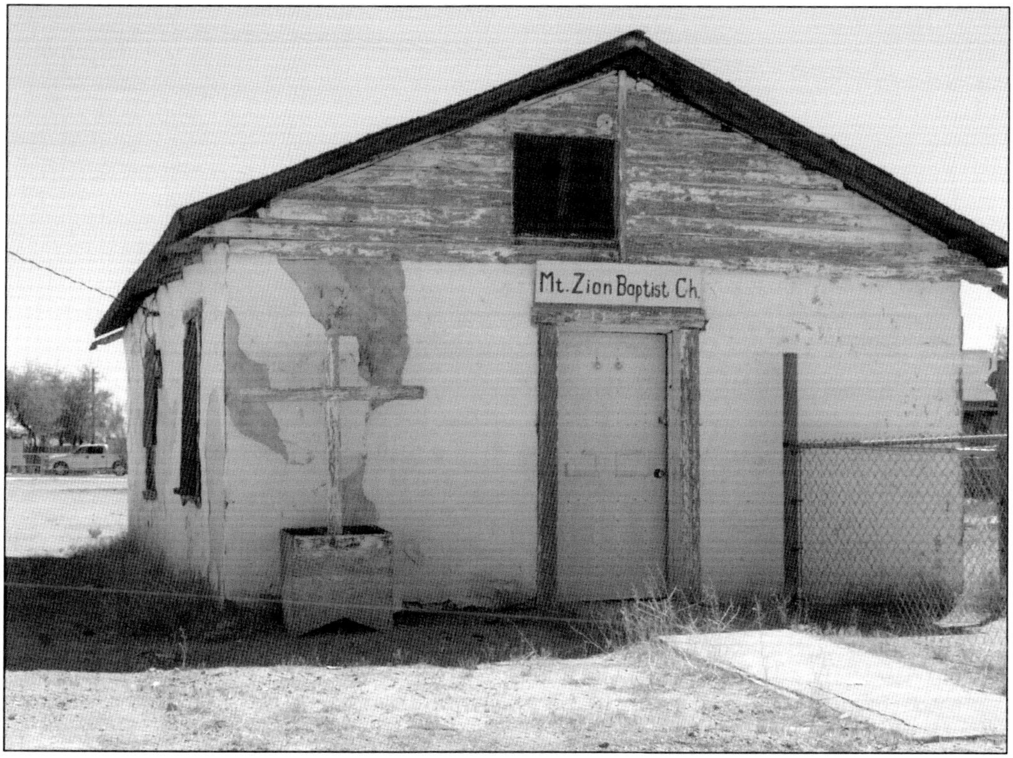

Once a place of worship, the Mt. Zion Church has now closed its doors. (Courtesy of Cyndi Eisenberger.)

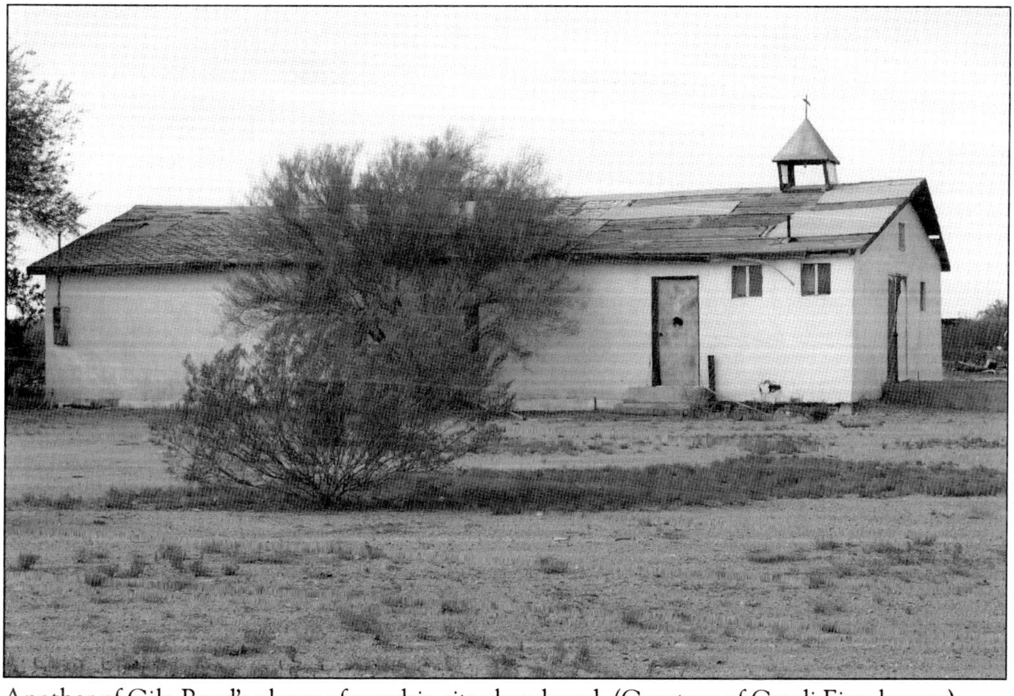

Another of Gila Bend's places of worship sits abandoned. (Courtesy of Cyndi Eisenberger.)

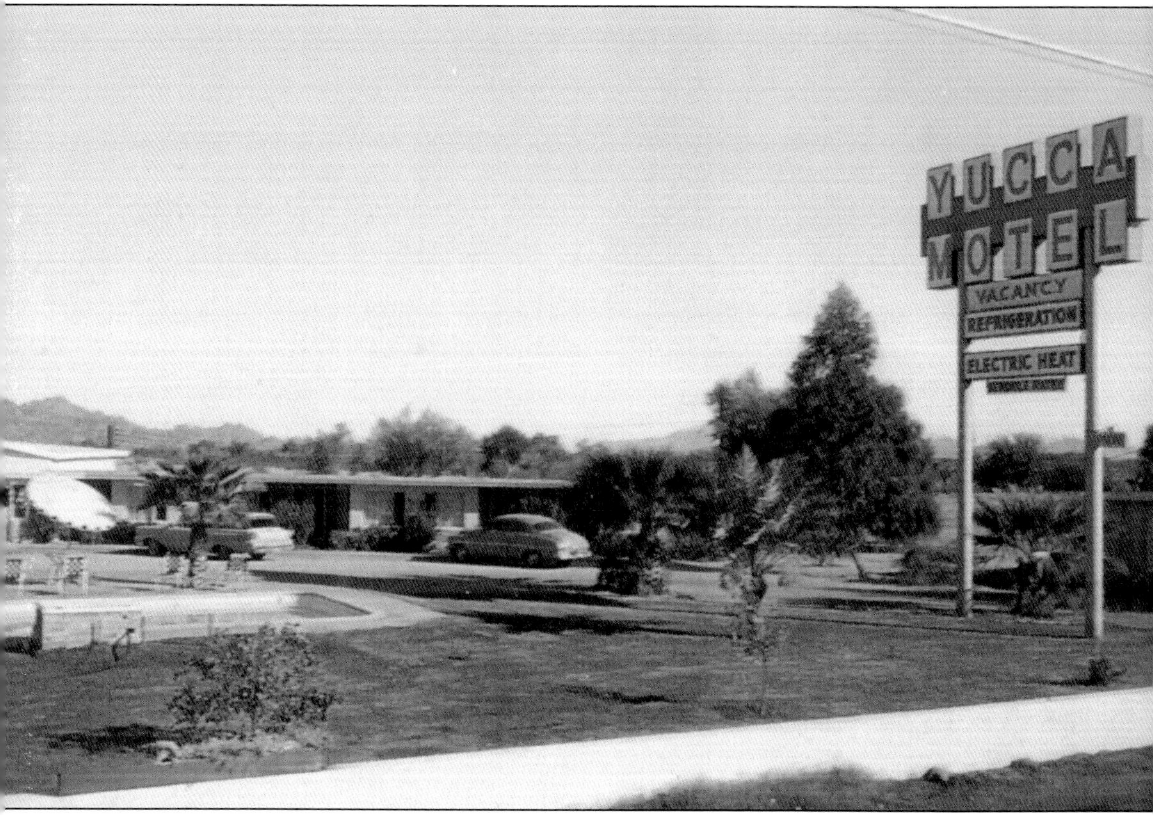

The Yucca Motel is an iconic American roadside lodging that has been operating since the 1950s. It has been under the same ownership and management since the 1970s. (Courtesy of Natu Bhakta.)

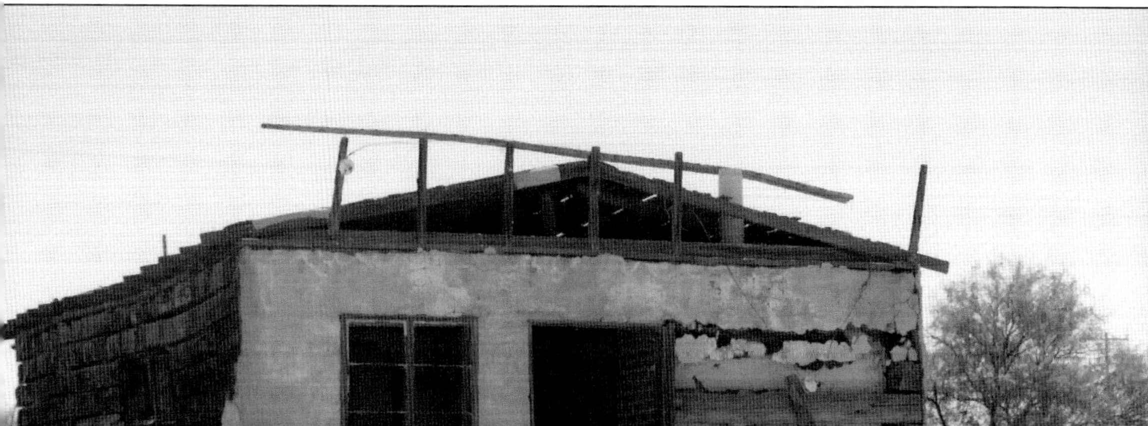

Gila Bend was once segregated like many American towns. African Americans lived primarily south of the railroad tracks. This is all that remains of the African American school, which was constructed in 1923. The schoolhouse was built almost entirely of railroad ties. (Courtesy of Cyndi Eisenberger.)

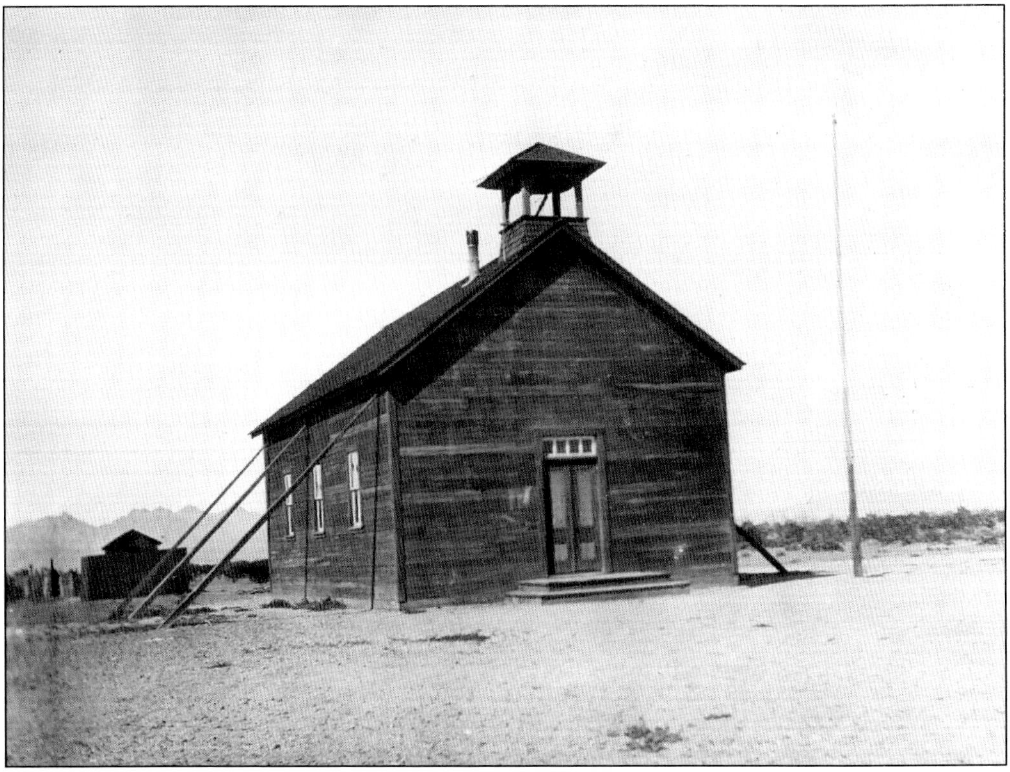

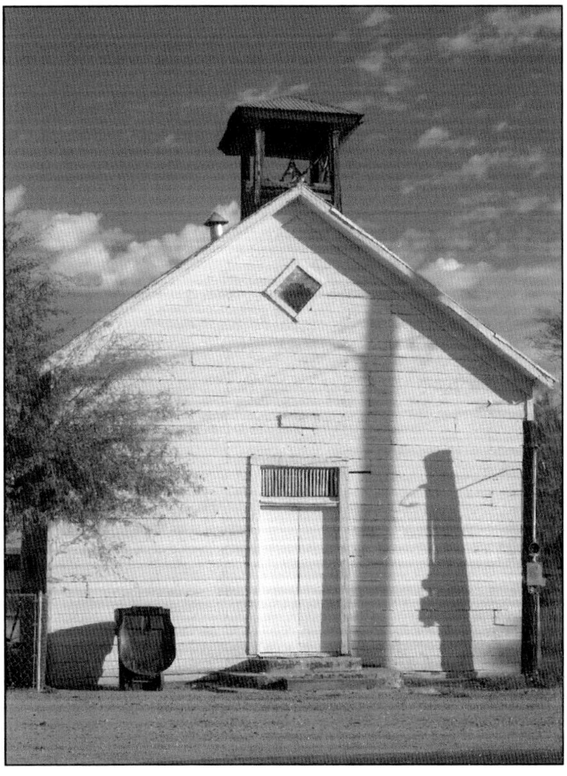

Pictured is the Gila Bend schoolhouse shortly after construction in 1896. (Courtesy of Johnny Laird.)

Seen here is the Gila Bend schoolhouse as it appears today. Shortly after construction, the schoolhouse was heavily damaged in a storm, having been lifted off of its foundation and deposited in a nearby alley. To prevent future *Wizard of Oz*–like episodes, the parents and teachers anchored the building with narrow-gauge rails. (Courtesy of Cyndi Eisenberger.)

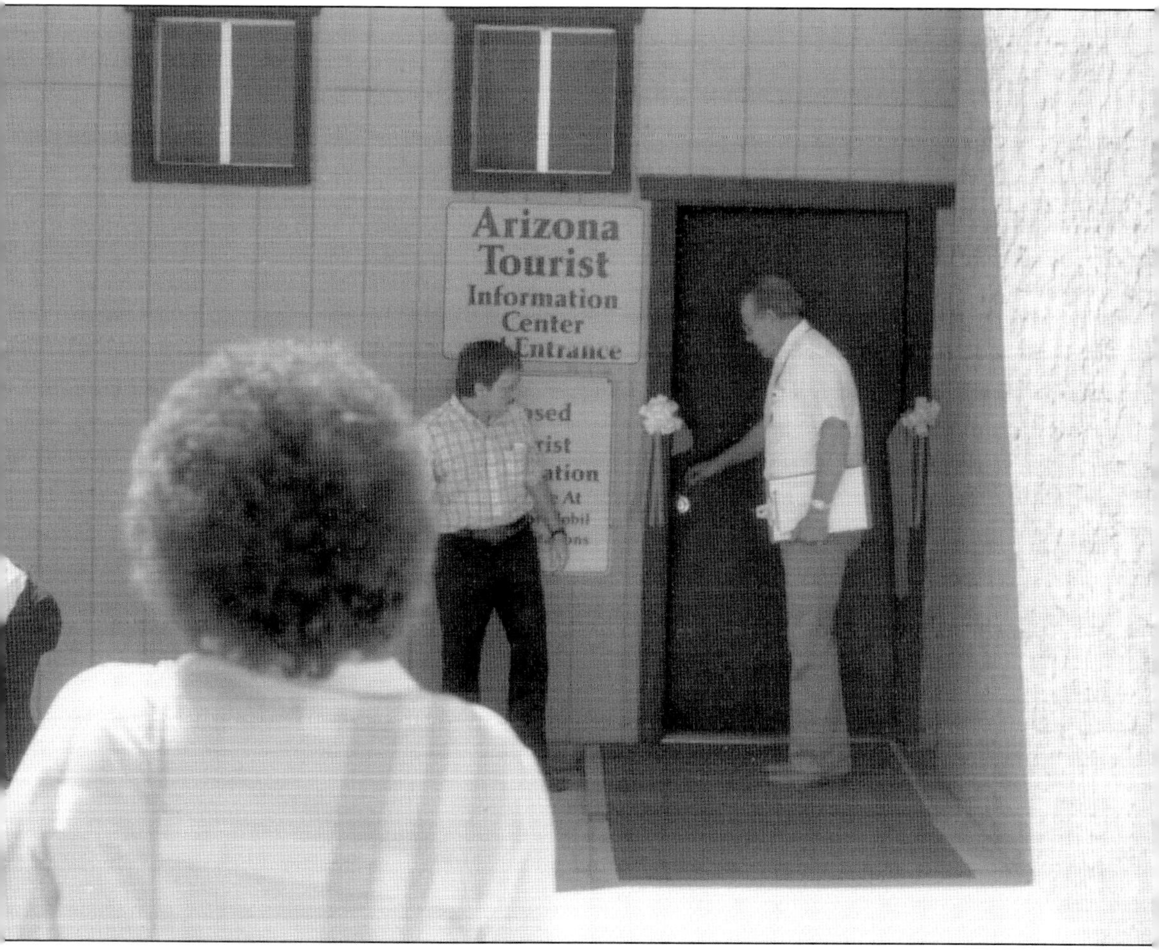

On March 26, 1988, the Gila Bend Museum opened and was dedicated to the citizens of Gila Bend. The museum continues to be operated by the Town of Gila Bend. Its collection focuses on the town and the surrounding area and includes Native American artifacts, basketry, artwork, historical photographs, and other items of interest. (Courtesy of the Gila Bend Museum.)

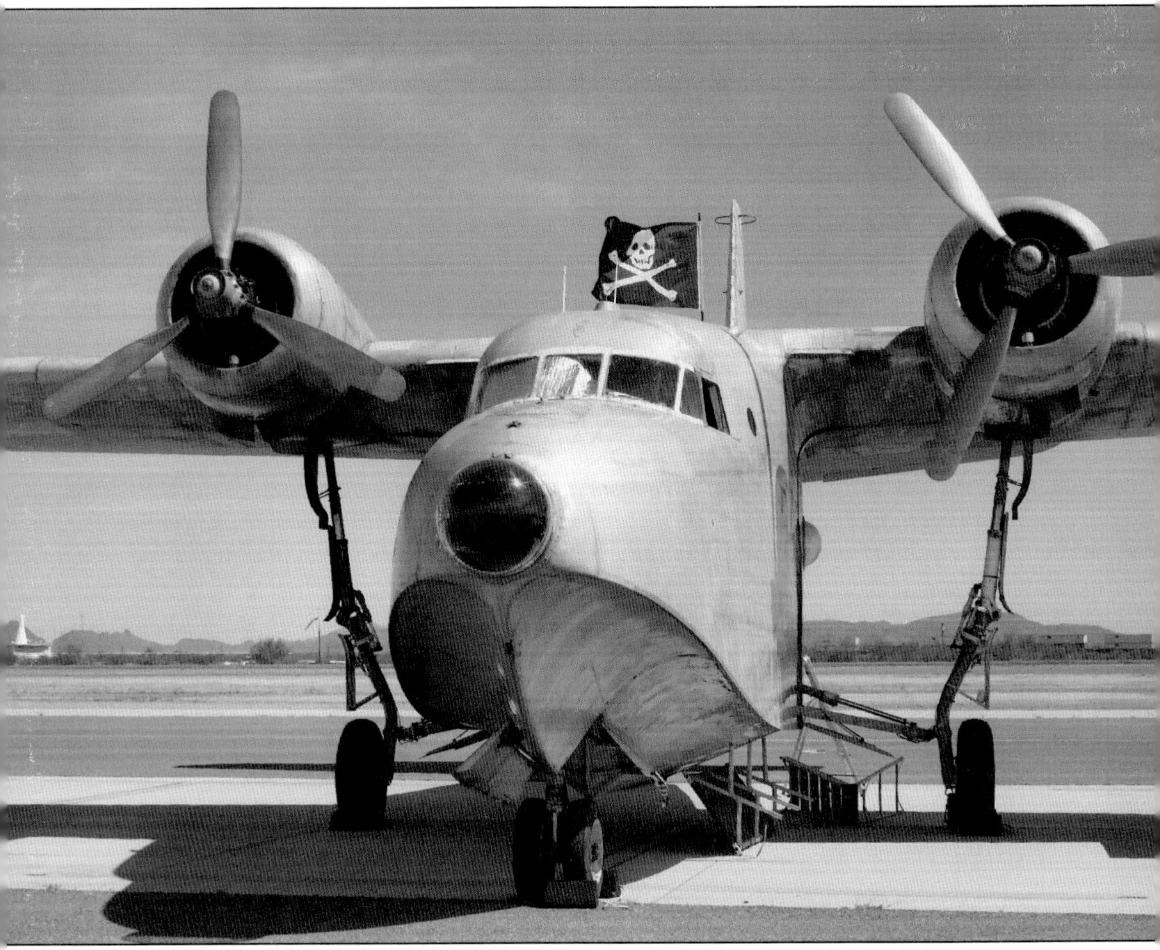

This seaplane graced the desert for the first annual Gila Bend Air Fair in 2009. (Courtesy of Cyndi Eisenberger.)

The Gila Bend jailhouse is one of the oldest extant buildings in town, as attested by this photograph from 1911. While the roof is newer, the adobe walls already show its age. (Courtesy of Gary Miller.)

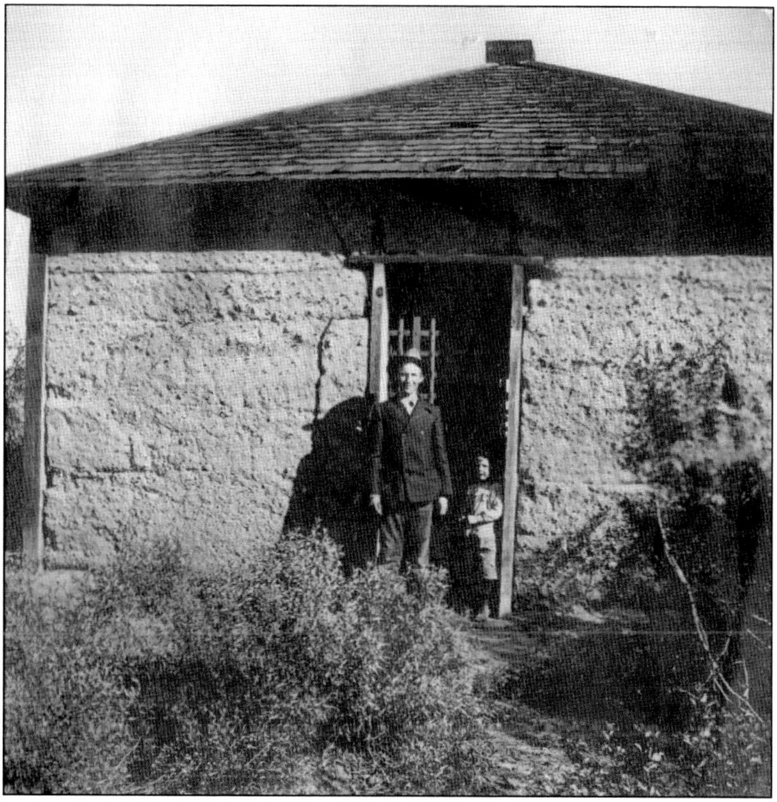

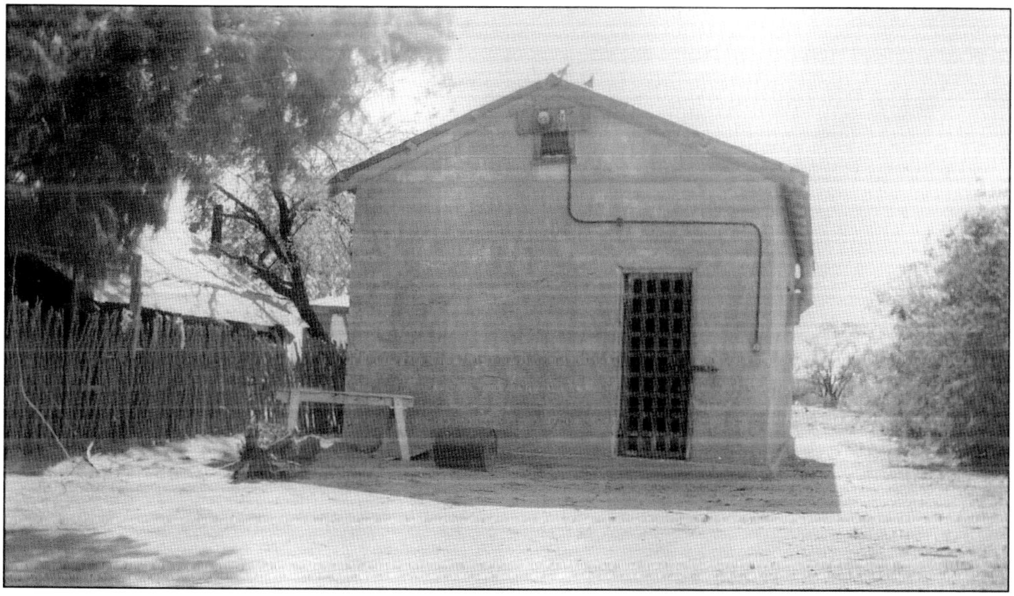

Pictured is the Gila Bend jailhouse after a more recent remodel. (Courtesy of Gila Bend Museum.)

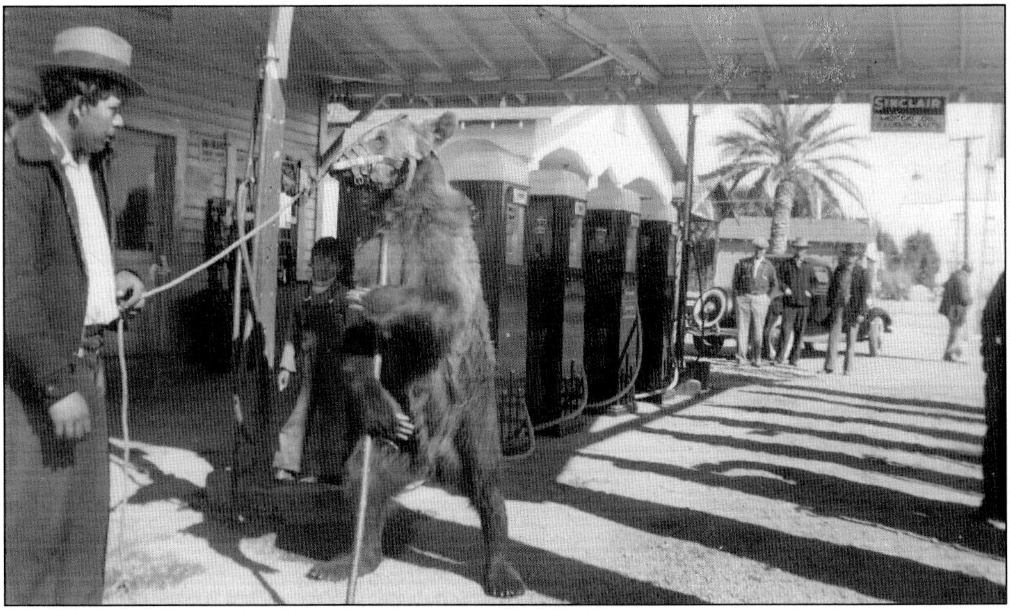

A dancing bear provides entertainment at the Gila Auto Court around 1940. While many found animal acts such as this amusing, the animals were typically starved and beaten as part of their training. Now considered cruelty to animals, dancing bear acts are seldom seen. (Courtesy of Johnny Laird.)

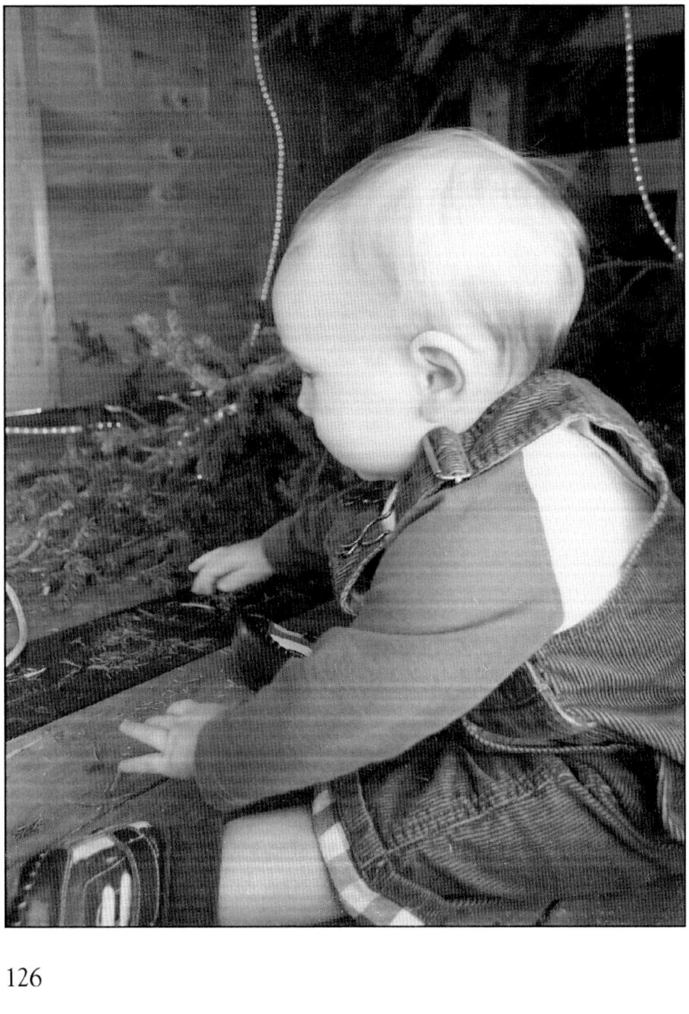

Eleven-month-old Aaron Doucette touches the US Capitol building's Christmas tree as it travels through town. In 2009, an 85-foot-tall tree was cut down in Arizona's White Mountains and paraded around the state before being placed on display in the Capitol. (Courtesy of Cyndi Eisenberger.)

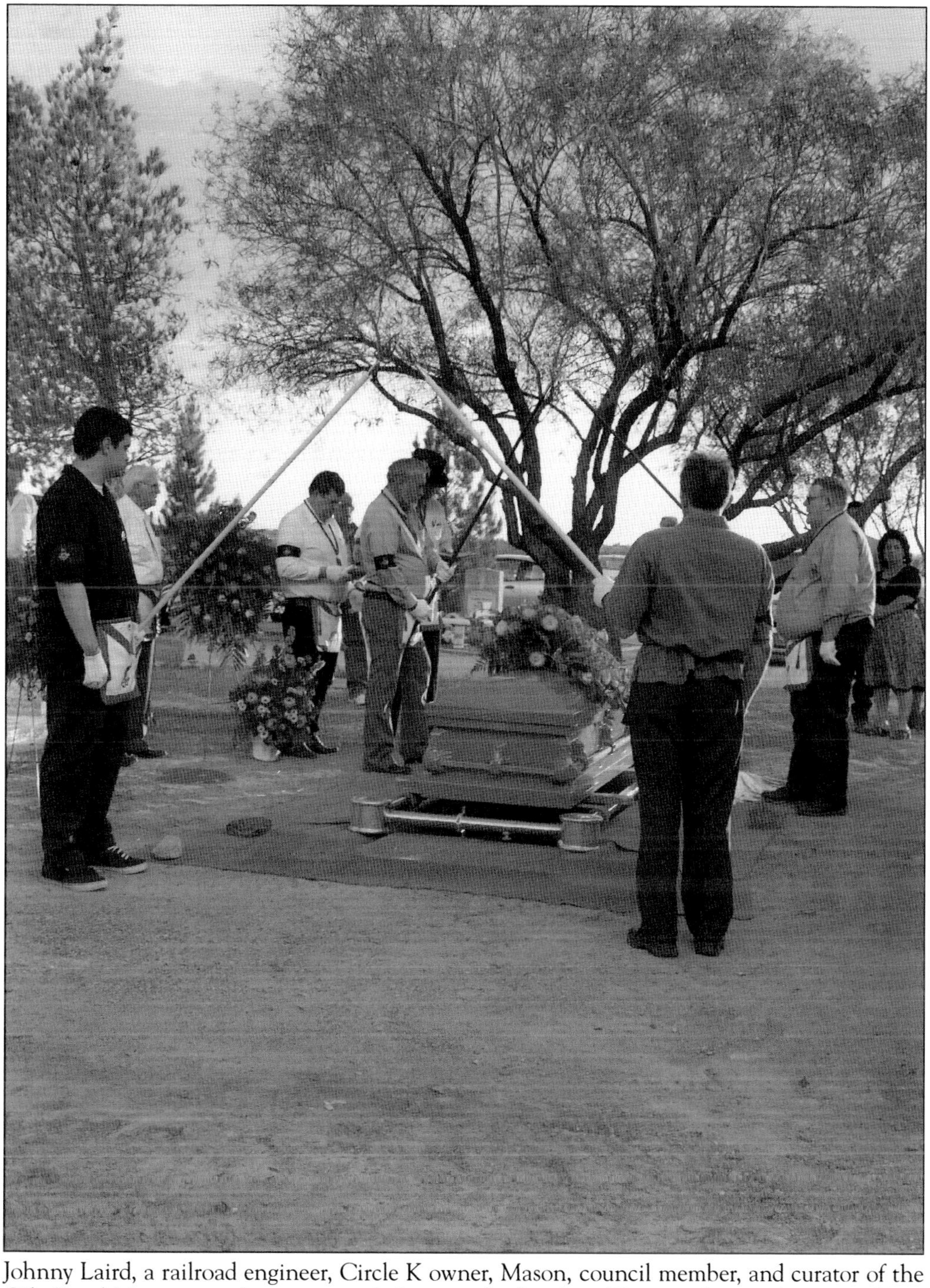

Johnny Laird, a railroad engineer, Circle K owner, Mason, council member, and curator of the Gila Bend Museum, truly represented the town he lived in. He passed away August 1, 2010. (Courtesy of Heather Goebels.)

Discover Thousands of Local History Books Featuring Millions of Vintage Images

Arcadia Publishing, the leading local history publisher in the United States, is committed to making history accessible and meaningful through publishing books that celebrate and preserve the heritage of America's people and places.

Find more books like this at
www.arcadiapublishing.com

Search for your hometown history, your old stomping grounds, and even your favorite sports team.

Consistent with our mission to preserve history on a local level, this book was printed in South Carolina on American-made paper and manufactured entirely in the United States. Products carrying the accredited Forest Stewardship Council (FSC) label are printed on 100 percent FSC-certified paper.

MADE IN THE USA